Services for Children and their Families

ASPECTS OF CHILD CARE FOR SOCIAL WORKERS

EDITED BY

JOHN STROUD

Assistant Director of Social Services Hertfordshire County Council

PERGAMON PRESS

OXFORD · NEW YORK · TORONTO

SYDNEY · BRAUNSCHWEIG

Pergamon Press Ltd., Headington Hill Hall, Oxford
Pergamon Press Inc., Maxwell House, Fairview Park, Elmsford,
New York 10523
Pergamon of Canada Ltd., 207 Queen's Quay West, Toronto 1
Pergamon Press (Aust.) Pty. Ltd., 19a Boundary Street,
Rushcutters Bay, N.S.W. 2011, Australia
Vieweg & Sohn GmbH, Burgplatz 1, Braunschweig

First edition 1973

Library of Congress Cataloging in Publication Data
Stroud, John, 1923–
Services for children and their families.

(The Commonwealth and international library. Social work division)
Bibliography: p.
1. Child welfare—Great Britain—Addresses, essays, lectures.
2. Social service—Great Britain—Addresses, essays, lectures.
I. Title.
HV751.A6S73 1973   362.7′0942   73–3343
ISBN 0–08–016604–0
ISBN 0–08–016605–9 Flexicover

Printed in Great Britain by The Anchor Press Ltd., Tiptree, Essex.

Contents

Editor's Introduction

WHEN this book was being planned it was known that the local authority social services in England and Wales were about to be amalgamated. This amalgamation was to be primarily administrative. From 1948 until 1971 the statutes relating to the care of children were administered by a specialist committee of the local authority to whom was responsible a specialist chief officer, the Children's Officer. At the same time, statutes relating to services for handicapped people were administered by another specialist committee known as the Welfare Committee, and, in most authorities, services related to the mental health of the community were controlled by a Health Committee.

Under the Local Authority Social Services Act of 1970, no change was made in any of the relevant statutes: the services to be administered remained the same. One committee only, however, was made responsible for their administration—the Social Services Committee; and one chief officer only was to be appointed—the Director of Social Services. Soon after this Act came into operation, a parallel change was made at central government level: whereas until 1971 the Home Office was responsible for child care services, this responsibility was passed to the Department of Health and Social Services where already lay the overall control of the mental health and welfare services.

Although at first glance this change appears to be only administrative—almost a "tidying up"—there lay behind it a considerable change in administrative attitude and in the practice of social work itself. During the period 1948–71 it became clear that there were considerable advantages in the specialized administration of what might be called "custodial care". Children's committees and their officers devoted great care and attention to, for example, the development of residential and foster-home care for

vii

children, and the administrative problems encountered were quite different from those appearing in, for example, the field of caring for elderly people. But social workers themselves became increasingly anxious to develop what was at first called a "preventive service". Put crudely, they wished to prevent children coming into care because they had observed that the separation of children from familiar surroundings often added to the children's problems or, at best, displaced the problem. More and more, social workers attempted to work with families in an attempt to solve problems in a community setting; and similar changes in approach went on in the fields of mental health and the care of old people.

As this sort of development went on, it became clearer that the fragmented administration of the social services was, in fact, disadvantageous. There was duplication of effort, and competition between services for resources; and confusion amongst families who did not know to whom to turn. In the view of the social workers, the separate administrative compartments perpetuated a system of dealing with presenting symptoms rather than with the whole problem of the family and its environment. It is hoped that the new local authority social service departments will not only administer the existing statutes more powerfully, more comprehensibly, and less wastefully, but that they will encourage the development of a service which is truly based on the strengths of the family and the local community.

At the time of writing, with social service departments barely a year old, it can only be said that in some areas there are distinct signs that these hopes may ultimately be fulfilled. The process will, however, take some years to complete. In some areas of the country amalgamation and reorganization has been, to administrators and social workers alike, a bewildering and, indeed, painful experience, and their standards of service achieved in the previously "specialized" settings seem to have been diluted.

It has seemed to the contributors to this book that however the social services are ultimately redeployed and however great the resources which are ultimately put into "preventive" or "community" work, there must remain a considerable number of children who are in care or at imminent risk of coming into care. Services for such children and the techniques of helping them have developed very slowly over a long period. Barely a quarter of a century ago, when the social services under the Public Assistance administration were organized on a generic rather than a specialized basis, children deprived of a normal family life were found to be considerably deprived and underprivileged even within the local authority's care. Such is the demand for attention coming from other groups, notably elderly people, those with handicaps, and those who are mentally ill, and such is the range of responsibilities shouldered by the new departments that resources are at present spread very thinly over the whole field, that there is the possibility that the needs of one small group of human beings may be overlooked or neglected.

This book is therefore an attempt to record the position achieved by the child care service on the eve of reorganization. It has been written by people who have been active in the child care service and have gained their experience and formed their opinions in the thick of the fray. These contributors have attempted to pass on to new entrants to the service some idea of their values and the opinions and philosophies which they have evolved. Naturally in doing so they have adopted different styles and have selected from a mass of material those aspects of the work which seemed to them most important and relevant. The result is not intended to present a static picture or indeed a collection of Holy Writ. Hopefully, the social services will never be static: hopefully, they will never be dominated by the dogmas of times past; and hopefully, new generations of social workers will inquire, challenge, formulate, and review as their predecessors, the specialist child care officers, have always done. Indeed, it might be said that one of the purposes of the book is to help the new entrant into the social services to comprehend what has gone on before and at the same time invite him to challenge and rethink the position in which he will find himself. Some of the contributors here draw more attention to problems than to solutions; by the time the book is published more problems may well have appeared, so fluid is the present situation. This is particularly the case where the society which itself throws up so many problems of law and order, of educational success and failure, of community disorientation, of power structures, and of value systems, struggles to readjust itself to the problems of the later twentieth century. Those painful struggles towards a reborn society are often most sensitively recorded in the attitudes of society towards its children. The task of the social workers—never easy—is much more difficult when they operate in a society in the throes of rapid evolution;

and their work is even more demanding when a part of it is to prepare the younger generation to face the difficulties and transitions of our society *au fin de siècle*.

In these circumstances the contributors to this book wish their successors well in the task that lies before them and hope that in these pages they may find much to stimulate, interest and, perhaps, to guide them.

CHAPTER 1

Changing Responses, 1870–1970

JEAN S. HEYWOOD*

EDITOR'S INTRODUCTION

When the new social worker first enters into his chosen field of study he may feel that he is fairly clear in his mind what duties he has towards children who are "deprived of a normal family life" and an idea of what the social agency has as its aims and objectives. Soon he will find, however, that no agency concerned with children exists in isolation. What the social worker does affects and is affected by what is being done by many other agencies. What is done by the Education Department? What is done by the health visitor and the associated medical services? What is done by the police? And, indeed, what environment is created by the planning authorities, the housing authorities, and the deep-flowing economic forces within the country that create the milieu in which he and the child have to live and to which to some extent they may have to adapt? What is more, all these other agencies and, indeed, his own social work agency, will have been much affected in their thinking and attitudes by events of the past. As the student goes deeper into the subject of what he is and what he stands for and what he wishes for the children for whom he is responsible, he will find that much of his thinking and much of his presuppositions have been shaped by the events of the last hundred years. The Victorians, who were also faced with a society in violent change and flux, made individualistic responses to the new social problems which were thrown up. Sometimes services were thus created, linked (it would now appear illogically) with a particular

* Director of Generic Social Work Studies, University of Manchester.

1

government or local authority department, with the result that in the early 1970s social work was often faced with a multiplicity of agencies' activities all concerned with some part of the growing child.

It is in an attempt to demonstrate to the social worker of the 1970s the extent to which his own attitudes and his *modus operandi* as a social worker may be affected by the events of the past, that Jean Heywood reviews the principal legislative developments of the past century as they affect the child and his family.

The last 30 years of the nineteenth century was a period of response to and consolidation of the great social developments which had taken place in the earlier years. People had lived through a social revolution on a scale never experienced before, and society had to develop ways of dealing with the change and the resulting problems. The industrial and social revolutions and scientific discoveries hardly need to be detailed, but a glance at them will show how far the old ways of living had become outdated by the 1870s. Railways had already opened up the country and screw-steamers had opened up the world; the Suez Canal, opened in November 1869, made the East accessible to trade. Faraday had died in 1867 having given the world the discovery of electromagnetic induction from which came the telegraph and incandescent filament lamp. Darwin, after publishing *The Origin of Species* in 1859, was in 1870 still working and writing on his thesis concerned with the survival of the most adaptable species. Pasteur, in 1865, discovered the cause of putrefaction to be a microbe and, after three further years' work on the diseases of silk worms, isolated the bacillus of two distinct diseases and found a method of preventing contagion by disease. From his discoveries, Lister in 1867 began to experiment with carbolized silk ligatures and, in 1869, to provide an antiseptic atmosphere for surgery. We should not under-estimate the climate of hope and adventure resulting from these discoveries, which was an essential part of the time.

The novelist Hardy has chronicled with love the lives of country people of this period, whose destinies were reflected in the natural cycles of the countryside and country labours; but England was already in the process of changing from an agricultural to an industrial nation, and with this came unfamiliarity, the problem of living together in cities, industrial dirt, drainage, sewerage, housing, and ignorance of public health, which resulted in epidemic disease and increased infant mortality. The first Public Health Act of 1848 had established the concept and structure of a central health department, and in 1864 the Ladies' Sanitary Reform Movement (the origin of the health visitor service we know today) was started in Manchester to help mothers and families with the care of young children by preventing the spread of infection and, by teaching better budgeting, attempting to reduce the amount of secondary poverty. Women were now beginning to make a significant contribution to social change. It is not inappropriate to note that the higher education of women had begun about this time. Girton and Newnham were founded in 1869 and 1871, and the first Education Act of 1870, with its school boards and powers to make attendance compulsory, brought to many women as well as men their first experience of local administration and widespread insight into the needs of children of different social groups. Thus an awareness of the social rights of children was born.

The last quarter of the nineteenth century was a time of emancipation and loosening chains. The trumpets perhaps had earlier sounded from hidden battlements with the publication in 1847 of Karl Marx's work *Das Kapital.* In 1883 the Fabian Society was founded; in 1887 the Independent Labour Party. In 1886 there was a royal commission on the Housing of the Poor; in 1888 a select committee on Sweating.[1] The dock strike of 1889, the engineers' strike of 1897, and the South Wales coal dispute of 1898 all emphasized the growing strength and struggle for emancipation of the industrial worker. Booth's study of the *Life and Labour of the People* (begun in 1886), with its factual disclosure of the appalling amount of poverty (30 per cent) existing in London, the richest city in the world, shocked thinking people. Rowntree in 1899 showed a similar proportion of poverty to exist in York, a representative small town. Finally, at the end of the century, the medical examination of recruits for the Boer War revealed such poor physique among young working-class adults that a committee on Physical Deterioration was set up. The state of the physical health of children needed for the country's future, and the high infantile mortality of the time, shook complacency and precipitated the movement for social justice for children.

Previously the care given to children in need had been shared beween the

[1] That is, "sweated labour" or the extreme exploitation of certain groups of workers.

Poor Law and the voluntary organizations. The Poor Law was concerned with the destitute child of the pauper family; the voluntary societies with those who needed protection and rescue because of their inadequate families. From 1870 the Poor Law Board had begun to experiment with boarding-out as a means of caring for pauper children who were orphaned, deserted, or illegitimate, setting up certified committees of voluntary workers to find suitable homes and subsequently to place and visit the children. In 1885 the Local Government Board appointed a woman inspector, Miss Mason, to inspect the work of the boarding-out committees and visit all children boarded outside their own unions. The Poor Law authorities learnt much from many of the ideas and developments of the voluntary organizations, who were the real pioneers in methods of care. The voluntary organizations began as rescue movements, first in the "ragged schools", for vagrant and delinquent children of the streets. It was here that both Mary Carpenter and Dr. Barnardo served their apprenticeship. Mary Carpenter realized that the ragged schools were not sufficient to meet the real needs of these delinquent children, who were already hardened by prison sentences. She it was who developed the idea of reformatory schools, based on continental experiments, where the boys lived and worked with the staff in "families" —a "cottage village" of boy-families, with workshops and dwelling-houses, a little chapel, a wash and drying house, a printing office and a bakehouse. Her work was crowned by the passing of the Industrial Schools Act 1854 and the Reformatory Schools Act 1857, which gave courts powers to order convicted juveniles to be detained in these schools instead of in prisons, and enabled local authorities to contribute to their establishment. At this time, too, the educational influence of Friedrich Froebel was being felt. One HMI reported in 1854: "This system treats the child as a child, encourages him to think for himself: teaches him gradually to tell his own story and to listen to that of others . . . whatever is said and . . . done is totally and altogether such as belongs to a child." Yet the lessons in schools did not live up to this vision. "Well conceived, but ill-conducted", Herbert Spencer described them, and education had a long road to travel.

The work of Dr. Barnardo and Dr. Stephenson, founder of the National Children's Home, represents at its best the great voluntary movements for homeless children in the nineteenth century. In 1870 Dr. Barnardo opened the first home for destitute boys at No. 18 Stepney Causeway, for children who had no homes but the roofs and gutters of London streets. He, too, based his work on the family system and on the power of a new environment. "If the children of the slums can be removed from their surroundings early enough and can be kept sufficiently long under training, heredity counts for little, environment counts for everything." He established the principle of the ever-open door, founded schools on his home premises in which he equipped workshops with craftsmen in charge to teach the boys a trade, and, for girls, he ensured a careful domestic training lasting 3 months before placing them as servants or nannies with respectable families.

Dr. Stephenson opened his first home in 1869, taking his children from the streets of Lambeth, from warehouses and wasteland, wharves and casks covered with tarpaulins which the homeless boys had made their own. There, when the police turned on their bull's-eye lanterns, the boys "swarmed from their holes like rats from a sewer". He described his work very simply: "They needed a friend and a home—someone to tell them of God and to teach them a trade."

All the pioneers of the voluntary movements based their work on the principle of rescuing the children from the old environment and providing a new one where, working together as a family, they had a sense of belonging and could own something, do something, be somebody. They developed systems of emigrating selected children, mainly to Canada, but also to Australia, New Zealand, and Rhodesia, where there was a large demand for boys and girls as workers and domestics on the farms. Special receiving homes were set up in the overseas countries, where the children stayed to get acclimatized and to get to know the agent who would supervise them in their new homes.

All these methods of care, by changing the environment and ensuring the ability to work, reflect the social conditions of the time, the prevalence of poverty, and the absence of supportive social services for the family. The Poor Law adopted from the voluntary organizations the idea of cottage homes and then developed from these the scattered-home system—isolated small homes in localities of their own selection near to denominational schools with receiving homes instead of the workhouse, where children went first on admission, for care and selection for the different kinds of home.

The whole position of children was of gradual emancipation during the last quarter of the nineteenth century. Their defencelessness in an impersonal industrial world called for legal protection, and this was developed through successive legislation. This was seen first in the protection of unwanted, illegitimate children from their own high death rate, a problem brought out into the open by the emphasis of the new public health movement on the prevention of mortality. The Government set up a select committee which reported in 1871 and recommended legislation to protect illegitimate children against the abuses of baby farming and infanticide. The Act of 1872 for the better protection of infant life ensured that professional foster mothers were brought under inspection by registration; and, in the same year, the Bastardy Law Amendment Act made it possible for unmarried mothers to claim from the father more financial support for their babies through the courts. The declining birth rate and high infantile mortality rate were very significant factors in the concern for infant welfare. The birth rate fell from 35·5 live births per 1000 population during 1870–5 to 29·3 live births per 1000 population in 1896–1900, while in 1899 out of every 1000 children born 163 died within the first year of life. This change in the balance of population set a premium on the life of children which began the emphasis of the public health movement on maternity and child welfare, but this also had repercussions in the care of even the most neglected children. So we see the growth of voluntary societies dealing with the prevention of child cruelty and the passing in 1889 of the first Act for the prevention of cruelty to and better protection of children in response to the work of Benjamin Waugh and his followers. Here was the beginning of state protection for the inarticulate child. The Act contained important new powers: the right of any person—believing a child to be suffering—to obtain a warrant on sworn evidence to remove such a child to a place of safety, and the power of the courts to remove a child from his parents and commit him to the care of a fit person.

The great social changes of the time had fostered concepts of emancipation, entitlement, and inductive thinking from factual observation, while the scarcity value of children emphasized their individuality. They were no longer chattels but individuals with rights. As studies revealed the extent of poverty and its crippling physical effects, we see the beginnings of early tentative legislation to deal with the relief of poverty among children.

The Education (Provision of Meals) Act of 1906 made school meals possible, the Education (Administrative Provisions) Act of 1907 inaugurated the medical inspection of school children and the School Health Service. The infant welfare and health visiting movement was extended as a result of the passing of the Notification of Births Acts of 1907 and 1913, which enabled the public health departments to be notified by the Registrar of all births. It was in this atmosphere of reaction against the anarchy of the industrial revolution that the Children Act of 1908—the Children's Charter as it was called—was passed. This Act strengthened the provisions intended to prevent cruelty to children, extended the regulations governing infant life protection, and set up remand homes and special courts for juveniles. Now, for the first time, the courts were seen as agencies for the rescue of children as well as for the punishment of the delinquent act.

Meanwhile, the Poor Law was itself working towards the emancipation of the child. The royal commission on the Poor Laws of 1905–9 was concerned in both its minority and majority reports to free him from the stigma of pauperism and the principle of less eligibility. The minority report advocated that the care of pauper children should be taken out of the hands of the Poor Law and that the education authorities should be entirely responsible for them. Although no legislation followed the deadlock produced by these two irreconcilable reports, the minority report had a profound influence on social thinking and reform, and led over the next 40 years to the emasculation and eventual death of the structure for poor relief as England had known it for 300 years. During the 1920s the Poor Law authorities worked hard to abolish the stigma associated with their name. They pursued the policy of extended boarding-out, removed children from the workhouses, and they provided scattered homes with a central emphasis on the education of the child not as a preparation for work only but, following now national educational trends, related to the aptitudes of the child. As the child's social rights were extended we see the beginning of an understanding of his entitlement to emotional rights too. The heralds of the struggle for emotional rights had also sounded from hidden battlements 50 years or so before when children's literature moved from death-bed scenes and an excess of moralizing into the realms of fantasy and imagination. The nonsense writers—Lear *(A Book of Nonsense* in 1846) and Carroll *(Alice's Adventures in Wonderland* in 1865)—explored in disguised ways the hidden feelings of children about "them", about "authority", about the grown-up world, the muddle of change, and rules and confusing adult values, while the women writers, the true forerunners of our psychologists today, entered into the child's mind and explored his loves and fears and his ability to cope with the task of growing up. "Mrs. Molesworth", said a contemporary literary critic, "is an almost infallible guide to the eccentricities of child nature and analyses the workings of a child's brain in a manner that explains doubts which the child either is incapable of or afraid of attempting." Sometimes, as in Lear's poems, these writers expressed childhood's cry of pain, its feelings of hatred against conformity, and the adult world which rejects their spontaneity. Sometimes they entered without reserve the child's world and indulged in pure delightful fantasy and fun. These were the nineteenth-century public sensitizers, working in hidden ways, while the educationists worked more openly. But true developmental psychology, based on scientific observation of children, was to be a twentieth-century phenomenon.

By the end of the First World War many services previously unified in the Poor Law were becoming diversified and divided among different local authority departments. This was especially true of the new social service which developed for children. The economic distress and unemployment of the twenties and thirties and the financial stringencies of the times gradually reduced the efficiency of the Poor Law care of children. The main developments took place elsewhere—in the reformatory and industrial schools for example, with their extension of the principle of boarding-out of young delinquents and their establishment of a relationship with parents while the boy was still in school. It was these schools which began constructive work to restore the child to his family. Throughout this period of poverty and depression, the falling birth rate was again giving rise to serious alarm about the capacity of the population to maintain itself, and concern was felt about the balance of intelligence and mental health in the population and about juvenile delinquency. These alarms emphasized the importance of the child's psychological development and mental and physical health, and thus brought about an increase and expansion (though not dramatic) in special educational services—school health, school milk and meals, child guidance, special schools, school attendance officers, care of the feeble-minded. The case for family allowances was put forward by Eleanor Rathbone in a book published in 1924. The first child guidance clinic was started in East London in 1927 by a voluntary body, the Jewish Health Organization, and gradually, as the value of the work was established, local education authorities grant-aided similar voluntary bodies or established clinics of their own. The education of blind, deaf, epileptic, and defective children had been provided for by Acts of Parliament in 1893 and 1899, but the Education Act of 1921 imposed on local education authorities the duty of ascertaining the numbers of mentally and physically defective children in their areas and of making special provision for them. The concept of collectivism and community support had begun to grow again as the Poor Law died, and as the concept of entitlement was underlined by the first National Insurance Acts of 1908 and 1911.

Perhaps the most important factor behind the response to the children's services was the development in understanding of their psychology. The growth here was very great and included the work of such different masters as Cyril Burt in the field of psychometrics, and MacDougal, Freud, Jung, and Adler, who, in their individual ways, dealt with the springs of action. The concepts of the American educationist Dewey were also significant; they were introduced into English primary education by Professor Findley of Manchester in his book, *The Children of England*, published in 1923. Dewey held that a democratic society is based on co-operative activity. This led to a liberation of primary education from subject divisions and to an emphasis on projects and learning together through discovery. Piaget's work in Europe drew attention to the manner in which young children think and showed how their thinking differed from the conceptual thought of mature adults. By his work he has helped teachers to relate their teaching to the child's stages of development. The child's nature became truly differentiated from that of adults and respected in its own right. From these seminate thinkers stems the growing literature of child guidance and care today.

Education, therefore, began to be seen as something new—the opposite of adjustment, something which took place in harmony with the developmental stage of the child, emphasizing experience and relationship, a fulfilment of the individual's potential through control of the environment in a vast complex of interactions and relationships. It was in this atmosphere that the Children and Young Persons Act of 1933 was passed, following two departmental committees concerned with young offenders and children in need of care or protection. The 1933 Act forged still closer the link between the work of education authorities and the condition of delinquent and neglected children, placing upon the Education Department a primary duty to intervene in cases of neglect or delinquency, to bring the children before the courts, and to care for them after committal. The courts were therefore seen as instruments of rehabilitation through educational insights rather than instruments of punishment, for the Act contained the memorable words "The Court shall have regard to the welfare of the child". It was this Act, too, which required magistrates to be specially selected for the juvenile court on grounds of experience and interest. Nevertheless, the concept of rehabilitation was limited in that it applied only to the child. There was nothing in the Act to encourage family rehabilitation and support, and this again is a reflection of the poverty of the family social services of that time. Such changes did not come until increasing general economic prosperity, with its underpinning of full employment and social security, bred the realistic hope and expectancy that family and individual difficulties could be overcome and family and individual potentials fulfilled.

This change began, paradoxically, with the Second World War, which, by the widespread disruption of family life by conscription and the evacuation which both preceded and followed aerial bombardment, brought home to the British people the precious value of personal attachment, security and possessive care, so central to family life. The hardships of the war, and the experience of fair sharing by the rationing of the basic necessities of food and clothing, also conditioned the British people to a different outlook, a refusal to go back to conditions which would in any way resemble the poverty and inequalities of the years of depression in the twenties and thirties. Beveridge's plan for social security, adopted by the Cabinet and put into legislation by Attlee's post-war government in 1946, was based upon the idea of "fairer shares" through a redistribution of income by insurance and taxation. The Family Allowances Act of 1945, the National Health Service Act of 1946, and the Education Act of 1944 similarly attempted to provide comprehensive coverage for basic human needs. However, it was left to a private individual, Lady Allen of Hurtwood, who on 15 July 1944 wrote a letter to *The Times* to point out that thoughtful consideration was being given to many fundamental problems, but in reconstruction plans one section of the community had, so far, been entirely forgotten. She referred, of course, to children in public care, and showed that the quality of this care was generations out of date. Further correspondence in *The Times* underlined her case, and called for a government inquiry which was, in fact, precipitated by the death of just such a child: in January 1945 a boy had been removed from his neglectful parents by the courts and committed to the local education authority who had boarded him out in another area. Here he died as a result of lack of proper care. A public inquiry was held and an interdepartmental committee was set up to examine and make recommendations about the public care of children (the Curtis Committee). This committee recommended, on ground of efficiency and better skills and management, a complete re-casting of the legislation and administrative machinery, and led to the passing of the Children Act in 1948. This Act concentrated the relevant powers covering children in public care into one central government department—the Home Office. It set up one specialized committee in each local authority to be known as the Children's Committee with its own specialist children's officer to be responsible for all children removed from their homes whether because the parents were dead or sick or unable to care, or because the children were offenders or in need of care or protection or beyond control. Important and new in the legislation was the emphasis on the natural family and the duty laid for the first time on the local authority to try to restore children received into care to their own families. This duty was a reflection of the better conditions prevailing in the community and the extended family support available because of full employment and rising economic prosperity and the extended social services they made possible. The appointment of specialists to the children's officer posts and the development of departments with staff trained as professional social workers had a dramatic effect upon the direction forms of care were to take. With a professional understanding of the background of deprived children, the service began to move from its protective, child-centred base towards working with the family in order to prevent the need to remove the child from home at all. In 1963 a revolutionary step was taken when the Children and Young Persons Act of that year laid a new duty on local authorities—to make available the sort of advice, guidance, and assistance which could promote the welfare of children by diminishing the need to receive or keep them in care or to bring them before a court. In other words, the Act entitles all children to an experience of good parenthood, and children's departments had to work to ensure this. Since 1963, therefore, the child care service has acquired a preventive emphasis by working with children and parents at home, providing in practice a service for families. This has enabled the problem of deprived children to be contained for the moment. The latest figures of children in care are 70,188 in England and Wales, an increase of 324 over the previous year, compared with 61,580 in 1959. But these figures must be seen in the light of the increasing problems of illegitimacy, juvenile delinquency, migrant population, and drug abuse which are present. The existence of these problems, while the overall standards of living and of education are rising in the country, is a cause for particular concern, and juvenile crime has been the subject of one report—the Longford (Labour Party Study Group) report of 1964—and three White Papers, *Children and Young Persons Scotland* (Cmnd 2306) (Kilbrandon 1964), *The Child, the Family and the Young Offender* (Cmnd 2742, 1965), and *Children in Trouble* (Cmnd 3601, 1968). The proposals in this last White Paper were carefully tested by public opinion and professional conferences before they were finally embodied in the Children and Young Persons Act of 1969. This Act is historic in correlating delinquency with deprivation and ensuring that measures to deal with it should be varied and flexible. The legislation is really a response to the sociological and psychological theories that our physical and emotional well being are vulnerable to environmental hazard, particularly in childhood, and particularly among boys with their longer period of growth in puberty. This Act abolishes the concept of punishable offences for any child under 14 and requires offenders, if parents need help, to be brought before a juvenile court not as offenders but as in need of care and control. Between the ages of 14 and 17 prosecution will take place (except on charges of homicide or other special circumstances) only after consultation and discussion with magistrates, police, probation officers, and social workers. The Act provides that these changes in the law will be brought about in stages at the discretion of the Government. At the time of writing, the "age of criminal responsibility" remains at 10: in other words, children above that age may still be brought before a court as offenders. It is anticipated that this age will rise to 12 during 1973. The approved schools— which had their origins in the enlightened concepts of Mary Carpenter's industrial and reformatory schools—now cease to exist, and children who need to be removed from home can be removed only by committal to the local authority. Provision is made for new kinds of "intermediate" treatment at home, under supervision by social workers, to be used as an intermediate measure between supervision at home and committal to care. The whole pattern of residential care is in future to be planned on a regional basis to meet the needs of regional areas and their children, concerned no longer with custody but with social and psychological diagnosis and plans for help, tailored to the needs of the individual child, and the solution of his problem rather than to the symptoms of his deprivation.

The developments have been immense, the changing responses great. In the nineteenth century three factors lay behind the history of reform in child care: the economic consequences to Britain of a falling birth rate and rising infantile mortality; the fear of unchecked pauperism; and the humanitarianism of the voluntary organizations. The factors operating today can be seen in ideological pressures and the necessity for an educated, rational and informed democracy; our need to check the crippling problems of delinquency; our body of psychological knowledge about the development of children which has recognized their nature and emotional rights and so individualized them, enfranchising them from categorization.

The children's departments with their lay committees were important in the wide dissemination of understanding about deprived and delinquent children and their problems. They stimulated a better public understanding of social and psychological needs and so to a new and enlightened legislative response. Much experiment and research is now needed to find out more about the proper treatment of the child with problems through the provision of appropriate relationships and experience, in harmony with his stage of growth and development.

CHAPTER 2

Supportive Services to the Family

ROBERT HOLMAN*

EDITOR'S INTRODUCTION

As was stated in the introduction to Chapter 1, a multiplicity of
agencies, both statutory and voluntary, grew up over the last century
and dealt sometimes in an *ad hoc* way with various aspects of childhood
and family life. It might be said that these developments came about
during three peak periods: the first was in the last quarter of the reign
of Queen Victoria; the second was after 1918 and through to the years
of the depression in the early 1930s; and the third was in the immediate
post-war period of 1945–50. These three periods were all, of course,
marked by massive social and economic changes which in themselves
affected the functioning of families. As far as social work was concerned all three periods were marked by great activity both in the
statutory and in the voluntary fields, and it is interesting to draw
parallels between 1970 and 1870 when we look at the numbers of new
voluntary societies which were active at both times. When society is
under stress not only does it throw up its problems but it throws up
many new leaders and persons of goodwill who initiate and pioneer
new responses to them.

The result of these periods of change has been the appearance in the
field of child care of new agencies with whom social workers of today
have to relate in some way or another in the course of their daily work.
The work is, of course, much affected by economic changes, patterns
of social security and national insurance, patterns of employment,
utilization of land, and other environmental factors. As Robert

* Lecturer in Social Administration and Social Work, University of Glasgow.

14

Holman says in his opening paragraph, activities which provide support for the family and, indeed, social activities which affect the functioning of the family, are so numerous that it is impossible to record them all in a book of this length. Taking as his basis, therefore, the child care statistics which until reorganization were prepared by the Home Office, Robert Holman has looked at those agencies with which social workers in child care are likely to be most often in touch and whose resources may be of considerable practical value to them in their daily work.

From 1948 to 1971 children's departments had the primary responsibility for children needing—or likely to need—public care. None the less, in various ways other services have worked to support families in their own homes and within the community. Activities which do provide support are so wide and diverse that they could be said to embrace economic services affecting the cost of living, employment prospects, taxation levels, etc., as well as the social services provided by central government, local authorities, and voluntary societies. To pursue this argument would fill the chapter with a catalogue of names and no more, so two decisions have been taken to limit its scope: firstly, arbitrarily to select services for mention, and, secondly, to take as a guide the major reasons why children enter public care and to discuss some of the social services which may help to prevent such breakdown in family life.

Temporary Absence of Mothers

In the year preceding 31 March 1970, 22,845 children (44·3 per cent of the total) were received into care because of temporary absence of a parent, usually the mother.[1] Some mothers had received short-term treatment for mental illness, for recent developments in psychotherapy have decreased the chances of permanent hospitalization while increasing the incidence of short-stay "in-and-out" patients. Other mothers entered hospital for

[1] The source for the statistics relating to 1969–70 in this chapter is *Children in Care in England and Wales, March 1970*, HMSO, London, 1971, unless otherwise stated.

confinement. Of course, many fathers can cope alone for a short period or can call on relatives or friends. But research indicates that certain vulnerable families lack these capacities and resources.[2]

The social services can sometimes operate to prevent the development of these situations which cause mothers to leave home. Skilled social work may relieve the pressures on some mothers vulnerable to mental illness. Local authorities have a responsibility under the Mental Health Act 1959 to provide services for the mentally disordered and, in particular, employ mental welfare officers to give reality to a policy of care within the community rather than in institutions. They may also run day care and training centres as well as hostels, though development in these directions is still slow. Unfortunately, referrals to social workers are often made only when entry to hospital is imminent, while the number of qualified officers in post has not kept pace with that in other branches of social work.

Hospitalization due to pregnancy or physical illness can sometimes be averted by home care from midwives and home nurses employed by local authority health departments. They do not function as social workers nor for child care, but the resultant presence of the mother at home may encourage the father to cope. The availability of such personnel varies throughout the country as the Seebohm report made clear.

Domestic help is made available by local authorities in the form of home helps. Theoretically such help could enable fathers to keep their children at home, but in practice home helps work mainly with the elderly, while one study showed that most parents of children received into short-term care were ignorant of their existence or found their rigid hours "an insuperable obstacle".[3] A recent government report, *The Home Help Service in England and Wales*, shows that not only could it be expanded to two or three times its present level but that astonishing disparities of provision occur between local authorities.

Even if services fail to keep children at home all day, they may prevent longer separations. Local authorities may maintain day nurseries where fathers can leave pre-school children while they are at work. These will be discussed later but it is worth noting, firstly, that the unpredictable nature

---

[2] H. Schaffer and E. Schaffer, *Child Care and the Family*, Occasional Papers in Social Administration, Bell, London, 1968.
[3] *Ibid.*

of short-term absences makes it difficult to line up vacancies at already overcrowded day nurseries and, secondly, that voluntary societies are beginning to initiate day care centres. Unable to get official help, father may turn to daily minders—who care privately for children for payment—or to neighbours. Even here the social services are involved, as doubts have been cast on the quality of many daily minders,[4] so it is fortunate that local authorities have a duty to supervise them. The strengthening of neighbourhood ties with a consequent readiness to help others can result from community activities. One voluntary body, an adventure playground in a "twilight" zone, reports that mothers drawn together through the play needs of their children stepped in to help when one mother deserted her family.

Desertion by Mothers

By taking time off work, father may cope temporarily, but the strains become intense over a long period. Maternal desertion frequently means long-term or permanent family break-up, and in 1969–70 some 5241 children (10·2 per cent of the total) were received into care for this reason.

The possible serious effects on children of long-term separation makes preventive work even more important. As many desertions appear to stem from unsatisfactory marital relationships, the supporting services logically should offer aid before the final break occurs. Where mental illness contributes to marital disharmony, mental welfare officers and, where available, psychiatric treatment through hospital out-patient departments, may help. More general marital casework is provided by the voluntary marriage guidance councils and by probation officers. Psychological therapy is not the only means of strengthening a marriage. Sometimes financial or housing hardships are the weights breaking the relationship bonds. Sometimes coping with children, especially a large family, impose too many strains. In these circumstances, pre-school play groups provide not only stimulation for children but also a break for their mothers, possibly spent away from the confines of overcrowded homes and in the

[4] S. Yudkin, *0–5, A Report on the Care of Pre-school Children,* National Society of Children's Nurseries, London, 1967.

company of other women. The Pre-school Play-groups Association has encouraged growth, but statutory bodies have no duty to maintain play groups. Even voluntary ones are frequently concentrated in middle-class suburbs although one body, the Priority Areas Playgroups Project, promotes them in "twilight" areas.

A mother having deserted on a long-term basis, the supportive services are hard pushed to keep the child with the remaining parent. Day nurseries can cope daily with pre-school children, but once at school a time gap exists between the hour school ends and the father's return from work. Occasionally, a father remains at home and acts as mother while drawing income from state benefits. However, many will need to work for social and psychological as well as economic motives. Further, there is pressure from society, and perhaps from officials of the Supplementary Benefits Commission, on fathers not to be dependent on the state.

Illegitimate Children

"Child illegitimate, mother unable to provide a home" accounted for 2709 receptions into care (5·2 per cent of the total) in 1969–70. Presumably most, although not all, of the mothers were unmarried. In regard to preventive work, the role of the supporting services appears twofold: to prevent unwanted births occurring and to enable mothers, who so wish, to keep their children rather than relinquishing them to public care.

Local authorities have powers both to give contraceptive help directly to the unmarried and to finance voluntary bodies like the Family Planning Association and the Brook advisory centres. However, evidence suggests that the use of these powers varies widely throughout the country. Theoretically, abortions can be obtained in certain circumstances under the National Health Service, but in practice they are obtained far more easily in some parts of the country than in others.

Before and following birth, social workers from the Church's diocesan councils for moral welfare or, less frequently, from local authority departments, may help expectant mothers decide whether to keep their children or to place them for adoption. Those who opt for the former will require adequate financial income, reasonable accommodation, and—if they desire or need to work—day care for the children. Studies suggest that many unsupported mothers lack all these,[5] but the present section will concentrate on the provision of day care.

Day care reduces the possibility of a permanent break between mothers and children by relieving pressures on the mothers while enabling them to receive social and economic benefits from employment. Local authority pre-school day care may be in the form of day nurseries, which have already been mentioned, or the Education Department's nursery schools and classes which cater for children between 3 and 5 years of age. In one study unsupported mothers were found to be most satisfied with the standards of these forms of care,[6] so it is unfortunate that they are in short supply. The numbers of day nurseries in England and Wales has actually declined from 1431 in 1945 to 445 in 1968.[7] Further, regional provision varies greatly from nearly 20 places per 1000 population to none at all.[8] No doubt single mothers receive preferential treatment from day nurseries; even so, in 1967 in Birmingham some 290 "priority" cases were still on the waiting lists. Nursery school places are equally hard to come by and as erratically distributed, with nearly every nursery school having a waiting list longer than its school roll.[9] The consequent difficulties in obtaining official day care combined with the short hours and short terms of nursery schools cause many mothers to turn to the private market. Usually unable to afford private nurseries or schools, they use daily minders. As indicated before, the worst of these may emotionally harm children, and it is the unsupported mothers—because of their low incomes—who are likely to use the worst.

The National Council for the Unmarried Mother and her Child and other voluntary bodies have long campaigned on behalf of illegitimate children and their mothers. But the record of the supporting services is still

[5] R. Holman, *Unsupported Mothers and the Day Care of their Children*, Mothers in Action, London, 1970.

[6] *Ibid.*

[7] This was stated by the then Minister of Health in March 1968, and is quoted in *Parliament and Social Work*, April 1968.

[8] J. Packman, *Child Care: Needs and Numbers*, Allen & Unwin, London, 1968, and T. Ryan, *Day Nursery Provision under the Health Service, England and Wales, 1948–1963*, National Society of Children's Nurseries, London, 1964.

[9] See both the Seebohm and Plowden reports for statistics relating to nursery school places.

not impressive, one reason being that powers to meet the needs of unsupported mothers have been distributed amongst too many departments. The result is that not infrequently a mother gives up after a few years. The child thus misses both an adoptive home from birth and a permanent relationship with his mother.

Homelessness

Some 2693 children (5·2 per cent of the total) were received into public care in 1969–70 because of their families' homelessness. Their plight is obviously associated with the availability of housing, but as Derek Stroud points out in *Penelope Hall's Social Services of England and Wales*,[10] it is also frequently associated with poverty. Greve, for instance, found that the homeless in London in 1961–2 largely could not afford accommodation spacious enough for children.[11] Parents unable to maintain rent payments have been evicted and their children taken into care. Further, both financial and housing deprivation can cause or aggravate relationship difficulties which end in family break-ups. It follows that the role of the supporting services is to ensure adequate income as well as accommodation.

The main bulwark against poverty is the Government's social security system, administered by the Department of Health and Social Security, which has three main wings. Firstly, family allowances, financed by the Government, are paid to all families for second and succeeding children. Secondly, the National Insurance scheme is intended to provide income during interruptions of earnings and particular "risk" periods such as sickness, unemployment, disablement, widowhood, and retirement. Benefits are also available for orphans, while maternity, death, and—in certain circumstances—redundancy payments are also made. The scheme is financed by contributions from the state, employers, and individuals. Originally, contributions were on a flat-rate basis, all persons paying and receiving equal amounts. The 1959 and 1966 National Insurance Acts introduced earnings selected pensions and supplements to other benefits combined with graduated contributions. A government scheme, effective from 1972, will guide benefits and contributions according to individuals'

[10] Edited A. Forder, Routledge and Kegan Paul, London, 1969.

[11] See J. Greve, *London's Homeless*, Occasional Papers in Social Administration, Codicote Press, Welwyn, 1964.

earnings and standard of living. For a discussion of the scheme the reader is referred to Lafitte.[12] Thirdly, the Supplementary Benefits Commission gives assistance to those not qualifying for insurance benefit or whose income, even with it, does not reach a "subsistence" level. Unlike National Insurance, which depends only on the payment of sufficient contributions, supplementary benefit involves a means test with payments according to defined scales plus the cost of rates and a "reasonable" rent. Officials also have discretionary power concerning grants for extra expenditure on clothes, furniture, etc.

Financial deprivation is further modified by central and local government schemes for subsidized or free welfare foods for pre-school children, subsidized or free school meals and school maintenance and clothing grants according to assessed need. Legal aid and council rent and rate rebates are sometimes available after a means test. Lastly, a multitude of voluntary societies and trusts may give financial help to individuals although usually of a limited nature.

The social security system admirably attempts to give comprehensive coverage while recognizing that children require extra financial support. However, it can be criticized at a number of points. Firstly, some writers believe that the level of family allowances is too low to affect radically the position of the poor. Brown wrote in 1969[12a] that they "had fallen in value, relatively, and . . . failed to meet the additional costs of keeping a child". Secondly, the insurance system, far from being universal, excludes those who have made insufficient contributions or outrun entitlement. Substantial numbers therefore have recourse to supplementary benefit which, to many, smacks of charity. Thirdly, the levels of supplementary benefits are open to the criticism that, although sufficient for a temporary crisis, they are inadequate for long-term dependence as with unsupported mothers and some unemployed. As Marsh says,[13] the levels seem directed "at the right to exist rather than to live the full life". Fourthly, complaints are sometimes made that officials use the discretionary powers in very diverse ways, that

[12] F. Lafitte, in R. Holman (ed.), *Socially Deprived Families in Britain*, Bedford Square Press, 1970.

[12a] In M. Brown, *Introduction to Social Administration in Britain*, Hutchinson, London, 1969.

[13] In D. Marsh, *The Future of the Welfare State*, Penguin, London, 1964.

they do not inform claimants of all the grants available, and that they display condemnatory attitudes. Fifthly, research has established that extensive numbers of families still receive an income below the minimum of supplementary benefit. They include those who do not avail themselves of benefit, those whose earned wage is below this level, and those subjected to the wage stop. The wage stop is applied to recipients of benefit where the level of benefit would have given them more than their normal earnings. It can be concluded that, although Britain has an extensive social security system, some families can still be left with very low incomes. The consequences can impair their prospects of decent accommodation and affect their social functioning in a host of other ways.

Turning to housing services, Brown points out that in England and Wales some 46 per cent of dwellings are owner-occupied, 28 per cent local authority owned, and 21 per cent privately rented. The central government makes little direct provision—save through the setting up of new towns— but it still has enormous influence. Its economic policies affect interest and mortgage rates, it sets council housing standards, and provides loans and subsidies for local authority building programmes.

Local authorities have a general responsibility of meeting housing need and abating overcrowding. Their housing departments not only provide dwellings but can also give grants to improve privately owned and rented accommodation. The local authority responsibility to cater for homeless families is discharged through social service departments. Homelessness frequently arises from non-payment of rent, and some housing departments employ housing welfare officers to work with tenants who get into arrears, others have an "early warning" system which refers them to other departments with caseworkers on hand to help.

Private tenants have benefited least from housing services, but during the mid 1960s machinery was installed to determine—on request—the rents of some tenancies. Legislation has also given some security against eviction without a court order for tenants of unfurnished and, for a limited period, of furnished accommodation.

Although the contribution of voluntary bodies in regard to direct housing provision is comparatively small, mention must be made of the increasing number of housing associations and societies, many of which cater for "needy" groups. Housing advisory centres have also been established, while Shelter has run enormous publicity campaigns both to convince society of the extent of housing deprivation and to raise money for the voluntary providers.

The housing services have made advances in reducing overcrowding, clearing slums, and providing accommodation. None the less, the distribution and extent of housing deprivation still handicaps many families. Spencer[14] demonstrates the great variability between local authorities in regard to council house building, methods of allocating dwellings and fixing their rents, and in use of powers to improve privately owned property. The progressive policies of some authorities towards the homeless and travellers must be contrasted with the almost barbaric methods of others.[15] It is Spencer who also draws attention to the fact that of a housing stock in England and Wales in 1967 of 15·7 million dwellings over 1·8 million were "unfit for human habitation". Over a quarter lacked some basic housing amenity. This type of housing becomes the lot of those with low incomes, the unsupported mothers, and the large families. Unable to afford the rents of reasonable private property or the deposit for a mortgage, often with little hope of council housing which is frequently allocated on the basis of a long residential qualification (or even according to housekeeping standards) rather than need; they may well end up in overcrowded, multi-occupied private rented property, sub-standard council housing, or hostels for the homeless. In short, many families still find themselves in the very conditions most likely to foster family break up.

Unsatisfactory Care of Children

Some 3074 children were received into care in 1969–70 because of "unsatisfactory home conditions", while another 3357 were committed through the courts not being offenders against the law (together they amounted to 12·4 per cent of the receptions into care). Amongst them were cases where the parents were unable to give the material, social, and emotional conditions which society deems a minimum for children. Supporting services exist to help the internal functioning of families so that neither the

[14] In R. Holman, *op cit.*

[15] See J. Packman, *op cit.*, and N. Swingler, Move on, Gypsy, *New Society*, 26 June 1969.

care given nor the behaviour of the children will warrant removal. Even where this objective is not achieved they may work to prepare the families for the children's return.

Many people requiring help from health, educational, and welfare services are in no way likely to part with their children. Yet as such families as those described above are particularly prone to sickness, physical handicap, and educational problems, it is as well to mention some agencies providing more general services. For instance, local authority social service, education departments, and voluntary bodies maintain homes, schools, and hostels for various forms of handicap. For many children the fact of attending special residential schools and returning home in the holidays means they do not experience the finality of a legal break sometimes associated with reception into the care of a social service department. Unfortunately, there exist long waiting lists for places at schools for the educationally sub-normal and the maladjusted. The same departments also emphasize "community care" with medical, recreational, and occupational activities designed to enable recipients to remain in their own homes. Generally speaking these services are not extensively developed, so the contributions of voluntary societies, outstanding examples being the Royal National Institute for the Blind and the Spastics Society, are as necessary as ever.

The departments frequently recognize that some families do require help of a more personal nature, help that works through individual relationships. No one local authority department has full responsibility for a casework service to families in difficulties, but specific needs, such as mentioned above, may well bring them into contact with departments who respond with a personal service for families with extra problems. Two examples must suffice: health departments employ health visitors who mainly concentrate on helping mothers with post-natal care of young children but frequently spend disproportionate time with more vulnerable families; education departments have educational welfare officers to visit homes of children with prolonged absences from school or who display other educational problems stemming from family circumstances. Three points must be made about these officers. Firstly, there is some debate whether they should attempt a casework service. The health visitor has been described as the "all purpose medico-social worker in the home where she should act for all departments of the local authority in any way concerned with health and welfare",[16] but the social work professions (and some health visitors) would see their role as having a medical rather than a casework orientation. Education welfare officers are still trying to escape from the shadow of their authoritarian predecessors—the school attendance officers. Secondly, doubts are expressed concerning their ability to give a casework service. Health visitors are not trained caseworkers, while the proportion of professionally qualified educational welfare officers is low. Thirdly, figures published with the Seebohm report indicate that the distribution of these workers per 1000 population varies greatly between authorities. Despite these limitations they are strategically placed, health visitors seeing all children under 5 years old and educational welfare officers having access to homes with school problems. They can therefore pick up symptoms of family malfunctioning and, if unable to provide a casework service themselves, can refer to an appropriate agency at an early stage.

The record of a number of voluntary bodies specializing in working with families whose child rearing and social behaviour patterns provoke society to intervene, is impressive. In a number of towns, family service units undertake intensive work through close relationships with a small number of families. Emphasis has been on helping emotional and practical problems through casework skills, but increasingly units encompass community work skills. Haringey Family Service Unit is a pace-setter which utilizes families' strengths by involving them in the agency's policy decisions. A family welfare association operates in a number of urban areas with caseworkers taking referrals from a large number of sources. The National Society for the Prevention of Cruelty to Children is shedding its "cruelty man" image as it dons a family casework mantle. Occasionally residential centres, such as Crowley House in Birmingham, link training in child care and home management for mothers accompanied by their children (and, in some centres, by husbands) with a casework service.

Once again it has to be reported that the benefits of voluntary enterprise are restricted to a number of favoured areas. Some large cities are without a family service unit or family welfare agency. The National Society for the Prevention of Cruelty to Children, as Packman shows, has comparatively few workers in the large, urban complex of the Midlands. Consequently,

[16] AMC, *Municipal Review*, Supplement 1954, quoted in J. Parker, *Local Health and Welfare Services*, Allen & Unwin, London, 1965.

many families in need lack the services and skills available to their counter-
parts in other areas.

Delinquency

An offence against the law accounted for the committal to the care of
children's departments of 1641 children (3 per cent of the total) in 1969–70.
This by no means represents all those separated from their families by a
court order. Others were sent to approved schools, detention centres, etc.,
without coming into the care of local authorities.

It is increasingly recognized that delinquency is but one symptom of
family malfunctioning or environmental deficiencies in society. It follows
that all the social services—in so far as they promote healthy functioning and
reduce social injustices—are a means of preventing delinquency. Services
to aid healthy child socialization in early years are particularly important in
areas of urban decay where children suffer so many social disadvantages. In
addition to play-groups, day nurseries, and nursery education, already discussed, adventure playgrounds, unattached youth workers, and youth clubs
can give stimulating experiences for children of various ages. The availability of these amenities leaves much to be desired. The Inner London
Education Authority's progressive policy of guaranteeing financial support
for established adventure playgrounds has to be contrasted with the one
playground in Glasgow and the two in Birmingham. The position of the
youth service in general has recently been discussed in the official report
Youth and Community Work in the 70's, while unattached youth work is in
but its infancy.

Conviction by a court does not necessarily lead to removal from home.
Probation officers, who are "servants of the courts", have long maintained
a casework service supervising probationers within the community. This
probation and after-care service has overlapped with children's departments
for both have taken children under supervision orders and carried out
approved school after-care. Now the Children and Young Persons Act
1969 has transferred more functions to the local authorities. Probation
officers will concentrate increasingly on older teenagers and adults, including parole supervision and prison welfare work. By helping adults whose
own detention could lead to their children being received into care or

whose pattern of life might pass on patterns of delinquent behaviour to their children, probation officers will still be fulfilling a preventive role.

This canter through the social services has left many gaps: hardly a word about education, little about the hospital, general practioner, and environmental aspects of health. Employment services have not been covered although the possibility of increasing earning capacity is of utmost importance to those in poverty. The writer can but refer those needing more information to the sources mentioned in the footnotes and in the suggestions for further reading at the end of this book, and conclude with some topical and general points about the supporting social services.

This chapter has stressed the differences in the availability of services—both voluntary and local authority—between various areas. Consequently, prospects of receiving adequate help often depend upon the chance of a person's residence rather than on his need. Frequently the distribution of services appears to bear no correlation with measurements of need; indeed, the reverse may be true. In particular, the north-east, the west Midlands, and a number of boroughs in the north-west appear at a severe disadvantage in terms of needs and resources compared with London and the south-east. Nor are deficiencies in one service compensated by strengths in another, nor local authority weaknesses by voluntary enterprise.

Some families are under-served because adequate services are not available. Others do not avail themselves of benefits intended for them. Evidence shows that many who are eligible do not claim rate rebates, welfare foods, educational grants, medical prescription reimbursements, legal aid, and rent reductions. Feelings of shame about means-tested benefits, ignorance of rights (often due to inadequate publicity), complicated application procedures, and even off-putting attitudes from officials, can prevent take-up, so reducing the effectiveness of services for the family. Undoubtedly, two of the greatest challenges facing policy makers is to devise means of equalizing the availability of services and enabling people to use them.

It is now recognized that families most in need of services are frequently concentrated in definable geographical locations characterized by old property, overcrowding, a lack of play space, high incidence of delinquency and child separation, and relatively high numbers of immigrants, unskilled workers, large and fatherless families. Concentration has one advantage—it makes possible the allocation of extra social resources to such areas. Accordingly, the Government's urban programme, educational priority areas, and community development projects have attempted to maximize the efficiency of educational, welfare, and health services in deprived areas. To date the priority programmes are small in expenditure and number, but their initiation indicates a promising new approach.

The continuance and expansion of voluntary bodies constitute a remarkable feature of the contemporary Welfare State. Traditional bodies have continued their work while sometimes changing their emphasis. The national children's societies, for instance, have developed boarding-out while continuing their residential facilities. New bodies have been born. Outstanding is the Child Poverty Action Group which rapidly became a national pressure group speaking for families in poverty. These developments continue the tradition of British voluntary work. Other publications classify and discuss such societies;[17] here three new and less-traditional developments will be noted.

Firstly, youth movements concerned to serve others—at home and abroad—have grown rapidly. Community Service Volunteers, International Voluntary Service, and Voluntary Service Overseas are well-established examples, while more recently the government-sponsored Young Volunteer Force has added a "whizz-kid" version. Youngsters have eagerly decorated for the elderly, supported the mentally ill, and undertaken a host of projects. If, at one time, a colonial air pervaded the movements—white socks and Oxbridge accents distributing middle-class goods to the heathen—a healthy reaction has occurred. Simultaneously, many students have turned to community service. Student Community Action, manned full-time by former students, not only stimulates community involvement but is prepared to analyse its principles and practice often with a firm commitment to the deprived.

Secondly, in deprived areas community action or self-help groups have arisen to provide services and promote radical change. Participants are to be distinguished from traditional volunteers who attach themselves to established voluntary or statutory bodies as described in the Aves report.[18] They

---

[17] For instance, Central Office of Information, *Social Services in Britain*, HMSO, London, various dates.

[18] *The Voluntary Worker in the Social Services*, Allen & Unwin, and Bedford Square Press, London, 1969.

are residents or persons fully identified with residents, often politically involved, who regard improvements to their neighbourhoods as a right and form self-governing bodies to achieve their objectives by militant methods if necessary. The various activities in Notting Hill are well known, but other groups have mushroomed often basing themselves on one activity like an adventure playground or tenants' association. The growth of the latter has been especially rapid, usually on council estates and tenement blocks which form natural units for organization, rather than amongst the private tenants of houses.

With the boom in community action, professional community workers have been more in evidence, stimulating growth. Although needed, they may bring some dangers. Community workers, wishing to justify their existence, and often attached to short-term projects for which they feel they must get results, sometimes undertake a "numbers" policy, creating as many playgrounds and groups as possible without the impetus coming from local residents. A powerful and articulate community worker is as likely to impose his or her standards on a neighbourhood as a caseworker on a client.

In what ways do these groups support families in need? By enabling members to obtain more control over their environments they enhance the quality of life in neighbourhoods as well as encouraging action by individual families. Further, they constitute a voice for sections of the community who are rarely heard. Parker puts forward the view that voluntary bodies and local government are desirable in order to prevent a concentration of power in central government. But it may well be that Members of Parliament, councillors, higher civil servants, local government officers, and members of traditional voluntary bodies consist of persons from similar backgrounds and with similar attitudes who are not representative of society as a whole. Community action groups can be a voice for the deprived, representing their interests and winning services which they think appropriate to their families and areas.

A third feature has been the development of client or consumer organizations. The Birmingham Claimants Union, for those in receipt of social security benefit, and Mothers in Action, composed of unsupported mothers, have led the way both in their rapid growth of membership and their militant frame of mind. Mainly, they operate to improve existing services to families. For instance, they ensure members get their full rights by advocating for them before supplementary appeals tribunals, rent officers, etc. In addition they constitute group support for members with similar problems.

Implicit in the work of community action groups and client organizations is the intention to create societal changes, especially in the power structure controlling the social services and other resources. Herein is an alternative philosophy to that which underlies much contemporary social work. For running through much of the latter is the assumption that deprivation springs from individual inadequacies. Brown writes: "But some families do not seem able to take full advantage of the services offered and despite the basic provision they do fall into poverty and sickness . . . sometimes it is, in a sense, the fault of the families."[19] The answer, it is concluded, is for even better services to enable families to function more effectively, and so benefit. However, another view is that poverty inheres less in individual families, but, to quote Kramer, "in the social and economic systems and persisting because of the 'powerlessness' of the poor".[20] The deduction is that the poor or deprived will only change their situation as they organize and win power for themselves.

A significant feature of present-day social services in general, Parker points out, is the desire to preserve family relationships. This chapter has examined various services in relation to preventing family break-ups caused by children being received into care. Even the short comments offered on each of the services serve to demonstrate that in terms of distribution, outreach, and availability, they have many limitations. Fortunately, the services—be they central, local, or voluntary—are experiencing the dynamic of change. New functions have been taken on, existing services improved, and their overall organization thrown into the melting pot. Significantly, the changes arise not only from the greater attention given to their structure by the Government and social work bodies but also by non-professionals. Volunteers, residents of socially deprived areas, clients, are indicating that their voices must be heeded concerning the social policy decisions which so affect their own families. Their involvement threatens the existing power structure of the social services, so that the resolution of their demands remains a question to be settled in the next decade.

[19] M. Brown, *op. cit.*

[20] R. Kramer, *Participation of the Poor*, Prentice-Hall, 1969.

CHAPTER 3

Personal Service to the Family

PAULINE HAMMOND, APSW*

EDITOR'S INTRODUCTION

In the previous chapters some account has been given of those influences—in part historical, in part economical/geographical—which create the environment in which the social worker operates and of whose influence he should be aware. Nevertheless, as a social worker, while he may have a responsibility to comment upon these environmental factors affecting families and children and perhaps do his best to change them where they appear to be deleterious, he will in the mainstream of his work be using his own personal skills and qualities to help the individual person who may be in need. One of the traditional tools of the social worker has been "casework". Many books have been written on the nature of casework itself, the casework relationship, the techniques which are used, and so on; and while at one time casework with an individual client was considered to be the only tool available to the social worker, much thought has been devoted more recently to other techniques such as group work and community work. The one common element to all these techniques, however, is the way in which the social worker can use his own personality in a conscious and planned way to effect change in the client and change in the client's immediate environment as measured by a pattern of relationships. Pauline Hammond singles out those principal elements in the casework process which the social worker will need to harness and to use in whatever milieu he operates, irrespective of the social factors. However much our society may change and however rapidly group work and community work may

* Senior Adviser (Training), Social Work Services Group, Edinburgh.

31

develop, it is likely that personal service to the family and to the individual member of the family will remain the social worker's primary and unique responsibility. At this stage in this book we begin to move towards the study of that immediately personal involvement.

(Views expressed in this chapter are not necessarily the views of the Social Work Services Group in which Miss Hammond is a senior adviser.)

In Britain personal social services to the family have grown up in response to the need for specialist services for its individual members. A child in need would, between 1948 and 1971, have been referred to a children's department; the social problems of a sick member to a medical or psychiatric social worker; a delinquent to a probation officer. Increasingly, over the past 15 years or so, social workers working in different situations have come to realize that, whilst the service for which they had had a particular kind of preparation had certain aspects which were peculiar to that service, the basic principles of social work and the body of theory from which it derives, its knowledge and expertise, are fundamentally common to social work wherever it happens to be practised. This realization has been reflected in patterns of training, and there has been an increasing move to teach on newly designed generic courses the basic principles of social work which were a common element in specialist courses and, in addition, to provide within such a course learning opportunities in the skills needed in practising social work in different settings.

Gradually, legislation has also reflected new thinking, and the Local Authority Social Services Act 1970 (relating to services in England and Wales) and the Social Work (Scotland) Act 1968, both represent a restructuring of the ways in which families can obtain the help they need from a body of people who share the same basic professional ethics, knowledge, and skills, viz. the profession of social work.

That social work is a new and developing profession, that there are still large numbers of people within it who have not undergone the appropriate training, does not invalidate the objectives of the profession which are accepted by it as a whole and for which, increasingly, suitable training is demanded.

In the past, services have been provided through a large number of agencies, statutory and voluntary—e.g. the children's department of a local authority, a social work department of a hospital, or an independent organization such as the Family Welfare Association. Statutes reflected the piecemeal growth of personal social services and often defined function quite rigidly. The Social Work (Scotland) Act 1968 illustrates the new approach: section 12(i): "It shall be the duty of every local authority to promote social welfare by making available advice, guidance and assistance on such a scale as may be appropriate for their area, and in that behalf to make arrangements and to provide or secure the provision of such facilities (including the provision or arranging for the provision of residential and other establishments) as they may consider suitable and adequate. ..."

The form in which people expressed their needs was often determined by the legislative framework in which services were offered. New legislation has not yet been in operation long enough for us to see new patterns, but the following may give some idea of the range of problems which come to social workers: social needs in relation to housing or finance, problems associated with the effects of ill health—mental or physical; difficulties which may occur following situations of deprivation, e.g. a child whose parents cannot care for him, an elderly person with no relations; people who are unable to meet the demands of society—the delinquent, the deviant; and people whose difficulties show themselves primarily as problems of interpersonal relationships—marital problems, a rejected child, a "wayward" adolescent, or a "difficult" elderly person. In practice clients' difficulties are seldom confined to one area of their lives, and usually there is a combination of factors involved.

If we examine the methods of help which are available we find that in Britain the most highly developed method of social work help is that known as social casework, but in the last few years the use of social group-work method is becoming increasingly important and is now normally included on most training courses. Community work as a method of social work is still more talked about than carried out, but over the next few years one would expect to see a greater interest developing in this method of work. In the United States casework, group work, and community work have in the past been seen as three separate specialist branches of social-work method, but in Britain it seems to be fairly generally accepted that the basic principles of social work are common to each method of work, and training patterns reflect this assumption.

For the purpose of the remainder of this chapter, reference will be made to the method of social casework on the assumption that the basic approach, knowledge, and attitude of social workers are shared by all, whichever method of practice they use, although, of course, the choice of method will be affected by the kind of problem to be tackled, the setting in which it occurs, and the knowledge, skill, and experience of the individual social worker.

Social casework is a method of offering help to people in which the relationship made with the client is the main medium through which the diagnosis and treatment of the problem is carried out. The sorts of communication which occur during an interview of this kind are very varied: verbal communication (including the manner in which this is conveyed and also what is not said); non-verbal (facial expression, gesture, etc.); behaviour during the interview (manifestation of aggression, distress, etc.); and what is technically called the "transference" phenomenon. This means the transfer of expectations, attitudes, and behaviour from an earlier life situation, sometimes inappropriately, to the here and now. The phenomenon occurs to us all at times, particularly when we are in a situation of stress. The more emotionally mature the person the less likely is transference to occur to a marked extent, but the social worker uses such evidence as a means of identifying and understanding the client's problems. For example, a client's earlier experiences of authority figures—parents, teachers, and so on—may be transferred to all people who may appear to him to carry an authoritarian role, and his expectation and reaction may occur regardless of the reality of the situation.

The social worker will handle the relationship with the client in a variety of ways—sometimes by observing and using such observations to help him/her to understand the client's problems; sometimes by encouraging the client to see for himself what is happening in the interview situation; and sometimes by making direct transference interpretations, i.e. verbalizing for the client what seems to be taking place between him and the social worker which had its origins elsewhere. Such techniques are designed to help the client to develop self-awareness, which will in certain circumstances be a necessary first step if he is to be able to overcome some of his problems of relationships with other people.

Other clients may need an experience of a certain kind of relationship as a first step to growing emotionally. For example, an adult client who has had childhood experiences in which he was very deprived of affection and security, may need, for a time, to experience a dependent relationship with a social worker before he can begin to function as a responsible adult.

Not all clients need, or could benefit from, "insight-giving" procedures, but the social worker will still be alert to what is going on so that he/she can help in the most appropriate way. For example a client who needs help with financial problems and who is also an immature and dependent person is unlikely to be able to plan to solve his problems in the same way as a very independent but penurious elderly person. It may be that the social worker will have to meet some of the dependency needs of the first client and to help the latter to see that acceptance of help does not necessarily mean a confession of failure before either is able to begin to look at ways of overcoming the problems which brought each to the social worker in the first place.

When offering a personal social service there are three main factors to be taken into account: the role of the family in society; the uniqueness of the individual; and the interaction between the individual, his family, and the society in which he lives. By definition, then, the social worker is immediately faced with a situation of conflict in which the needs, rights, power, or opinion of an individual may clash with those of other members of his family, or where a pattern of family functioning may be at variance with the norms of the society in which it operates. Furthermore, in Britain, almost without exception, social workers operate within an agency setting (a local authority service, a hospital, a voluntary organization), and they are, therefore, responsible for carrying out the policy of the agency which employs them. This can be difficult at times: for example, a hospital whose primary task is to cure or alleviate illness will not always define the needs of a patient and his family in the same terms or in the same order of priority as a social worker; a community worker may be endeavouring to help a group of local people to become critical of and to take action against the agency which employs him.

If one sees the social worker's job as being concerned with change, one must ask in which direction such change should aim—to meet the need of the individual? To maintain group cohesion? To uphold the values of the society in which both client and social worker live? Consider the example of a family living in an area in which a wide range of delinquent behaviour forms part of the norms of that neighbourhood. As a social worker should one be trying to change behaviour so that it conforms to the standard of society as a whole? In such a case, if one were successful, the client would then be seen as deviant within the subculture in which he operates. Should one seek to help an individual to readjust his way of life? In so doing he may then be placed in a position of conflict with the value system of his family. Should one then seek to change the values of society as a whole? This raises much wider issues and demands knowledge and skills for which the social worker is not necessarily employed or trained.

Consider the needs of a family in which one member suffers from a chronic mental illness. Conflict is inherent in that the needs of the sick member, his wife, his children, and perhaps the neighbourhood, will not coincide. Which of the conflicting needs should take precedence? In which direction should change be orientated? In the past the service within which a social worker operated to some extent defined the task. If one was employed by a hospital the patient was the prime focus; if by a children's department it was the child; and so on. This gave guide lines (although social workers were also only too well aware of this limitation of goal and function). Section 12 of the Social Work (Scotland) Act 1968 quoted above, no longer allows such nice, neat solutions to what are inherent problems of conflict, and decisions about their resolution will now be firmly laid in the lap of social workers and the local authorities which employ them. It is, therefore, even more important that we continue to develop a body of soundly based concepts which can guide us to ask the right questions of ourselves, to use the cumulative knowledge and skill of others, and to test out and evaluate the effectiveness of work done.

Social work is not, of course, the only profession which offers personal service to families: teachers, lawyers, doctors, and many others have their particular contribution to make. What is peculiar to social work is the wide theoretical framework from which it draws its knowledge and the specialized way in which that knowledge is used. Perhaps as a social worker one really does attempt to see people as a whole, operating within a complex network of relationships, expectations, and pressures which is the hallmark of an advanced industrialized society.

There are five main disciplines from which we draw our concepts: social administration, sociology, psychology, medicine, and psychiatry. The first two are concerned with the structure and fabric of our society and their effects, e.g. on the child-rearing practices, the educational system, housing policy, employment policy, and so on. Psychology and psychiatry are concerned with the norms and the deviances of human behaviour, their methods of assessment and evaluation, and, where appropriate, with the treatment of people who are defined as "sick". Medicine enables us to identify norms of physical growth and behaviour and defines malfunctioning and malformation.

One of the problems of drawing from a multi-disciplinary framework is to keep abreast of new knowledge, to identify what might be of value to the practice of social work, and then to see that it is applied appropriately. There was a time when social workers valued the knowledge derived from psychoanalysis so highly that they also adopted its methods in a rather uncritical way when applying it in a social work context. As a result, concentration on a client's intra-psychic problems was so great that at times there was a tendency to ignore other kinds of difficulty in his life situation. Today there is a far greater awareness of the importance of knowledge derived from sociology and psychology as well, and the balance is more rounded. Naturally some practitioners have a leaning more in one direction than in another, and, indeed, some problems are more susceptible to study and resolution within one theoretical framework than within another. What is important is that social workers are sufficiently familiar with a variety of approaches to enable them to explore, assess, and operate over a wide area of knowledge and skill.

Social work owes much to the concepts derived from a variety of other disciplines, but it has also developed a body of knowledge and techniques of its own. It is only relatively recently, however, that attempts have been made to define, test out, and validate hypotheses in a rigorous and systematic way. This is an essential step in the development of a body of theory from which future growth—both conceptual and applied—can be derived, and this academic discipline is the hallmark of a soundly based discipline. Florence Hollis[1] has attempted to classify the process of the relationship

[1] Florence Hollis, *Social Casework—A Psycho-social Theory*, Random House, New York, 1960.

between the client and the social worker, e.g. the use of such techniques as sustaining or supporting the client, helping him to ventilate feelings, clarification of the situation with the client, and so on. Perhaps the handling of aggression might illustrate the point. Within the caring professions aggressive feelings, attitudes, or actions are not uncommon amongst the clients served whether they show themselves overtly or remain covert. Usually such phenomena will be tolerated, ignored, or reacted to, but seldom are they used as a central part of the treatment process. The social worker, however, will help the client to express the hostility, perhaps directly against himself; he will attempt to understand its origins, which may be due to external or to internal causes, and he will try to react in the most helpful way for the client in the light of the assessment he has made. This reaction may be a simple non-judgemental acceptance of the hostility, or perhaps reassurance that such feelings are appropriate in the circumstances, or are a "normal" response to the client's perception of the problem; it may include an exploration with the client of the origins of the aggression and a consideration of the interaction between himself and the social worker or the effects which may result from similar interaction with other people relevant to the client's life situation.

Social workers "know" that the relationship they establish with the client is a valuable tool in the helping process, they "know" that there are similarities in the relationships and ways of handling them shared with other of the helping professions, but they also "know" that there are some qualities which are unique to the professional skill of the social worker. What must now follow is the development of techniques of assessment and validation of the work that social workers do and the testing of the "hypotheses" from which they operate. Again methods of investigation and research used in the field of medicine, psychiatry, sociology, and so on, have relevance, but there are also problems which are peculiar to the field of social work which will necessitate new methods of investigation and validation. E. Matilda Goldberg's book *Helping the Aged*[2] is perhaps the most exciting advance in the field of research method in social work, and it illustrates the kind of problems which have to be faced and overcome before we have really effective tools with which to handle the particular questions which arise from the practice of social work. In the meantime we

[2] E. Matilda Goldberg, *Helping the Aged*, Allen & Unwin, 1970.

use validated knowledge from other disciplines (although this, of course, constantly changes and expands); we develop our own particular areas of knowledge and expertise derived from our own practice; and a small but increasingly accelerating start has been made on a more rigorous definition, evaluation, and quantification of the concepts and practice of social work.

The basic tool of the social worker is the use that is made of the "to-and-fro" which takes place between any two or more people who are met together to consider a problem. This coming together need not always be a voluntary decision on the part of all concerned, e.g. a young man about to be placed on probation by a court is asked if he is willing to accept this form of help, but when the other options open to him are all less desirable, the question of real freedom of choice is, at times, somewhat academic. However, the social worker is very much concerned with the unexpressed feelings, attitudes, and consequences which may follow. One can take a horse to the water but to make him drink is a problem of another dimension. To impose, coerce, demand, or even to assume a complete desire for help on the part of any client ignores a good deal of the teaching concerning the complex motivation which is part of all our functioning.

To take a simple example: a "simple" request for help from, say, our bank manager. Which of us has not at such times become aware of a wider range of feeling than one might have expected—of anxiety, of guilt, inadequacy, anger, resentment, and so on, just because one is placed in such a position. Some of us would, of course, prefer not even to recognize such an uncomfortable state of affairs, but we may express ourselves unwittingly through our actions, "forgetting" the appointment, being late, complaining of the inefficiency of the manager or of the system, blaming other people for the situation in which we find ourselves, or perhaps just simply taking it out on the wife or children before or after the event.

In social work, the situations in which clients find themselves are often far more complicated than the apparently simple request for help from a bank manager. Their value and dignity as human beings may seem to them to be in question and, indeed, may be labelled as such by society, for example, parents who are unable or unfit to care for their children, the physically or mentally disabled who cannot manage in a competitive society. The social worker has to develop skill in applying knowledge about the ways in which human beings react and function under stress. Awareness of the attitudes of society to certain kinds of situation, to differing norms between, for example, different ethnic groups or social classes, the kinds of psychological defences we all employ to protect ourselves from hurt, anxiety or other unpleasant experiences, are a vital part of the equipment of the social worker. It is also important for him to know how to handle them, when to observe and leave well alone, when to help the client to become aware of and to attempt to understand or modify what is happening. The social worker is concerned to work with the client in attempting as far as possible to involve him in defining, assessing, and eventually finding solutions to the problems with which he is faced. It is a task which presupposes a give and take on both sides, in which there is essential trust but which, at the same time, can enable the handling of a wide range of feeling, sometimes conflicting, sometimes positive, sometimes negative, and often painful.

Perhaps the most effective way of illustrating the method of a social worker will be the use of a case example. Mrs. X, aged 24, has written asking for help: "My marriage is breaking up, I want a divorce, but I suppose it's my fault really and there are times when I hate my child." Let us leave aside the setting in which the social worker was employed—indeed, such a problem could have arrived on the doorstep of a range of social work agencies, although the problem as presented might have been phrased in slightly differing ways depending on the avenue through which it had reached the social worker.

Although Mrs. X had herself asked for help, one cannot assume that the asking was easy. Indeed, she showed this clearly quite early on in the interview by implying that she expected the social worker to despise her for her failure to manage and by behaving as if she expected a long harangue on her inadequacies. Although such observations were made by the social worker, she made no overt reference to them at first, but took them into account in the way in which she approached Mrs. X, received any information which was offered, and attempted to involve her as an adult person in defining and considering the problem facing her.

Mrs. X had been married some 5 years, she had a son John aged $3\frac{1}{2}$ years and baby Peter aged 4 months. For the last year or so she had found it increasingly difficult to manage John and at times would "beat" him for no really good reason. Since the birth of the baby things had become acute, and

Mrs. X felt that the only solution would be for her to go out of the lives of her husband and her children "because I am no good to them and cannot feel for them as other people do". The manner in which this information was given was of significance in that Mrs. X constantly tried to put herself in a position in which she appeared stupid, of no importance, and where one might have expected the social worker to have reacted by being the one who knew and who would tell her what to do, rather as one might tell a small child. Eventually the social worker commented on this and immediately Mrs. X launched forth into a long and bitter tirade against her parents, particularly her mother, who had always assumed she was stupid and who treated her as an irresponsible child and who even chose her husband for her.

Thus the observation of patterns of reacting or behaving during the interview itself gave clues to areas of painful and difficult feeling which it was important to identify before the client could even begin to define the real nature of her problem. Similarly, in discussing John's behaviour, Mrs. X showed a strength of feeling which did not entirely match up with the circumstances she described. A sudden outburst of bitter tears revealed in no uncertain terms the depth of inadequacy Mrs. X was experiencing as an adult, a mother, and a wife. It was not without significance that her problem had become more prominent since the birth of her younger son, and one suspected some degree of the kind of depression which not uncommonly follows childbirth, but Mrs. X's difficulties had been present well before this, and, indeed, presented a much repeated pattern of behaviour throughout her personal history.

Mrs. X's home was pleasant but not luxurious though she made it plain that she did not know, or indeed wish to know, any of her neighbours. Observation showed that her standards and expectations of her home were different from those of the immediate neighbourhood which raised queries in the social worker's mind as to the meaning of all this. It later became clear that Mrs. X had, indeed, cut herself off from the neighbourhood, not because she felt superior but because she feared that as her husband had been brought up in this very house and knew everybody, she might not be considered acceptable because she was an outsider. This reflected many earlier experiences when as a child she had had eleven changes of school and found it very hard to make friends and feel part of a group.

In discussing her feeling about her marriage, Mrs. X's attitude varied greatly from moment to moment; at one time she was vitriolic in her attitude towards her husband and the next was taking total blame for all the difficulties. She commented, sadly, "you see we cannot live together, but we also cannot live apart as neither of us really knows how to cope with people". This later turned out to be a pretty accurate description of the problem; both Mr. and Mrs. X had experienced considerable deprivation in their early years and each was attempting to get from the other the security and affection that was felt to be lacking from the past—each was asking the impossible from the other. This problem was further exacerbated when John reached an age when his emotional needs were too close to those of his parents, and thus he became the scapegoat of them both.

How, then, could one help? The problem clearly involved all the members of the family. Mrs. X had asked for help and during the course of the first interview had showed that she could use such help. Her husband, whilst being willing to discuss the problems, was unable to accept any formulation of them except in terms of "my wife is overwrought". This always presents problems for the social worker when one member of a partnership implies that the difficulties all lie with the other person. This is seldom so. A marriage partnership always involves a system of checks and balances in which each partner gives and takes in a variety of ways—conscious and unconscious. In helping one partner one will almost certainly alter the balance of need and satisfaction between the two, and usually it is therefore desirable to involve both partners in the process.

In the case of Mr. and Mrs. X, John's position was also important. His needs were in direct rivalry with those of his parents. As far as one could see he had not yet begun to react in unhealthy ways to the situation, but one would anticipate that if the problem remained unsolved it would merely be a matter of time before he began to feel and show the strain. A similar situation might also arise in relation to Peter as soon as his needs came into competition with those of his parents.

In fact Mrs. X agreed to accept help for herself. It was made plain to Mr. X that whilst one had to accept his decision not to become closely involved, it was expected that he would be willing to consider the position again in the light of any changes which occurred. Arrangements were made for John to spend some time daily in a play-group as a means of relief both for him and his mother.

Work with Mrs. *X* was concentrated on helping her to see and understand the ways in which she was using present situations to try and meet unmet childhood needs. Her ability to separate the past from the present gradually increased, and she began to value herself as a person. It was at this point that Mr. *X* ran into difficulties as Mrs. *X* was no longer willing to accept the role of the "overwrought wife" but wanted to talk out with her husband the problems which were contained in their relationship together. Mr. *X* reacted violently because of the implication that he, too, had problems. For many months he maintained his stand but gradually came to realize that to admit to difficulties did not necessarily imply weakness, and he agreed to participate in joint discussions.

Whilst some progress was made, Mr. *X* found it much more difficult to consider his problems and to accept that his wife was no longer the weaker, less-adequate partner in the marriage. However, in many other ways things became easier. The family found a variety of other outlets for their needs, thus making fewer demands on one another which could not be fully met. Relationships with the children improved out of all recognition, and one felt that the family would probably weather at least the normal ups and downs of life.

Thus the process of helping involves a study and diagnosis of the problems (involving as far as possible all the people concerned) and an awareness of the implications that changes may have on the others concerned. One needs to make an assessment of the strengths as well as the weaknesses of the people and the situation in order to know how far and in what direction change might be expected to occur. Throughout the process of working with clients, a continuing reassessment will be taking place with them of what has been achieved, what still needs to be done, and the limits of help which can be offered. Such considerations may be primarily in the area of interpersonal relationships as illustrated above, at other times they may be concerned with the material resources of a family or neighbourhood, or the health resources or those with limitations of ability or most probably of a combination of any or all of them. Often, too, the skills and services of other agencies or professions will also need to be employed.

Social work must always be aware of the many aspects that go to make up the resources, needs, and aspirations of human beings. It is this which brings both its greatest challenge and its greatest rewards.

CHAPTER 4

The Children's Department and the 1963 Act

SYLVIA WATSON, OBE, MA★

EDITOR'S INTRODUCTION

Just a hundred years have passed since a little-remembered
Victorian social worker named Ellice Hopkins first coined the phrase
"Were it not a thousand times better instead of sending our ambulances to the foot of the cliff we should build a fence at the top?"
Since that time Ellice Hopkins's phrase has become very well worn
and has been used in numerous different contexts. As far as social
work is concerned, however, the point she made is still very relevant.
To what extent ought we to regard the social services as casualty
services—the ambulances which come along and scrape up the social
casualties from the road? And to what extent should they rather be
regarded as "the fence at the top" which prevents people ever
becoming social casualties in the first place? As far as the child care
service was concerned it very soon became apparent after 1948 that
however good the children's homes and however well selected the
foster homes to ensure that children already in care were looked
after as well as possible, nothing could really recompense the child
for the dreaded experience of being separated from parents and home
and of coming into care. This was the cliff over which many children
tumbled, and the well-appointed ambulances at the foot could often
do very little to provide more than immediate first aid. Early in the
1950s, therefore, the growing volume of opinion amongst child care
officers was that greater power should be given to local authorities to
build their "fences at the top"—in other words a preventive service

★ Director of Social Services, Cambridgeshire and Isle of Ely.

44

aimed at preventing children from coming into care. As Sylvia Watson points out, between 1963 when the Children and Young Persons Act came into operation and 1971 when the children's departments were disbanded, an enormous change in the allocation of resources took place and far more staff were engaged on preventive work than on "ambulance" work. It is likely that any civilized social service must attempt to deploy its resources somewhat in this proportion; and, therefore, it would seem that new entrants to the social services are likely to find themselves attempting more family casework in a preventive role than work with children in care. It is very probable that the other social services will develop in the same way and that in the field of mental health, for example, far more attention will be given in the future to the prevention of breakdown situations than to remedial work in hospitals. What Miss Watson has to say may therefore be of wider relevance than the child care aspects of social work.

The child care service was 15 years old before it was given legal sanction to work to help children receiving unsatisfactory care in their own homes. Before that, the official policy was that of "the fresh start". A child who was neglected or ill-treated or who had committed an offence punishable in an adult by imprisonment could be removed from his home by court order and placed in the care of a children's department. Children's departments wishing to help parents who were prevented by incapacity or other circumstances from providing for their child's proper care could only do so by receiving the child into care. The doctrine was that of rescue from an unsatisfactory environment and compensation by the provision of a substitute home in which the child would be given wise and loving individual care "to further his best interests and to afford him opportunity for the proper development of his character and abilities".

The Children Act 1948 was an enlightened piece of social legislation which attempted to give orphans and children who had suffered from poor parental care as large a share of the good things of life as other children. Its great contribution was its recognition of the right of each child to be considered as an individual human being. Its limitation was that it legislated for the individual child in isolation. Children's officers soon found that attempting to wipe the slate clean and rebuild a child's life was rarely satisfactory and that substitute home care, however kindly, was but a pale shadow of the real thing. The Act did not give children's departments the right to retain children in care against the wishes of parents, but neither did it give power to help parents improve their home conditions so that children could be restored to them. So long as children were separated from parents there was no limit on the amount of money which a benevolent local authority could spend on their upbringing, but officially it was not until 1963 that children's departments could use the ratepayers' money to prevent family breakdown or rehabilitate a family so that children could return home.

The 1948 Act was too narrowly based because it followed the pattern of English social history of providing a specialist service to meet a specific need without considering the reasons why the need arose or relating the need to the wider social scene. Its progenitors, the members of the Curtis Committee, were bound by their terms of reference to consider only the needs of children in public care, but they drew attention in their report to the fact that many children living in their own homes were suffering from neglect or other evils. They pointed the way for the future by expressing the hope that the welfare of these children would receive serious consideration. At the same time, the Women's Group on Public Welfare published a report, *The Neglected Child and his Family*, in which they recommended that children's committees should, from their establishment, be empowered to provide a comprehensive family casework service for all children in their area. Many people have expressed regret that their recommendations were not adopted in 1948, but it is easy to be wise in retrospect. It may be that children's departments were not adequately equipped in 1948 to establish a comprehensive service and that the experience of providing a service for children in public care was needed before that service could effectively be extended to cover homes from which children were in risk of having to be removed or to which they could be returned after separation.

What was it that convinced children's officers that extension of their service was necessary? Above all it was the children themselves who, in their search for personal identity, uttered their sad cry "Who am I?" and showed that most of them felt that where they came from was where they belonged. "The child who has no past, has no future" was too often shown to be true.

One remembers a young man of 22 years who visited his ex-child care officer and said: "I've got everything I ever wanted—money, a good job, a girl friend—but it's nothing, I'm still alone." Once a child has lost his own home he is in danger of feeling a lodger in the world all his life.

So children's officers welcomed warmly the opening clause of the Children and Young Persons Act 1963 which gave them a legal right to work to prevent family breakdown and to help a child within his own home. The clause reads as follows: "It shall be the duty of every local authority to make available such advice, guidance and assistance as may promote the welfare of children by diminishing the need to receive children into or keep them in care under the Children Act 1948, the principal Act or the principal Scottish Act or to bring children before a juvenile court; and any provisions made by a local authority under this subsection may, if the local authority think fit, include provision for giving assistance in kind or, in exceptional circumstances, in cash."

Overnight the children's service—from being a curative and rescuing service—became, in addition, a service with the almost limitless aim of promoting the welfare of children by helping the family as a whole as well as a service charged with the task of attempting to combat incipient juvenile delinquency without recourse to the juvenile courts.

What effect did this have on children's departments? The most striking factor was the growth of departments. On 31 March 1963 there were 1549 full-time child care officers in post in England and Wales. On 31 March 1969 the figure had risen to the equivalent of 3591 full-time officers, an increase of over 130 per cent in 6 years. The growth had not been without pain. It was impossible for training courses to expand quickly enough to meet the demand, and local authorities vied with each other to attract qualified staff. The Central Training Council in Child Care did an outstanding job in encouraging the establishment of new courses, and it was very much to their credit that in a time of rapid expansion the number of professionally qualified child care officers—instead of falling—rose from 27 to $38\frac{1}{2}$ per cent. Nevertheless, the advance was uneven, and some local authorities not only had difficulty in attracting qualified staff but were unable to fill in any way a significant proportion of posts in their establishment.

Increased size altered the character of departments. Many older workers felt that something precious had been lost, and that from being a close-knit band of workers united in a common aim, departments had become large, amorphous conglomerations with diffuse aims, where size and rapid turn-over of staff made individual workers feel mere cogs in a machine. Communication is more difficult in a large organization and more important. Departments had to work out new patterns of working and new ways of communicating. Decentralization became essential, and through decentralization area teams built up new loyalties. These individual cells of worker-bees had to be woven together into a total organization which maintained common aims and common standards while allowing the maximum flexibility possible for each team. The new work altered the role of child care officers. Some found it hard to adjust to work with no obvious statutory limits—very different from their closely defined duties under the 1948 Act.

Now, even after some 7 years' experience, and in spite of reorganization, problems continue. On what basis should cases be selected? Is there a basis on which cases can be rejected or should an attempt be made to deal with every application for help? Should we attempt to give intensive help to a few families or more superficial help to a large number? Is it more profitable to concentrate on short-term help to families which are basically sound and with such help could become independent or is it better to put most of our energies into helping multi-problem families who may never function satisfactorily but who without long-term support might break up alto-gether? It is certain that if we help 100 families there will be 100 more who could be helped. Selection is inevitable and for the sake of workers, clients, and other agencies, definition of aims must be attempted or we shall merely become a human dustbin of lost causes. But let no one think that definition is easy or that rejection of referrals can be done without anxiety and heart-searching.

In this work there is anxiety about the families which are helped and anxiety about the families which cannot be helped. There may be criticism from other agencies, criticism from the local community. Rescuing children from poverty, degradation, and suffering is regarded as a noble activity, "wonderful work" which brings praise for the worker and sympathy for the child. But there is nothing dramatic about work under the 1963 Children and Young Persons Act. Families are referred who have been the despair of local residents for years, with low material standards, uncontrolled and neglected children, immoral, improvident, and delinquent habits, about whom someone should DO SOMETHING. And the local authority appears to do nothing—endless visiting but no action. And, perhaps, one day a child dies or is injured through a parent's carelessness or neglect, and the worker feels guilty and is criticized for failing to protect the child.

For some workers it has not been easy to find as great a satisfaction in their new role of giving indirect help to children through supporting parents as in their old quasi-parental role of working directly with children as provider, protector, and home-finder. Supporting adults whose immature behaviour resembles that of overgrown children and helping them to be good parents demands of the worker great resources of maturity and tolerance, and the satisfactions derived from such work may be neither immediate nor obvious.

While the worker has been learning to adjust to a new role, colleagues in other departments have had to adjust to it too—to this growing, sprawling organization which has come out of its enclosed patch into work in the community and with the family where other departments and other agencies are already operating. Initially, there was suspicion of empire building and a feeling that the children's department wanted to monopolize family work. Gradually, other departments and agencies have come to accept that there is more than enough room for all services but that co-ordination is needed if overlapping and gaps are to be avoided. The social services department is not wanting to take over general services provided by such agencies as health and education departments and the Ministry of Social Security. It is providing a personal service for those individuals who cannot, without help, make full use of general services: it acts as an interpreter, an intermediary, and an advocate. A family does not need the help of the social services department if it can manage independently with the assistance of the general community services nor if it has need for personal help but is receiving it from some other source. The responsibility of the local authority is to ensure, in the interests of the children, that personal help is available for families who cannot without such help function satisfactorily.

Local authorities can exercise their duties under section 1 of the 1963 Act as they think fit. These duties can be interpreted widely or narrowly according to local needs and local whims. Some have interpreted their duties very widely indeed, while in other areas the response appears to have been minimal. Because there is no national pattern, any account of work done must be fragmentary. No national report has been compiled, and the writer's information is based on personal experience and knowledge gleaned from colleagues. National statistics for the years ending 31 March 1967, 1968, and 1969 record the number of families who were given advice and assistance for each year and the number of children involved:

    1967   54,458 families involving 133,687 children;
    1968   65,458 families involving 161,339 children;
    1969   78,460 families involving 182,478 children.

Statistics before 1967 give only the number of cases where reception into care was averted by action under section 1 of the Act and do not include those where appearance before a juvenile court was prevented or where children were returned home after separation as a result of help given. It is interesting to compare the figures of children received into the care of children's departments during the 3 years and the total number in care.

Received into care	In care at 31 March
1967 53,381	69,405
1968 50,938	69,358
1969 51,262	70,188[a]

[a] But decrease recorded in number of children in care of voluntary organizations.

It will be seen that children's departments were by 1969 supervising well over twice as many children living in their own homes as separated from parents and in public care. To these figures might be added the number of children still in the legal care of local authorities but living at home under supervision, those being supervised at home after leaving approved schools, and those in respect of whom courts have appointed local authorities as supervisors under matrimonial orders or orders made under the Children and Young Persons Act 1933—an estimated total of some 14,000. In all these cases, the children's department was giving the kind of advice and support which it gives under section 1 of the 1963 Act in an effort to help the family function satisfactorily and to avoid family breakdown.

It was the expressed hope of the Government that work under the 1963

Act would lead to a reduction of the numbers of children in public care and an overall saving in the cost of the child care service. There has been a decrease in the combined numbers of children in the care of voluntary organizations and local authorities during the last 3 years, but the decrease is marginal and it would be unwise to relate this directly to work under the 1963 Act because factors which influence the number of children in care are extremely complex.

There is insufficient evidence to judge whether the cost of the new service bears any relationship to its effectiveness and, indeed, it is difficult to decide by what criteria effectiveness can be judged. Even if the narrow yardstick of reduction of numbers in care is used, it could still be claimed that reception into care on a short-term basis can sometimes ease family pressures and thus prevent total family breakdown and long-term reception into care. If a broader and more positive standard of judgement is adopted, then how can one judge whether a child's welfare has been promoted and whether parents have been helped to function more effectively? One can assess externals such as competence in paying rent and not running into debt, keeping the house and children clean and out of trouble with the police, but how can one assess emotional factors? How does one know whether a social worker's help has, in the words of Lady Allen of Hurtwood, "enabled a child to lead a fuller and happier life"? Such judgements are qualitative and cannot be recorded in statistics. And yet if one believes that the act of separating a child from parents is nearly always emotionally damaging and that most homes are worth preserving, surely money spent on attempting to keep a family together is money well spent in emotional and in economic terms? The average cost per week of maintaining a child in care in 1968–9 was £8. 1s. 9d. (£8·09). At that rate a local authority might spend £7–8000 on bringing up a child. It is therefore interesting to consider how much local authorities are in fact spending on attempting to keep children out of care. The main expenditure is on social workers' salaries, and no statistics are available showing the proportion of social workers' time which is being spent on this work compared with other child care work. Statistics are available, however, which record the amount of money spent on financial assistance during the year ending 31 March 1970 covering such things as cash grants and loans, payments of fares, arrears of rent, household necessities, and fuel. The expenditure is surprisingly small. Out of 174 local authorities in England and Wales only 23 spent more than £3000, and the highest recorded was a London borough which spent just over £8000; 22 spent less than £100; 11 spent nothing at all. Astonishing, when the alternative to spending a little money may be so very much more expensive. Perhaps some local authorities see the powers given under section 1 of the 1963 Act as so limitless that they hold a tight rein on their officers' power to act lest the flood-gates once opened should overwhelm them. Of course, considerable use is being made of money obtained from local and national charities as an alternative to local authority expenditure, but there is no information available to show which local authorities are most active in tapping all available resources. It may be that those local authorities which themselves spend most are also those most likely to take the initiative in mobilizing the community to help itself so that requests received by local authorities can be channelled back to the community.

The impression should not be given that spending money or giving material aid is the heart of work under the Act. It is only valuable if it forms part of an overall plan to support, encourage, and build up the confidence of a family so that its members may be helped to function more satisfactorily as parents and citizens. In the last resort, no one can solve a family's problems but the family itself. Their material needs and emotional needs are interwoven. They may fail because they feel failures, and a social worker who attempts to take over their problems by paying off debts, cleaning the house, and providing new furniture or clothes for the children may merely increase their sense of inadequacy and make them less capable of managing their own affairs. Very rarely does a family need help with a single, isolated problem. The reasons for which help is needed are complex and deep-seated, and a worker can only be of service if he attempts to understand the hidden needs of each individual and, through showing concern and support, aims at relieving pressures so that the individual can carry on and eventually find his own way out of his problems. Ultimately success depends on building up a relationship of trust in which individuals feel safe to talk about their underlying anxieties with a professional worker who neither criticizes nor condemns but who holds a mirror so that the individual may look at himself and the motives for his actions.

What kind of families are being helped? It may be the family with poor material standards where there is debt, dirt and child neglect. Some are large families where the father is an unskilled worker earning too little for his family needs. In some, the parents are of low intelligence, in most they are not using their full intelligence because of emotional factors and their own confusion and anxiety. Some are struggling with poverty because of illness or physical or mental handicap; some are single parents who are unmarried, deserted, divorced, or widowed. In some the income is adequate but it is lost through alcoholism or gambling, while in others there is no financial or material problem. In all but a small minority the roots of the problem lie in emotional factors—disharmony between parents, tension and lack of understanding between parents and children, loneliness, frustration, self-centredness. Many parents themselves had unhappy childhoods and are for ever chasing a mirage of happiness and self-fulfilment through fleeting personal relationships in which they take but are unable to give. So we have young people from unhappy, dreary homes who seek glamour through early sex experiences, drugs, or delinquency, and repeat the pattern of the last generation by setting up families in which children are deprived of consistent love and care because the parents have not themselves had an experience of good family life with stable relationships. The task of the social worker is to give such parents an experience of a stable, reliable relationship in which their needs are understood and sympathy and concern are demonstrated by sticking to the family through thick and thin and giving them time, encouragement, and reassurance. To such parents the social worker may become a parent figure who, in order to move them towards independence and maturity, must sometimes allow them to be dependent for a period and must at times cajole, direct, and persuade in an effort to help them assume responsibility and face reality.

Help with personal problems and practical problems go hand in hand. A rent guarantee may be given to avoid eviction; a worker may assist a family to sort out its debts and work out priorities for payment. Debtors are kept at bay by promises of small, regular payments with the worker acting as intermediary. In some cases, families are advised and helped to go bankrupt or to obtain an administration order by which a county court takes over responsibility for collection and disbursements of debts. Second-hand furniture may be made available to prevent a family entering into hire-purchase agreements which are beyond their means. A mother with a large number of children may be provided with a washing machine, either free or at small cost, while another is given a sewing machine with which to make clothes for her children and sometimes even augment the family income by making clothes for other people. A work-shy father who says he cannot get up in the mornings is given an alarm clock or arrangements are made for a neighbour to wake him; and one who says he lacks transport to get to work is given a bicycle. Loans are often used rather than grants in an effort to encourage a family to be independent, and some loans may be for substantial amounts. One family, for instance, was given a £2000 loan for a house mortgage so that a father could provide accommodation for his family. Electricity, water, and gas payments are an everlasting problem. Should a family which mismanages its finances and which rifles the gas or electricity meter be left to suffer the consequence of its action where there are young children left without water, cooking facilities, heating or light ? The position may be alleviated by the provision of primus stove, paraffin lamps, and candles, but is this too great a safety risk to take if a parent is mentally subnormal or unstable? The giving of material and financial aid poses fundamental questions. Non-payment of rent and debts is often the result of a family's attitude and lack of maturity rather than of actual poverty. In some families the withholding or mismanagement of money is used by one partner as a means of hurting the other. Some families live in a fantasy world and cannot—or will not—appreciate that certain actions will have certain results. A rent guarantee or payment of debts may confirm their fantasy that they will be protected from eviction and that they have no obligations to other people or to society. If we condone non-payment of rent and debts, we shall not help a family to gain maturity and we will condition the children to have the same attitude when they become adult. Should we therefore let such families break up?

In a few cases the solution may be to give the whole family a period of intensive care in a rehabilitation centre. Such centres have in the past been run largely by voluntary organizations, but increasingly local authorities are setting up centres themselves or using their homeless families hostels for the purpose. The family which finds that it has not been protected from eviction after repeatedly failing to pay rent, but at the same time is not abandoned but is given accommodation and support, may at last be accessible to constructive help. The help is given jointly by the staff of the centre and the social worker. It consists of casework help to sort out personal and emotional problems through the giving of time, the demonstration of concern, and the building up of a professional relationship. It consists of practical help in sorting out money tangles, helping with budgeting, giving day-by-day guidance on child care and household tasks, getting the man employment, and then ensuring that he goes to work regularly. It consists of group help through seminars in which the family talk out their problems and gain strength from each other and in which they themselves make decisions about the running of the centre, or a group in which the women are given simple instruction in cooking or sewing or the men taught simple carpentry or car maintenance. It consists in helping the children and through them the parents. A nursery for children under school age, a club for the school-age children, and an adventure playground give opportunity for creative play and self-expression. On admission, many of the children have pathetically little idea how to play; they are tense, anxious, and frightened. And the parents, who have often missed out on their own childhood, will sneak in and play with the toys and equipment themselves. The nursery groups are often run with the help of the mothers and are a means by which indirect guidance can be given to them in the management of their children. So inch by inch the families grow in strength and gain self-respect and confidence. When they have demonstrated progress by paying debts and rent arrears (sometimes through the local authority or a charity paying £1 for each £1 they pay), they may be moved to intermediate accommodation where they will still receive fairly close supervision, and the ultimate aim is to persuade a housing authority to rehouse them.

The kind of methods used in a rehabilitation centre are used with families who remain in their own homes both for the prevention of short-term and long-term family breakdown. Some social service departments run nursery groups to relieve overburdened mothers and to help the children. Some run play-centres for school children in the evenings and during holidays. Some take children for adventure holidays or arrange outings for them. Use is made of nurseries, nursery schools, play-centres and other facilities provided by other statutory agencies or by voluntary organizations. A number of local authorities have a visiting housemother scheme which enables children to remain in their own homes when mother is ill or in hospital; the most famous of these is Cornwall's Flying Angels scheme.

Cornwall's Flying Angels are equipped with dormobiles which they use for transport and in which they sleep. They claim to have reduced to a third the number of children received into care because of a mother's short-term illness or confinement. In the country as a whole, approximately 50 per cent of receptions into care of children in any one year are the result of a mother's illness, and schemes such as this are therefore of vital importance. Some local authorities use visiting housemothers to help in rehabilitation work with families, while others depend on the home help service for domestic help in temporary family crises and for giving guidance and assistance to inadequate mothers in household management. An alternative is the use of a good-neighbour or day-minder scheme by which a local authority pays a neighbour to care for the children while father is at work or to clean the house, wash the clothes, and cook.

An interesting development has been the use of children's homes and residential nurseries to assist in work with families. Residential nurseries have sometimes taken in a mother with her young children for a period of training; sometimes families have been accommodated in a cottage in the grounds of a children's home and the staff of the home have given them support and supervision. Other homes have offered day care for children to relieve mothers and to give children opportunities for play, creative activities, a bath, and a good square meal. Reception into care for short periods or for some members of a large family can also be useful as it not only relieves overburdened and overstrained mothers physically, but also gives the social worker an opportunity in an atmosphere of decreased pressure to help parents sort out feelings of resentment, hostility, or rejection, and to work out priorities in their way of life. The principle of placing children in boarding schools on grounds of social need was established in the Education Act 1944, though it has not been widely adopted. Rightly used, it can be of constructive help to child and parent. For some children, perhaps we should reverse the process, leaving them at home during term-time but taking them into a residential establishment in the holidays, while others might spend weekdays in residential care and return home each week-end.

Nothing has been said about the duty of local authorities under section 1 of the Act to diminish the need to bring children before a juvenile court. It is almost impossible to separate such work from other work to promote their welfare. Police, probation officers, and schools increasingly refer young people to social service departments because of behaviour problems such as staying out late at night, sexual misbehaviour, drug-taking, minor delinquencies, or truancy. Parents seek advice, particularly about their adolescent sons and daughters, some of whom they allege to be beyond control. Some young people themselves seek help in sorting out their problems. The social worker acts as a listener, confidant, interpreter— attempting to help under voluntary powers whenever possible in preference to bringing the young person before a court. Sometimes temporary placement in a residential establishment is suggested for a period of assessment and relief of tensions: sometimes, for the young person who needs a respite away from home, lodgings or residential job are found. Drug-taking is becoming an increasing hazard, and at least one local authority has appointed a detached youth worker to work with young people on the fringe of delinquency and in danger of becoming drug addicts. Such a worker has the support of the social workers in the department but a great measure of freedom to operate independently. The young people he seeks to help are drifters—in and out of jobs, often sleeping rough, unacceptable in orthodox youth clubs. The worker has to seek them out in coffee bars and shelters and attempt to gain acceptance by them through identifying with their way of life while remaining apart from it. Young people get support from each other, and many social workers are having to learn new skills in acting as leaders for a variety of groups—adolescents searching for their place in the world, often confused, anti-authority, aggressive, or parents with a whole range of human problems each one unique to the individual but with elements so similar to those of his neighbour.

   This need for flexibility in approach, willingness to experiment with new methods, and humility, are the most important lessons children's departments learnt from their work under section 1 of the 1963 Act. Social workers act as catalysts, mobilizing a family's own strengths to combat its weakness, guiding a family to use fully the resources of the comminity, and trying to interpret its needs and behaviour to the community. So far under the 1963 Act the work has been largely personal work with individual families, helping a family to develop its full potential and to live the best life possible according to its individual circumstances. We have concerned ourselves little with social policies which in many cases determine the circumstances in which families live. Is this right? Would it, in some cases, be a fair criticism to say that social workers are attempting to help families to tolerate the intolerable? Is it our job to salve the community's conscience by exercising compassion towards those to whom society does not give justice? Or have we a duty to work to change social conditions and not accept the *status quo* when we find that society is denying basic needs to some of its citizens?

If we have a duty to act as social reformers, it is a duty which, in the last decade, we have performed sparingly. The 1966 Ministry of Social Security survey showed that 160,000 families with half a million children in them had incomes below Ministry of Social Security scales. Since 1966, family allowances have been increased, rent and rates rebates have been extended, and wages of low-paid workers have increased. A recent publication, *Socially Deprived Families in Britain*, edited by Robert Holman, shows, however, that there has been no real advance, and that as a result of a rise in the cost of living the poor are relatively poorer than they were 10 years ago. This same book records that more than 1,800,000 dwellings in England and Wales are unfit, which by definition means that structurally and because of lack of amenities, they are not just unsatisfactory but are below tolerability standard and should be rendered fit or demolished. Should social workers content themselves with helping families living in conditions of financial and social deprivation to make the best of a bad job and accept their lot? Is our philosophy "The rich man in his castle, the poor man at his gate, God made them high and lowly and governs their estate"? Or is it just that we see ourselves as concerned with individual trees but not with the shape of the wood?

There are indications that social workers are beginning to see themselves as community workers and shapers of social policies, and that they are becoming conscious that a personal service for individuals and families in need which ignores burning social problems is of limited value. If our work is to be really preventive and promotional we must aim at remedying defects in the social structure as well as helping individuals. At present, the number of families receiving help from local authorities is little more than a sample of families who are socially deprived. Are we selecting the right families to help and are we giving them the right help?

Undoubtedly progress has been made since 1963, but the gap between the work actually done and the potential work that might be done is immense. In the future we must think widely and concern ourselves with the causes of social deprivation as well as with the alleviation of individual suffering. We must work in partnership with voluntary organizations, with education, housing, and health services, with politicians, and with the press. We must be the advocate of the inarticulate who are not able to speak effectively for themselves, and must convince society of their needs. Ultimately success depends on the community's own willingness to stretch out a helping hand to families in need.

CHAPTER 5

Incidence of Need

JEAN PACKMAN*

EDITOR'S INTRODUCTION

As has been stated in the previous chapter, any enlightened social
service must devote a great deal of its attention to the care of those
who inevitably have needed shelter and help away from their own
homes, but it must at the same time try to develop a preventive
service. In attempting to be effective in this latter sphere it is obviously
necessary to try to study the reason for a certain type of situation
breakdown; and—in the context of the present book—it seems
logical for us next to study the reasons why children have come into
care—why they have tumbled over their particular cliff. Jean Packman, who has done pioneer work in this sphere of investigation,
summarizes some of the information which is now available to
social workers and social administrators concerned with the development of a preventive service. This chapter points the way to those
areas where considerable further study is required and where also
perhaps some rationalization of the resources available ought to be
attempted in the next decade.

Despite all the supportive services for families that have been described,
some children cannot live with their own parents, and substitute care has to
be provided for them. They may require such care for a relatively short
period of time, for some years, or for the whole of their childhood. Their
need may arise because their family has disintegrated for one or more of a

* Lecturer and Tutor in Social Work, University of Exeter.

60

variety of reasons. Parental illness, incapacity or death, marital difficulties, homelessness, and illegitimacy are some likely causes. Other children, because of their own mental, physical, or emotional handicap, cannot be contained in their own homes even if these are undamaged and secure. In some circumstances a child's handicap and a family's problems interact and combine to produce breakdown. For many mentally and physically handicapped children and for some of those who are emotionally disturbed as well, there exist special residential educational and medical services which will be described in subsequent chapters. For deprived children, whose need for substitute care springs largely from family circumstances, a new child care service was set up in 1948. It is with the children coming within its ambit that the present chapter is concerned.

Many questions may be asked about these children who slip through the net of preventive services and who require some form of temporary or permanent substitute care. How many are there? Why do they have to leave home and for how long? Is the problem growing or diminishing? Which age groups seem most vulnerable? Do all parts of the country share common problems or are there regional differences? Can growing preventive effort be shown to have affected numbers in care? The answers to most of these questions can be derived from annual statistics which are kept by local authority departments and collated by the Home Office. With their aid some estimate of the size of the problem of child deprivation in England and Wales can be attempted.

In terms of the number of children who are admitted each year to the care of local authorities it is a problem which has grown steadily and consistently since the new service was set up, and it is only recently that it has shown any signs of decline. Table 1 shows the number of children admitted to care in England and Wales in each year since records were kept. The growth in numbers does not merely reflect the rising child population, but represents an increasing proportion of that population as well. Whereas 3·3 children per 1000 of the population under the age of 18 years (the population "at risk") were admitted in 1952, the peak figure for 1965 was 4·1 per 1000, and in 1969 it stood at 3·8 per 1000.

Some reasons for this prolonged upward trend and the more recent decline can be suggested. A new service had been set up in 1948 expressly to meet child care need at a more generous level. It was perhaps inevitable

TABLE 1. ADMISSIONS TO THE CARE OF CHILDREN'S DEPARTMENTS:
ENGLAND AND WALES, 1952–69

Year ending	Number of children admitted	Year ending	Number of children admitted
30 November 1952	37,977	31 March 1962	47,471
30 November 1953	39,300	31 March 1963	48,479
30 November 1954	39,498	31 March 1964	51,810
31 March 1956	38,120	31 March 1965	54,659
31 March 1957	39,096	31 March 1966	54,471
31 March 1958	40,021	31 March 1967	53,381
31 March 1959	40,319	31 March 1968	50,938
31 March 1960	42,048	31 March 1969	51,262
31 March 1961	45,203		

Source: _Children in Care in England and Wales, 1952–1969_, Home Office.

that cases of child deprivation should be recognized more swiftly and readily, and action taken in consequence. The 1963 Children and Young Persons Act, though embodying powers to _prevent_ admissions to care, seems initially to have had a similar effect to the earlier legislation. By involving children's departments in yet more situations of child care need, admissions to care rose again. It is perhaps only since 1966 that the hoped-for effects of the new preventive clauses have begun to take hold.

When we turn to examine the _reasons_ for admissions to care, other factors which influence the total admissions rate emerge. The circumstances which can lead to a child's admission to care are very varied and often complex. Any categorization of causes is liable to be arbitrary and over-simplified, and comparisons over the years are made difficult by the changing and expanding classification used in the Home Office statistics. A substantial proportion of admissions occur because of a mother's confinement or the temporary illness of a parent. Nearly 24,000 admissions in 1969 were for these two reasons alone, for instance, and involved children in only a short period away from home. Such admissions were largely unanticipated consequences of the 1948 Act—the "ambulance service" aspect of child care which had scarcely developed before 1948. Some causes of admission have declined in importance over the years. Tuberculosis incapacitates parents in only a few cases each year now. In contrast, other causes have gained in significance; the committal of offenders on Fit Person Orders for example (1276 cases in 1964 and 1541 in 1969) and the admission of illegitimate children to care because their mothers cannot provide for them adequately (2308 cases in 1964 and 3302 in 1969).

The pattern of reasons for care over the years therefore tends to be kaleidoscopic in character. It shows shifts of emphasis according to changes in the law or its use, in the incidence of need-producing circumstances (the upsurge of homelessness in the late 1950s and early 1960s leading to increased admissions, for instance) and in the particular breakdown of reasons for care used in the records. It is therefore difficult to generalize about the past or to predict future trends. Since 1948 the tendency appears to have been to admit children to care more readily, but for shorter periods of time; to apply first aid at an early stage of breakdown in order to prevent more lasting damage and deprivation. This will become clearer when we look at the total number in care at any one time and relate this to annual admissions. Whether the more recent decline in admissions means that a more advanced stage of prevention has now been reached whereby first aid can be administered in the home setting without recourse to admission to care, remains an open question. The next decade may produce some hard evidence on this.

One further aspect of admissions that is of interest is the *age* of the children concerned. Any child under the age of 17 is eligible, but it is clear that some age groups are more vulnerable than others. Children under school age (the under 5s) have always been at greater risk. In every year they account for over half of total admissions, and in the early years of children's departments the proportion was even larger (58 per cent in 1962). The reasons for this are not hard to find. Very young children need constant attention and care; they are not easily helped by part-time props if a family's stability founders. Further, their demands are more likely to tax a vulnerable parent and lead to breakdown. "Problem" families often achieve some degree of stability and competence once all their children reach school age, and the lives of unmarried mothers can be at their most stressful and restricted when their children are totally dependent on them.

In contrast, few adolescents of 15 and over are admitted to care, though the number has crept up steadily since 1952. In that year only 895 out of

37,977 admissions were of children over 14 (2·4 per cent), whereas in 1969 the figure was 2283 out of a total of 51,262 (4·4 per cent). This is certainly a reflection of the increasing involvement of children's departments with disturbed and delinquent teenagers—an involvement which must go on growing now that the 1969 Children and Young Persons Act puts prime responsibility for dealing with juvenile delinquency on the local authority.

One important piece of information that the child care statistics do not reveal is how many children are likely to be admitted to care at some time in their lives. We know the annual incidence of the problem of deprivation, but not its true prevalence. For this we would need to know how many admissions in each year are *first* admissions and how many children are in fact re-admitted. Some evidence on this point is to be found in Appendix Q of the Seebohm report.[1] By comparing an early study of the child care service by Gray and Parr[2] with data from the National Child Development Study[3] it suggests that approximately 80 per cent of admissions each year may be first admissions. When this figure is linked to average annual admission rates over an 18-year span, it suggests that around 5 per cent of the child population will be in care at some time in their childhood—a figure ten times greater than the total of children in care at any one time.

One final set of figures which helps put admissions to care in some perspective is the record of applications received and, since the 1963 Act, the combined total of applications and all other referrals for help. The increasing involvement of children's departments with families at risk is made clear through these figures. In the year ending 31 March 1962, for instance, applications for care were made on behalf of more than 104,000 children of whom only 47,471 were actually admitted. In the year ending 31 March 1969 the number of children who were referred for admission or for help was 308,076 but in the same year there were only 51,262 admissions. By far the larger part of the case-load in any children's department was, in fact, made up of children in their own homes.

Examination of the pattern of admissions is only one way of looking at

[1] See the suggestions for Further Reading at the end of this book.

[2] P. G. Gray and E. Parr, 'Children in Care and the Recruitment of Foster Parents', *Social Survey*, p. 249, November 1957.

[3] In a report prepared for the Seebohm Committee.

the problem of child deprivation. Another method is to study the total number of children in care at any one time. This figure, which is generally presented as a proportion of the number of children at risk, gives a snapshot view of the child care service's caseload and really highlights its long-term work. At any one time about 93 per cent of the children in care are there for a minimum of 6 months and many of them have been, or will be, in care for many years. They may therefore be regarded as truly "deprived" and merit special concern in consequence.

The proportion of children in care has changed slowly but significantly over the years. There was a predictable sharp upward movement in the years immediately following the foundation of the service in 1948. This reached its peak in 1954 when 65,309 children, or 5·6 per 1000 of the population under 18, were in care (Table 2).

Thereafter there was a slow decline both in the number and proportion of children in care despite the steadily mounting admissions rate. Short-term work was expanding but long-term cases were apparently held in check. Only in the 1960s was the trend reversed and the figures climbed slowly upward again, though never reaching the proportions of the early 1950s. The figures for 1970 are not yet available, but scrutiny of data for a small selection of individual authorities suggests that the situation has changed very little since 1969.

Some of the reasons for these changes in the total figures have already been explored in discussing admissions. The 1948 Act widened the limits of eligibility for care, and the new service was bound to respond more generously to need in its early years. Hard upon this response, however, came pressures from within and without to *prevent* children from coming into care. Child care workers, operating the new Act, soon began to express the view that more effort should be expended in keeping families together in the community, and a few authorities appointed special "preventive" workers or allowed child care officers to spend part of their time working with families whose children were *not* in care. This trend was reinforced by financial considerations, for as the Select Committee on Estimates 1951–2[4] pointed out: "Much frustration and suffering might be avoided if more attention were directed towards the means whereby situations that end in domestic upheaval and disaster might be dealt with and remedied before the

[4] On *Child Care*, Cmd. 235, HMSO, London.

TABLE 2: NUMBER OF CHILDREN IN CARE IN ENGLAND AND WALES,
1949–69

Year	Number	Rate per 1000 population under 18
1949	55,255	★
1950	58,987	★
1951	62,691	★
1952	64,682	5·6
1953	65,309	5·6
1954	64,560	5·5
1955	62,948	★
1956	62,347	5·3
1957	62,033	5·2
1958	62,070	5·2
1959	61,580	5·1
1960	61,729	5·0
1961	62,199	5·0
1962	63,648	5·1
1963	64,807	5·1
1964	66,281	5·1
1965	67,099	5·1
1966	69,157	5·3
1967	69,405	5·3
1968	69,358	5·2
1969	70,188	5·3

★ No comparative figures available.

Source: *Children in Care in England and Wales, 1952–1969*, Home Office.

actual breakup of the home occurs." Money was to be saved by the same process, and numbers did gradually decline.

The rise in figures in the 1960s is a more intriguing phenomenon. Despite the ever-growing emphasis on prevention and the legislation of 1963 which gave greater powers to local authorities in this respect, the upward trend has not been checked. Some reasons have already been suggested. New legislation uncovers new needs. Further, the 1963 Act had a twofold aim—to prevent admissions to care and to prevent the appearance of children before the juvenile court. These aims are not always compatible, and there was a

steadily increasing involvement on the part of children's departments with
delinquent youngsters, some of whom had to be admitted to care. In
addition, the incidence of other causes of need has been increasing. Illegitimacy rates have risen, and homelessness has been a special problem. In fact,
many indices of social pathology have been rising sharply since the end of
the 1950s, and it may be that increased local authority powers to support
families have yet to keep pace with apparently growing need.

The pattern of numbers in care over the whole of England and Wales is
not, perhaps, as interesting as that in individual local authority areas. The
national average conceals startling regional variations, and there has been
an attempt to explain these.[5] At 31 March 1969, when the proportion of
children in care in England and Wales was 5·3 per 1000 under 18, less than 2
out of every 1000 were in care in Solihull and Montgomeryshire, but more
than 20 out of every 1000 were in care in the London boroughs of Tower
Hamlets and Kensington and Chelsea. These enormous variations follow
some faint patterns. Numbers tend to be higher in the south and east than in
the north and west, and higher in boroughs than counties, but such generalizations are beset by exceptions. Neighbouring authorities frequently
have very different proportions of children in care (Oxfordshire 7·4 per
1000, and Buckinghamshire 4·0 per 1000; Cornwall 5·1 per 1000, and
Devon 2·7 per 1000). Towns of apparently similar character have markedly
dissimilar rates (Bournemouth 9·1 per 1000, Eastbourne 6·3 per 1000,
Torbay 4·8 per 1000, and Southport 3·3 per 1000). Parts of the same
conurbation present a contrasting picture (Kensington and Chelsea 23·3 per
1000, Southwark 11·5 per 1000, and Richmond 4·0 per 1000).

Reasons for these variations are complex. There seems little doubt, for
instance, that "need" varies and that some children's departments are bom-
barded with more problems than others. An analysis[6] of thousands of
families referred to over forty children's departments in a six-month period
highlights some of the circumstances which contribute to breakdown and
the admission of children to care. The incomplete family, whether affected
by death, desertion, divorce, or separation, is inevitably closely associated
with child care need. The working classes, particularly manual workers, are
at special risk, and families that have moved home and are without relatives

[5] In J. Packman, *Child Care: Needs and Numbers*, Allen & Unwin, London, 1965.
[6] *Ibid.*

or friends around them are also vulnerable. Following on from this, immigrants are also at special risk. Families of unemployed fathers appear to be in particular danger of breakdown, and poor housing conditions are closely correlated with child care need. Illegitimate children are much more likely to be admitted to care than others (over a third of all children in care are illegitimate). We have already seen that babies and very young children are more likely to be admitted to care than their elder brothers and sisters. Clearly these factors are interrelated in a most complex way. Unmarried mothers often leave their home area, for instance, and in attempting to set up in a strange new environment may be forced into cramped, inadequate accommodation. Unskilled manual workers are liable to face periods of unemployment more often than skilled or white-collar workers, and will have little money to spare to make private arrangements in an emergency. They may also be less reluctant to approach a local authority in time of trouble; less conscious of "stigma".

Whatever the exact relationship between the factors associated with family breakdown and the need for children to be admitted to care, there is no doubt that some parts of the country harbour more potential problems than other areas. There are a number of crude indices which can be used to measure these differences; illegitimacy rates, housing indices, migration rates, social class composition, and so on. However, attempts to relate these measures to the variations in numbers in care have met with little success. Simple correlation exercises produce no relationships of any significance whatever,[7] and even more sophisticated analysis[8] reveals only slight positive relationships between factors associated with need and rates in care. Variability of "need" is, in fact, only one cause of the variations in rates between different areas, and its effects are heavily overlaid by other factors.

Some contributory factors lie in the multiplicity of preventive services that have already been described. Supportive work with families is not the province of one service alone nor of the statutory services in isolation. Many voluntary organizations on a national or purely local scale are engaged in providing help in cash or kind or by means of personal advice or assistance. The spread, vigour, and effectiveness of all these many statutory and

[7] *Ibid.*

[8] Bleddyn Davies, *Social Needs and Resources in Local Services,* Allen & Unwin, London, 1968.

voluntary services are uneven and patchy, and this affects the burden placed on individual social service departments. The home-help service is just one example. In some authorities health departments developed the service in a flexible and far-reaching way. Domestic assistance was made available at all hours of the day and at week-ends too. Experiments with resident home helps were launched, and training for special aides who will tackle work in the most depressed "problem" families was attempted. In such areas families in difficulties may be effectively held together without removal of the children from their home setting. In contrast, in other authorities, only a rudimentary service exists, hampered in some places by the rival attractions of well-paid industrial opportunities for women, or the existence of isolated communities with a poor system of public transport. In such districts a high proportion of children may well have to be admitted to care. Other statutory services which are equally variable and of equal significance in diminishing or increasing the pressure on social service departments are preventive and rehabilitative services for the homeless (including temporary accommodation) and day nurseries. The incorporation of these services in the new "Seebohm" departments under the 1970 Act may gradually whittle away this particular cause of variations in numbers of children in care. A single local authority service will henceforth feel the direct effects of economies or lack of initiative in its preventive services, and may be persuaded to reallocate expenditure and effort in consequence.

In addition to the many preventive services that exist (of which only a few have been mentioned), there are also alternative sources of substitute care for children which meet similar needs to those met by social service departments, and therefore have an affect on the latter's caseloads. The rationalizing legislation of 1948, which created a new, single local authority department with responsibility for deprived children, left voluntary societies for children intact. Large national organizations like Dr. Barnardo's Homes and the Church of England Children's Society, together with small local societies, still care for many thousand children. Legislation also left several categories of "special" children outside the control of children's departments. Children may still be placed privately with foster parents or in independent children's homes by their parents, and though subject to the supervision of local authorities they are not in care. Other children are placed in adoptive homes (the most permanent form of substitute care) and are only supervised by a local authority in the period before an adoption order is made. There are also certain categories of children receiving boarding education whose home circumstances and needs closely resemble those of children in care. "Maladjusted" children, for whom special education may be provided under section 9(5) of the Education Act 1944, are often thought to be the product of distressing or inadequate home surroundings, and may be indistinguishable in behaviour and background from disturbed children in care. Children in approved schools also have much in common with deprived children. Whether or not they share the problem of delinquent behaviour (and often they do), they frequently come from similar circumstances and may, indeed, be separated from the deprived only by a magistrate's decision. (A committal to care on a fit person order was, until the 1969 Children and Young Persons Act, an alternative to committal to an approved school for both offenders and non-offenders.)

All these alternatives to local authority care are used in varying degrees in different parts of the country. Voluntary organizations, for instance, are busy in some areas and relatively inactive in others—sometimes influenced by historical accident in the siting of their headquarters or residential establishments. Private fostering and adoption are practised to a varying extent in different localities, and such differences are accounted for in part by the number of families who are able and prepared to offer these kind of facilities, and in part by the number of parents who need or demand them. The use of special boarding schools for maladjusted children and of approved schools for children who have appeared before the juvenile courts is also immensely variable. If figures for maladjusted pupils at special boarding schools are taken at their face value, it would appear that most emotional disturbance in children arises in London and the Home Counties (with odd pockets of difficulty in such places as Southampton and Blackpool) while the stability of children in some stretches of the north of England is almost totally unruffled. In fact, of course, facilities are so sparse and so patchily distributed that provision bears very little relationship to need. Courts have also been responsible for very different practices regarding approved school orders. Not only do some have to deal with a much higher incidence of juvenile delinquency than others, but they have also developed different sentencing policies, so that approved school rates in some areas can be as much as twenty times higher than those in other parts of the country. All these variations in the use made of different forms of substitute care have an effect on the numbers of children for whom local authorities assume responsibility and are thus undoubtedly a contributory reason for variations in numbers in care.

The interrelationship between these different, and administratively separate, modes of caring for children away from their own families can be demonstrated by treating them as one and adding together the numbers of children in each category. The resulting figure, which could be termed an approximate total of *all* deprived children, can be estimated for each local authority area and can be set against the indices of need which were outlined earlier. The fact that a few relationships of modest significance then emerge[9] linking indices of rootlessness and mobility with numbers of deprived children suggests that there is some basis to the presumption that different forms of care are, indeed, alternatives to one another and tend to meet similar needs.

This relationship between systems of care that, hitherto, have been kept separate, is further illuminated by comparing the distribution of children within the different administrative categories over a 23 year period. In 1946 the Curtis Committee[10] carried out a major survey of services for children "deprived of a normal home life with their own parents or relatives", and the Children Act 1948 was a direct result of their recommendations. The committee took a wide view of deprivation and produced figures for children accommodated in all forms of substitute care. These figures, and particularly the proportion each represents of *all* deprived children, can be compared with similar estimates for 1969.

The total number of deprived children has risen surprisingly little. In fact, in proportionate terms, it has *declined*, for the 1946 total represents 10·6 per 1000 of the population under the age of 20 years (the nearest comparable population base available for that year), whereas the 1969 total represents 9·7 per 1000 of the population under 20 years of age (Table 3). If deprivation is looked at in its broadest sense, in fact, and despite the contrary pull of increased responsibilities for wider age groups, preventive measures have

[9] See J. Packman, *op. cit.*
[10] *Report of the Care of Children Committee,* Cmd. 6922, HMSO, September 1946.

TABLE 3: DEPRIVED CHILDREN IN ALL FORMS OF CARE:
ENGLAND AND WALES, 1946 AND 1969

1946			1969		
Type of care	Number	%	Type of care	Number	%
In care/local authority	40,900	32	In care/local authority	70,188	48
In care/voluntary organization (not local authority responsibility)	26,700	21	In care/voluntary organization (not local authority responsibility)	8,208	6
Private foster homes and institutions	10,700	8	Private foster homes and institutions	10,907	7
Awaiting adoption	2,400	2	Awaiting adoption	7,437	5
Approved schools	11,200	9	Approved schools	7,535	5
Remand homes	1,500	2	Remand homes	1,063[a]	1
Probation homes, hostels	700	1	Probation homes, hostels	677[a]	1
			Detention centres	300[a]	
Ineducable, institutions, foster homes	7,500	6	Ineducable, institutions, foster homes	10,069[b]	7
All handicaps, boarding schools	14,500	12	All handicaps, boarding schools	27,000[c]	20
Homeless evacuees	5,200	4			
War orphans (foster homes)	3,600	3			
Total	124,900	100	Total	143,384	100

[a] 1966 figures from *Child Care: Needs and Numbers*, table XXXIII.

[b] 1967 figure from *Report of the Ministry of Health*, Cmnd 3326, HMSO, 1967, table 47, part 2, p. 125.

[c] 1968 figure from *The Health of the School Child 1966–1968*, Chief Medical Officer of Health, Department of Education and Science.

Other sources: *Report of the Care of Children Committee*, table IV, p. 27, Cmd 6922. *Summary of Local Authorities' Returns of Children in Care*, Home Office, 1969.

apparently borne fruit, and proportionately more vulnerable children are now being helped within their home setting than was previously the case.

The most dramatic changes have occurred in the *distribution* of children between the different categories of care. Local authorities have greatly increased their role since the Children Act, largely at the expense of voluntary organizations, which have played a much smaller part in recent years. Adoption has increased threefold. The facilities for delinquent children, on the other hand (approved schools, remand homes, and so on), are less frequently used than in 1946. In contrast, institutional care for handicapped children has almost doubled. The similarity between the total figures for each year therefore conceals significant differences in the use made of the different services.

The future holds possibilities of further change. Under the 1969 Children and Young Persons Act, approved schools are to be absorbed into the local authority system of "community homes and schools", and children within them will cease to be listed separately in the statistics. They will swell the local authority total and, in the process, some existing regional differences in proportions in care will be diminished as scope for variations in policy towards delinquents is narrowed.

Different degrees of need and different combinations of supportive and alternative services have clearly contributed to the regional variations in child care figures that have already been explored. But the children's departments themselves, their policies and practices, also bear some responsibility for the lack of uniformity in numbers in care. Though most child care workers acknowledge, on the one hand, that separation of a young child from his parents can have distressing and damaging effects and, on the other, that some children come from such inadequate or positively harmful families that they *have* to be separated, they differ in the degree of emphasis that is laid on these two propositions—on preservation of the family or on protection for the child. They differ, too, in the amount of optimism or pessimism with which they view their own facilities and the effects of intervention. Some clearly see admission to care as virtually an admission of failure. Others believe that it *can* be positively beneficial, either as a rescue operation or as a form of additional parenting. These differences of attitude are reflected in admission practice.

Some authorities reject many more applications for care than they accept (a refusal rate of 70 per cent in some cases, for example). In other areas the reverse is true (only 19 per cent of applications were refused in another authority). There are also differences over particular categories of admissions. Opinions differ over illegitimate children; some think mothers should be strongly encouraged to opt either for adoption or for keeping the child themselves, with no third possibility of admission to care; others believe local authorities should play an active part in caring for illegitimate children. Delinquent children have also been viewed very differently by different parts of the child care service; some areas have been keen to admit them to care and others have not. The law has now set the seal on the former policy, and many of the special residential services for offenders will now be incorporated in the total system for deprived children.

From study of the statistics relating to the child care service a rough picture of "need", and its incidence begins to emerge. That it is, indeed, only rough and therefore open to further investigation has constantly to be borne in mind. "Need" is a slippery concept and, like beauty, often to be found in the eye of the beholder. It is clear, for instance, that child care workers have a large part to play in defining need (the law only provides guide lines) and they are not all agreed on its exact dimensions. Further, need and demand are not always the same thing, and it is the latter that is most readily measured: and demand itself can be expanded or restricted by the suppliers of the service. In addition it is rarely the case that one service alone is responsible for meeting a particular range of needs, and this is certainly so with child care. Demands for one service will therefore influence and be influenced by the demands on and responses of other related services. By focusing on one part of the system alone we may therefore get a distorted picture which can only be corrected by looking at all parts together.

"Need" can be explored at many levels. In this chapter it has been approached in terms of expressed demand and the response of various services to that demand. In searching for the causes of regional differences, some of the factors which contribute to the breakdown of families and put their children at risk have been highlighted. But these go only part way to explaining a phenomenon. As the Schaffers point out in their small study of short-term admissions[11]—underlying the immediate causes of admission

[11] H. R. Schaffer *et al.*, *Child Care and the Family*, Occasional Papers on Social Administration, No. 25, Bell, 1968.

(like illegitimacy, desertion, parental illness, and so on) are "circumstances of a much more subtle and elusive nature". These are to do with the quality of relationships between family members, which lead one family to apply for local authority care in time of crisis and another, faced with the same situation, to tackle the problem so that the children can be contained within the family network. Such differences cannot be pinned down by bald statistics, but need more subtle studies in depth. Nor will they be solved by environmental manipulation alone: hence the social workers. That child care workers differ in their interpretation of need and their responses to it can also be taken a stage further. Why do they differ? What effects, if any, do the personality and training of the worker have? Questions like these also need investigation and have, indeed, received some attention.[12]

Our picture of the incidence of child care need is, therefore, at best a blurred and partial one, and should be treated with the caution it deserves. With caution, however, it gives us some idea of the problems faced by the child care service and of how far we still have to go in our "preventive" efforts. In this sense it acts as a brake upon simple-minded optimism and helps set realistic targets for the future.

[12] B. Butler, A Study of the Criteria governing Decisions on Admissions to Care, an unpublished thesis, 1961.

CHAPTER 6

Fostering

GILLIAN BALLANCE*

EDITOR'S INTRODUCTION

In the two preceding chapters we have looked at some of the implications of what is meant by a preventive service; and the importance of this has been stressed and is indeed self-evident in Jean Packman's figures (Chapter 5). At the same time those figures also reveal how many children actually do come into care and have to be looked after. Any social service and any social service agency must devote a good deal of time to the care and welfare of those for whom the preventive service has failed. As far as children in care are concerned, one of the most important ways of helping them has been through a fostering or "boarding-out" programme—a policy which has not always had a respectable history in England. If the fostering system has, in spite of setbacks, worked generally to the advantage of children in care, it is largely because of the tight statutory controls and safeguards which have been imposed. Some of the Acts and regulations impose an inescapable duty upon the social worker not only to visit and watch over the interests of the child but to assign this task a very high priority. Almost all social workers in the foreseeable future will have to find themselves required to deal with fostering situations and the problems of foster children. Gillian Ballance's introduction to a subject which is both complex and fascinating is therefore of major relevance to the social worker.

By "fostering" we mean the care and upbringing of a child in a household of which neither of his parents is a member. By such a definition it is

* Lately Area Children's Officer, South Hertfordshire.

obvious that fostering is of considerable antiquity: from earliest times it is likely that the orphaned or abandoned child would have been fostered by neighbours, friends, or other members of the tribe, and perhaps such primitive fostering will always be represented by the legend of Romulus and Remus. What we are more concerned about here is fostering as a more formalized activity—instigated, arranged, and supervised by a properly constituted child welfare agency.

The formalization of fostering in this sense is, in England and Wales at any rate, a surprisingly recent innovation. (In Scotland the fostering of destitute children in Highland crofts under the general oversight of the Guardians of the Poor was a well-established custom by the mid eighteenth century.) In England, although there were one or two attempts to establish a fostering system in the eighteenth century, no notable headway was made until the last quarter of the nineteenth century.

In preceding decades, increasing concern had been expressed by two different groups of people. On the one hand, the boards of guardians of the poor were able to discern the stunting effects which a workhouse life had upon destitute children who grew up in institutional conditions: often the children were unable to do without the institution for the rest of their lives. On the other hand, the great voluntary societies which sprang into existence in the Victorian cities were concerned to "rescue" children from urban squalor, and such pioneers were enamoured of the idea of placing the children in clean little country cottages.

The proposals by some boards of guardians to develop a system of fostering were at first greeted by the central government with great suspicion, and approval was given only grudgingly. Suspicions of the motives of foster parents were keen—and, indeed, have never really been entirely dispersed. It was thought that the foster parents would neglect the children, or lead them into evil ways, or misuse the money sent for maintenance. In the late nineteenth century there occurred several horrifying trials of "baby-farmers"—women who undertook, by private arrangement, the care of babies, insured the babies' lives, and then let the babies die so that the insurance money could be collected. These trials increased the public and official suspicion of foster parents. Regulations were drawn up which by their very tone indicate that only "respectable" persons could be officially registered as foster parents, and the rather jumpy and nervous concern of the Government in this field was repeated in successive sets of regulations over the next 80 years.

Nevertheless, the children who were successfully fostered under this nervous regime gained so discernibly in health, happiness, and (above all) in self-reliance that the system spread. Destitute children in residential care were boarded (i.e. maintained) *in* the workhouse, while children in foster homes were boarded *out*; and gradually the term boarding-out for the fostering of children was universally accepted, so that as recently as 1955 the Home Office could issue a set of Boarding Out Regulations.

The voluntary societies were not quite so cramped by regulation, and so they took the lead in developing a fostering system. Edward Rudolf, of The Waifs and Strays, and Dr. Barnardo were two pioneers whose efforts proved that the system was beneficial. If, however, the societies were not cramped by regulations, they were still cramped by the opinions of their supporters and they too were cautious and suspicious in their selection of foster parents. It was the custom in a number of societies for children to be fostered during the years of infancy and then to be uprooted and brought back into homes and schools for "training".

Between 1880, when the system was fairly well established, and 1939 it may be reckoned that about a quarter of the children in the care of voluntary societies were living in foster homes, as were a slightly smaller proportion of the children in the care of local authorities. For various reasons the numbers declined during the Second World War. Nevertheless, when the Curtis Committee investigated the whole field of the care of the destitute child in the years immediately following that war, they were perfectly confident that in general terms a child who had been deprived of his normal family life would best be cared for in a foster home.

The report of the Curtis Committee was closely followed by legislation in the shape of the Children Act 1948; and section 13 of that Act states: "A local authority shall discharge their duty to provide accommodation and maintenance for a child in their care (a) by boarding him out... or (b) when it is not practicable or desirable for the time being to make arrangements for boarding out, by maintaining the child in a home. . . ." Boarding-out was thus put as the primary objective in child care. Fostering had become respectable (though still tightly regulated).

With the coming into force of the Children Act, local authorities appointed persons at first called boarding-out officers (later child care officers); and these officers enthusiastically extended the fostering system. In November 1949 19,271 children in local authority care were fostered; by November 1953 the number had risen to 27,536 and that in spite of such contemporary problems as a severe housing shortage.

By the mid fifties such writers as Roy Parker and Gordon Trasler, amongst others, were re-examining the concept of fostering, and it was becoming clear that the early enthusiasm to carry out section 13 of the Act was to some extent misplaced. To be sure, many children had been found excellent homes, but, on the other hand, there was a worryingly high rate of breakdown. Through the sixties, therefore, a more thoughtful approach was gradually adopted as it came to be realized that fostering was not a matter of simply substituting one mother–child relationship for another. The relationships in a foster home are special and they are not automatically to be learnt and accepted by any of the participants. With the more cautious approach the number of children in foster homes has declined, and the latest figures available for local authority services show that on 31 March 1970, of 71,210 children then in the care of local authorities, 30,284 were boarded out (42 per cent of the whole).

There has, nevertheless, always been a shortage of foster parents, and some writers on child care say that much less haphazard methods of recruitment should be used and campaigns in each district should be more thoroughly organized. As it is at present, recruitment is rather unmethodical. Articles are written in newspapers on fostering; social workers put in advertisements asking for help for a particular child. There are appeals on the radio and television and there are programmes geared to this particular social need. Sometimes television and press publicity is given to a child who has been ill-treated or found abandoned; such stories always provoke a flood of offers to foster or adopt the child, and those who offer are often inspired by sentimentality. "I want to make it up to her for all she suffered; I want to make her my own" is the sort of sentiment expressed. Such a sentiment, often very strong and passionate, may blind its possessor to the realities of the child's feelings. The fact that the child may not want to be taken over will not be taken into account, or if such a child were to repudiate the offer, the would-be foster parent all too easily experiences hurt, anger, and rejection, and retaliates by rejecting.

More satisfactory recruits to fostering are often those who come forward because of some previous acquaintance with its rewards or interests; those whose mothers have been foster parents or those who have been told about fostering by friends, who are already foster parents. Social workers find that on many occasions neighbours offer to help out. This is particularly important as they are the people who are known to the children, and perhaps in the best position to help the children through a time of crisis. Examples known to the writer include the two girls who lost their mother and whose father was chronically ill who were fostered long term by the two next-door neighbours; and the little 3-year-old girl who was withdrawing and becoming mute because she would not cope with living with strangers who, when placed with a friend of her parents, began to recover. Often friends of families in need do not realize that they are eligible for financial help by becoming temporary foster parents, and it is an important task of social workers to encourage community feeling in this way. Sometimes older children find their own foster homes, and this can be particularly useful for adolescents who are rebellious and anti-authority. Mary came into care when she was 14. Her mother had left the family years back, and she was kicking against her very rigid, unforgiving father. Two foster homes were found her by the social worker which broke down. She then proceeded to find herself a series of homes and lodgings, gradually gaining confidence in her own autonomy, until she was able to settle down and marry. If the social worker is able to approve the foster home it can often be a step forward in the relationship between herself and the child, as she is confirming and supporting the adolescent's own independent choice.

Many social workers have discussed and written about the role of foster parents in the child care service. Most have come to regard foster parents as colleagues in the joint job of serving the child. Many feel that the title of foster parent is misleading because it denotes "substitute parentage", whereas in the majority of fosterings this is not what is involved. In fact such a title may be a great hindrance to the child in solving any conflict of loyalties that he may have, and also may confuse the foster parents as to the nature of their task. Thought has been given as to whether foster parents need some kind of voluntary training to help them in their very difficult and skilled job. To judge from foster parents' discussion groups in one area, some gained a lot by sharing their difficulties together, and also were stimulated by talking about child care problems in general. Other foster parents did not want to partake, and many of these were equally successful with their foster children. They may not have enjoyed group meetings, but often with their warmth and intuition were extraordinarily well equipped anyhow.

There are formal requirements in regard to the selection and approval of foster parents laid down in the Boarding Out Regulations. The home and material conditions are investigated by the social worker; medical history checked upon; references taken up. However, the nub of the matter lies in the interviews between the social worker and the foster parents spread usually over a fair period of time. First of all the social worker will make an attempt to find out what the foster parents are offering, what their needs are, and what their conception of fostering is. In her turn, she will then talk about fostering in general and how as a professional worker she views it; she will outline the hazards and difficulties as well as the satisfactions, and make certain that there is some realization that fostering could profoundly affect the family and could call for quite big adjustments. If there is then a mutual wish to continue, the social worker will attempt to assess how best the foster parents' offer to help can be used. She will try to look at their life experience, how they have tackled difficulties, and she will look at their relationship together and as parents. Sometimes the motivation for fostering lies in very painful experiences that the foster parents have themselves gone through in childhood, adolescence, or early marriage. Perhaps their own parents may have been at loggerheads, they may have encountered mental illness, or themselves suffered the loss of a child. The arrival of a foster child in the home may well resurrect their earlier feelings. In that case the social worker will have to make a judgement as to whether to some extent, at any rate, the experiences have been digested and accepted, and that therefore a greater amount of understanding and security will be offered to the child, or whether there is too great an amount of guilt, anxiety, or even angry feeling left over. Many foster parents after bringing up their own children offer to foster because they want to serve the community in this enormously valuable way. The social worker will find that different qualities are needed in short-stay and long-stay foster parents. It is not the same task to take a series of children for short periods as to take one child for an indeterminate length of time. She will also find that some foster parents are better able to deal with one age group, others with another. One family may like to have a baby always in the house, another family may prefer school-age children, but not yet feel ready to take a teenager. There are foster parents who are able to look after seven or eight children at a time, or even more; others who take just one child at a time. Though the majority of foster parents are married couples, some foster mothers are spinsters, widows, or divorcees. (It is forbidden by law to board out a child with a man alone unless the man is a relative; though if a child is boarded out with a married couple and the foster mother subsequently dies, there is no legal obligation to remove the child.)

Inevitably, the worker will make errors of judgement in her selection of foster parents as so much prediction is involved and asessment is such a difficult and delicate task. It is easy to talk about the feelings that may be aroused in taking a foster child, but his actual arrival and presence can on occasions arouse totally unexpected reactions.

There are many kinds of fostering and in the following paragraphs we will look at their diversity.

Short-stay fostering makes up a large part of the work where children are placed in foster homes to see them through minor emergencies and crises that are happening in their own families. As mentioned in Chapter 2, nearly half the total number of children coming into care during the course of a year do so because of the temporary incapacity of the mother—usually because she has been admitted to hospital. Sometimes these situations arise with such short notice as to make them emergency situations; in most cases the children are placed within the immediate neighbourhood of their homes, and sometimes it is not possible to prepare the children for the experience or select ideal foster parents. Of those recently researching this field of temporary separation from mother, Dr. and Mrs. Robertson of the Tavistock Clinic in London should be mentioned. They have used film as the medium for recording the reactions of the children. They have acted as foster parents to young short-stay children, and their filming of them shows how very skilfully and carefully this job needs to be done. Even though some of these small children were away from their parents for only very short periods of time and came from relatively stable backgrounds, they had a great struggle to cope with their feelings about being away from their parents. The first few days may have been plain sailing, but after that a great deal of sorrow and anger set in, together with a falling back to earlier comfort habits. Children need all the help they can get to see them through such an experience. If it is at all possible the social worker arranges for the parents, foster parents and children to meet beforehand. It is of enormous benefit for the foster parents to learn about the child's home routine, and very important for the foster child to bring his own bits and pieces with him—particularly those things, perhaps just a bit of old rag, or a sucked and favourite toy to which he is especially devoted, which can somehow bridge for him his feeling of separation and loss. Constant visits to parents, or by parents to the foster home, are essential where this is possible, particularly with very young children who are unable to hold the image of their parents in their minds for very long and without which they suffer very great anxieties indeed—for this image is the nucleus around which their own personalities grow. Foster parents often help a great deal by talking to them about their own homes and the little familiar happenings so that in some simple way the children may feel able to grasp what is going on or get the feeling that it makes sense and that someone understands. Some foster parents find it difficult to put up with too many visits by parents because they have to witness the distress of the child when they leave. This is very understandable, and it is hard to realize that crying, with comforting afterwards, is a healing thing; whereas a withdrawal and a forced equanimity on the part of the child may mean that the experience lies painfully undigested inside him and is harder to help with. The tragedy is that often in emergencies placements have to be made with great speed and there is no time for preparations. None the less, small things, such as whether the social worker knows about the important things at home, maybe a cat or a budgie, and can talk in a simple way perhaps of why the parent is ill; how she is able to listen and help the children show their feelings during the car journey; and how the foster parents receive the child to their house, can be of enormous value.

Often it is impossible to calculate for how long a child will be fostered. Doris's foster parents were to have had her for 3 months; Charles's for a week. Both have been fostered for at least 10 years, with every prospect of it continuing this way. These indeterminate lengths of time can be an added burden for foster parents from whom very great flexibility is required. It is often impossible to predict, for example, how long a mental illness will last, or to know when or if ever unstable parents will be ready to set up home again.

Sometimes children are placed with foster parents with a view to adoption later on. Some come from difficult backgrounds, e.g. where both parents show signs of mental subnormality or abnormality, and are assessed at a later age by a paediatrician before the social worker allows adoption proceedings to start. The child perhaps may have been conceived by a girl out on licence from a local subnormality hospital by an unknown father, or there may be a history of mental or physical illness in the parents' families. Parents of other children may have decided against giving their consent to adoption. This may be quite right and absolutely legitimate, but there are also situations where a move from the foster parents to a natural parent who is too unstable to be able to see it through, can severely damage the child.

Of the 30,000 children boarded out in 1970, some 5000 were fostered with relatives. It often happens that a child is taken in an emergency by his grandparents, or by an aunt or uncle, or by an older sister or married brother; it is not uncommon for the unmarried mother to leave her child with her own mother and then vanish. If relationships are fairly sound it seems right that children should remain within the family. Broadly speaking, a child seems to manage better when he knows that his foster mother is also his grandmother—provided that he really knows, for there have been cases where the child was kept in ignorance, believed his grandmother to be his real mother, and had in the long term severe problems of self-identification. But generally the child seems able to understand and accept the hierarchy of the generations. Not all relatives thus "left holding the baby" are made into registered foster parents; it is not known how many carry on without help or seek help by other means, and the policies of different local authorities vary considerably. Nevertheless, by recognizing the relatives as foster parents and the child as boarded out, local authorities are able to give financial support; they are able to help with emotional problems if they arise; they can, in certain cases, arrange for the child's status to be legally protected and, should anything happen to the relative—should, for example, an elderly grandparent die—then the local authority can provide a continuum of care, concern, and support. All these things may be desirable. In practice though, sometimes the social worker may find it difficult to visit the child, say at his grandparents; her right to be there seems less obvious. It can be harder for relatives to accept the visits of an employee of a local authority and to discuss in any meaningful way such problems of child rearing as may arise.

A situation with somewhat similar components may arise where the foster mother is not related to the child. A parent in difficulties may place a child by private agreement with a friend or neighbour on the promise of regular payments for maintenance; but after a while the promise may be broken and the parent may disappear. The foster mother may not be able to afford to keep the child, yet the child himself may by this time have formed a relationship with the foster mother which it would be disastrous to break. Here again the situation may be protected by the local authority's registration of the foster mother.

The fostering of teenage children deserves a paragraph on its own. Adolescence has often been called the time for second chances, and if all goes well the hidden and real problems emerge which were left unsolved in childhood. They emerge combined with the welter of new and bewildering feelings that every teenager has to experience. Children who have suffered deprivation at earlier times, are in their teens sometimes able to regain these feelings and often act in violent or strange ways. Sometimes these problems can be resolved more fruitfully and with hope by foster parents reacting in different or more constructive ways to those which originally left the child so disappointed and distressed. It can, though, be a shattering time for them. Natural parents often feel shaken by the growing vigour and sexuality of their teenage children. This can be much more keenly felt in foster homes where these is no blood tie, and the foster parents may not have had the cementing and intimate experience of caring for the child when he was dependent and tiny. Foster-home breakdowns at this age, particularly if the child has been there for many years, can be a very distressing experience for all concerned.

Short-stay children, as we have indicated above, are usually fostered straight from their own homes, but long-stay placements are more often arranged from nurseries or children's homes. A decision is taken at a case conference consisting of both field and residential staff that fostering is in the child's best interests; and if the child is old enough his feelings will have been thoroughly sounded. When a foster home has been found by the

social worker there will be visits by the foster parents to the nursery or home
and often the child's nursery nurse—"his special and loved person"—will go
with him on his first visit or two to the foster home. If the nursery is a good
one there will be much talking done with him and by him between the
visits in order to help him to see what is happening, and to find out how he
is feeling about the new move he is to make. The move will finally be made
when the child is ready and asking for it. Caroline, a little 4-year-old who
was originally brought to the nursery by the NSPCC for the second time,
was in such a state of anxiety about being moved that she needed to be given
the absolute reassurance that she could stay there in the nursery for as long
as she liked. It was herself who at a later date chose to go to live with her
new "mummy and daddy". In some nurseries foster parents who are to
foster young babies are invited to stay overnight in order for the baby to get
used to the new way they will hold him, feed him, etc. These are intensely
personal matters, and to a tiny baby mean everything to him. No wonder
changes in touch, smell, and surroundings have to be imaginatively handled.

It must certainly be obvious from the preceding paragraph that fostering
is by no means a uniform process or foster parents a homogeneous group. In
fact one area children's officer paying tribute to foster parents in her annual
report wrote: "They could be said to be the longest established and most
varied group to provide voluntary service within the community." A
warning must be given against generalization in any discussion of fostering.
Having given the warning, we can nevertheless proceed to examine the one
element which is common to all types of fostering. The element is the
special relationship. Put briefly, that relationship is in the form of a triangle
—"the eternal triangle" of fostering. At the points of the triangle stand the
child, the foster parents, and the natural parents. Each participant in the
triangle has to relate to the other two; he, or she, has to come to terms with
the fact that there is an inevitable duality of relationship. Since this is not
easy to do, there is an essential fourth element, a person who must oversee
the process, namely the social worker. The hardest situation in fostering for
the child to accept is, of course, that where his own mother and his foster
mother are of the same generation, and where his relationship to his own
mother, to whom he "ought" to belong, is spasmodic and unsatisfying,
whilst his relationship with his foster mother, to whom he *ought* not to
belong, is warm and precious. This is the classic dilemma in fostering, the

dilemma which all the participants find painfully disturbing; the child fearful of his mother yet fearful of fearing her; the mother jealous of the foster mother yet unsatisfied by her own child; the foster mother protective of the child yet frightened of too close an involvement in case she should lose him.

To take first the child, the part of the triangle for whom the child care service exists to serve and whose needs and feelings are paramount; some of the problems faced by foster children emerge only over longer periods of fostering. At 5 or 6 the children are often wrestling with the problem of the "two mummies". It is the time when they start school when they realize their surname is different from that of their foster parents. Sometimes the young child is confronted by this problem in a very poignant way; on Mother's Day to whom does he give his card and his bunch of flowers? To the person he loves who has stood in as his mother for several years, or to his own mother who perhaps visits only spasmodically? When the child has clear recollections of his real mother and where, perhaps, after placement she has visited the foster home for a time before disappearing, then the problem of duality will be a very real and pressing one. A little 5-year-old girl whose mother did not visit, but who could remember being taken by her to cafés earlier on, was severely upset when a doll was sent out of the blue by her mother for Christmas. She clutched this doll to herself and became very destructive in the foster home. Sometimes she would call her foster mother by her surname, sometimes she would call her "Mummy". Often young children imagine that parents they have not seen are dead. It may be that something deep inside them needs to be brought alive, or in their imagination "being dead" is preferable to the irrational fears and monsters of childhood which may have been built around the actual happening. A boy whose parents were not dead but who came from an incredibly bleak and frightening background commented that it was a relief to know what had happened and that he had imagined it to be worse than it really was. Sometimes children who have been tremendously deprived in one way or another imagine their parents as fairy godparents, as all that is marvellous, who can do no wrong. The foster parents may find their love rejected and themselves rebuffed, at least until the child, if he is able, can become a little less insecure, and gradually drop the fantasy of perfect parents and accept human help.

Often foster children express their yearnings obliquely for those who can listen and pick up and answer underlying questions in their own language. A girl had been rejected by her stepfather, who was unable to acknowlege even her presence in his house—a place was not even laid for her at table. She talked about how a father guinea-pig had looked after someone else's family of guinea-pigs. A 12-year-old-girl who, though fostered for 7 years, had been fairly uncommunicative, made a formal appointment through the secretary with two other school friends to see her social worker. She had chosen as her project at school "Fostering" and actually asked her two companions to ask the questions she dared not pose herself. A teenage girl wrote an essay at school about a nurse whose parents were unknown to her and who were brought into the hospital dead. Sometimes children reveal their problems after a crisis. A 13-year-old girl was inadvertently brought to a foster parents' discussion group where some of the conversation, particularly about foster children being moved, disturbed her. She relapsed into physical illness for a day or so, but at least some of her fears previously hidden came out into the open and could be allayed. A 9-year-old boy, who was very withdrawn, broke into a house and was detained by the owner. When he was asked quite kindly by the owner about the break-in and why he was away from home, he quite suddenly crumpled up in tears and said it was because he was bad. He had carried within him, alone all those years, this image of himself. In fact his mother had rejected him.

Other critical points for foster children may be during the teenage years when the adolescent is encountering boy friend/girl friend relationships, or even considering marriage. In fact, all the times which call for tremendous change and growth in ordinary children may bring to a head the special difficulties of those who are fostered. There can never be any generalization, but often between the ages of 6 and 12 the problems of personality identification may lie dormant. The foster child starting school has to discover who he is; so does the foster child struggling with the onset of puberty; in those explosive struggles, painful though they may be, lie the probability of emotional growth. It has been the experience of child care officers that children who have been placed for the first time in foster homes between those ages, and who have seemed to settle, when they reach the teenage period appear to have laid down no roots at all.

It certainly cannot be assumed that the triangle does not exist because the natural parent is not physically present. Some children come into public care having had virtually no contact with their mothers; some come in with no memories. However, although the very young child who is fostered soon after birth is likely to establish an exclusive relationship with his foster mother, he is also likely as he grows up, and probably during adolescence, to seek out knowledge of his true origins and may want to trace and meet his "real" mother. At some point he needs to come to terms with duality. A 16-year-old crippled girl who had been abandoned at birth insisted that her mother should be traced. Although the mother refused to see her, the girl seemed satisfied that the mother had at least been interviewed by the social worker. An 18-year-old illegitimate boy, just out of care, needed help in trying to trace the birth certificate of his unknown father at Somerset House. He asked the social worker to go with him and whilst there addressed the envelope in which the birth certificate would be sent to her home. Perhaps he did not want to open all by himself an envelope containing the birth certificate of some strange man who was his father.

Adolescence is surely the time for the search for identity, which involves much experimentation and struggle. This is much more difficult for some of the children who come from shaky and insecure backgrounds. Jane, for instance, brought up in her childhood by a strait-laced and anxious grandmother, but who dreamt of her delinquent and gypsy father, whom she had never been allowed to mention, found this struggle for her identity almost overpowering. For example, after a visit to her grandmother, who insisted that Jane should borrow and change into tidy clothes, Jane refused even to get out of the car on the long journey back to the foster home, and also refused to eat. Her personality felt usurped because she had been compelled to wear clothes other than her own untidy ones. Yet at the same time she was troubled by the ragamuffin and delinquent side of her nature. A reconciliation between these two parts of her, finding out what she herself is and wants to be, will be very hard to achieve.

Finally, it needs to be said that it has been the moving experience of many social workers to meet people in middle age who have been in foster homes or children's homes before the child care service realized the importance of keeping in touch with the parents. Such people are still looking for their lost families. A married foster mother of over 40 with three children who had been brought up by a voluntary society, was still trying to trace her mother. She said she kept on having visions about her. Though we could not trace the mother we were able to get some information about the background. This was extremely painful to the woman, and she needed a great deal of support in looking at the bare facts. Yet in tears she said she did not know how to express her gratitude, and "thank you" was not the right word.

We need to consider the feelings of the foster parents who occupy another corner of the triangle. Very deep feelings are aroused in foster parents by their foster children. Perhaps short-stay fostering is not quite so difficult, although even then, if the natural parents are immature and inadequate, great apprehension may be aroused about the child's future well being. Foster parents can be subject to enormous stress. The child who lost his own home may at times be overcome with bitterness and anger. "I hate you, I hate you", he will scream at those who have charge of him. It can be very hard to take such an onslaught, and the foster mother may find it an affront to herself, her way of life, and to her family circle. Her own children may be bewildered, hurt, and even rejective because of this obstreperous cuckoo in their nest, and the foster parents may well be caught up in a conflict of loyalties. However, over longer periods deeper and very loving feelings often develop towards the child, and all the foster parents' parental instincts naturally become involved. In fact in a good fostering the child is "given to" wholly, for this is what he needs; yet the foster parents often have to return him to his parents, and in any case always help him to see and imagine himself as part of his original family. Is this asking too much of any human being? It is certainly asking of foster parents a very great deal. Perhaps it helps if they can in some way realize that to love a foster child involves some acceptance of his family, or else at some level the child himself feels rejected, and also that it may make all the difference to a child's survival and future humanity that at a time of stress he was cared for with love and under-standing. Sometimes the quality of imaginative understanding of foster parents is very marked; for example, the foster parents of a little coloured girl whose father is unknown but who are close friends with a Jamaican family have helped her, through them, to imagine what her own father was like. Another foster mother fostered a boy for 5 years. The boy had re-mained very loyal to the memory of his mother who had disappeared. The foster mother helped him to sustain this memory, and gradually picked up clues from his chatter as to how the social worker could trace the mother. She finally had the mother to stay so that the boy, by then 11, could get to know her again before returning to her care. It was a very great triumph that the foster mother whose parental instincts had become so involved was able to hand him back to the mother and become, as it were, his aunt. Perhaps the boy showed his appreciation by saying that the two photographs of them looked "alike", though, in fact, the foster mother was dark and the mother fair.

We need to consider the feelings of the natural parents who occupy the third part of the triangle. Even a short-stay placement is often a very anxious time for them. It is not easy to hand children over to foster parents who are not very well known, and all sorts of misunderstandings can arise. Particularly where children are fostered for indefinite periods of time, parents who have to relinquish them have strong feelings of guilt and failure, of jealousy and fear. To see her own child in somebody else's warm, cosy family circle may reinforce a mother's feeling that she is "the outsider"; that she is the inadequate one, the failure. Fearing that the affections of the child will be alienated—will be diverted to the foster parents, the mother may, consciously or unconsciously, wish the fostering to fail even though she is aware at the same time that failure will hurt or damage her child. Visits to the foster home can be very disturbing for the parent. Some parents at the last moment may not be able to face a visit, and so do not turn up, or if they do may have to put a brave face on it. In a desperate attempt to make up for their inability to give loving and consistent care, they may shower the child with a bewildering amount of toys and sweets. It is by no means unknown for a parent visiting a foster home to arrive drunk, having needed Dutch courage, or to arrive supported by a number of large and jovial friends. However, these are descriptions of extreme situations, and there are many fosterings where such frictions are minimal. It is useful to have an understanding of the kind of feelings parents may have to experience to a greater or lesser degree. Natural parents vary, of course, as much as foster parents, and generalizations are just as misleading. One remembers, for example, the couple who were quite warm and loving parents but were feckless in other ways—the father did not work for long periods and the mother was a bad manager. They were evicted from their house and the family had to be separated for 8 weeks. Then there was the mother with a very low IQ who was permanently in a sub-normality hospital, who talked incessantly about her baby, but in a way that a little girl might about a doll; another mother who, though unable to take her baby home, caused scenes in the foster home because of jealousy; and yet another who some-how knew she could not offer her child loving care and asked for him to be found a long-term foster home. She then disappeared. Perhaps it was her very deep wish to be a good parent. Yet, because of personality difficulties she was not able to be. Rather than watch other people doing it better than herself she removed herself from the scene.

The position of the social worker, that fourth element, not part of the triangle yet involved in it, needs to be looked at. She has an inspectorial duty as laid down by the Boarding Out Regulations, for she is there to see that the welfare of the child is being served by the foster parents. She will seek, though, to accomplish a great deal more where this is possible. Although her feelings to serve the child may be deeply stirred, she will also be the most objective person in the fostering situation. She will therefore be in a position to try to feel herself into the shoes of child, parents, and foster parents. She must attempt to see that the relationship between two points of the triangle has not been formed to the exclusion of the third. She will help with interpretation and will try to help the foster parents to understand the feelings of the parents—and vice versa—for the benefit of the child. Above all she must see that the difficult nature of a dual relationship is not proving intolerable to him. Some writers on child care have wondered whether it may not be too difficult for one worker to work and have sympathy with all three, keeping steadily in mind all the time the welfare of the child which is by no means always a clear goal. In some situations it can be comparatively easy: the fostering may be short term, or there may be no particular conflicts arising for long periods of time. On the other hand, there may be situations where, for example, the social worker may have misjudged a foster home and later have to remove the child knowing full well the damage her misjudgement will have done him; where the points of view of parents and foster parents seem irreconcilable, and where in carrying out what is best for the child she has to watch one side suffer; or where she has to witness some cruelty done to a child, whether physical or mental, by a natural parent, yet bear in mind the dilemma and despair of that parent and his inevitable future importance to the child as an inescapable part of the triangle. All such situations will tax her to the uttermost and very great strain may arise for her as a person. In fact the fragile civilized shell of professionalism can at times wear thin, and she will certainly need the help of colleagues in discussion in order to retain her objectivity and understanding.

The social worker will have a direct relationship with the child, though with the very young ones her visits will be more to the family as a whole. She will perhaps become a familiar person to the child, playing with him and doing things like taking him for rides in her car as he gets older. If the child happens to be wrestling with the problem of the two mummies, because the foster mother is so vital a part of the situation, it may be easier for the social worker, being an outsider, to talk about it with the foster parents and child together during her visits as the occasion and need arises. The worker may be the person who brought the child to the foster parents, and in this case she will already be connected in his mind with his past and what has happened. She may literally be the last link with his lost world; she may be welcomed by him or else may be viewed with fear and mistrust, or be associated with some painful move. Whether or not she was actually involved in the placement she will try to be for him the trustee of his past and help him, according to his age, gradually to bring together the scattered pieces of his life. The way children use the social worker will differ according to all sorts of factors. There are certainly times when the relationship may be dormant or almost non-existent, though as a general rule it is more meaningful at times of growth such as the age of school entry and adolescence. Like many other teenagers, teenage foster children often need an outside person, other than their foster parents, with whom to work out their feelings. Two foster homes were doing extremely valuable work with a couple of teenage girls. Because of earlier difficult experiences that both girls had had, the relationships in both foster homes were stormy, but with the prospect of constructive outcome. The job of the social worker in both cases seemed to be to allow the girls to talk out their very strong feelings about the foster parents; to clarify the issues; and, as one deputy children's officer put it, "to siphon off some of the feelings" that otherwise might have rocked the foster homes to pieces.

The social worker's relationship with the child needs to be explained to the foster parents, otherwise misunderstandings can arise. Her job will be to support and "enable" foster parents, and somehow to convey to them, particularly during difficult times, what a tremendous and life-giving job they do. The social worker will want to help the foster parent to see the child and his behaviour in the light of his upbringing and of what has happened to him. They may be able to work out together how best to respond to him and sometimes to his quite startling behaviour problems. She will want to get across her understanding that the stresses of foster parenthood like anything else involve bad as well as good feelings, and to be the recipient of these, in such a way that hope can never be abandoned. She will need to discuss the feelings of the natural parents, of their significance to the child, which will mean in many situations working out the practical details of visits and the feelings which these arouse. The needs and abilities of foster parents vary enormously. Some are able to talk directly and warmly to the child about his background, others find it necessary to use the social worker; some find their bad feelings about the natural parents overwhelming; others have more intuitive understanding than the social worker and just require the facts to work on. The social worker has to try to be very sensitive as to where she can help and to the different things that are required from her. More often than not she has to accept that because of limitations in her own and the foster parents' personalities, some of the desirable things in a fostering cannot be achieved, but yet there is something there which is of value to the child. It can be extremely difficult for new social workers to take over supervision, as it takes time and care to build up relationships of trust. It is not uncommon for one child to have had a series of workers in a short space of time. This can be very perplexing for everyone concerned, and maybe the foster parents will not feel inclined to confide very easily. There is a large grain of truth in the theory that a continued relationship with the agency is what matters. Continuity is important, and probably each relationship is unique.

The social worker will, where possible, be in touch with the natural parents to discuss and involve them in the fostering of their children. The variety of parents has been mentioned, and she will need to work very differently with each one. She may, for example, have to try to persuade parents to visit the foster home even though they may be hoping to avoid distress to the child by not seeing him; she may on occasions have to arrange for a natural parent who may be very disturbed to visit the child at her office away from the foster home; she may have to help the over-protective domineering mother of some teenage girl to leave the child alone for a while, and not to try to see her so often.

It may well be asked whether, if the eternal triangle is so difficult to accept and tolerate, there are really any advantages in fostering.

The alternative to placement in a foster home is a placement in some form of residential establishment. In ideal conditions the latter mode of placement might have advantages: carefully selected, skilled, trained professional staff operating with small groups of children would be able to give the warmth, the opportunity for identification, and that degree of detachment and interpretative skill which the child deprived of his own home seems to need. However, in Britain at the present time the conditions are far from ideal, and so far as is known they have never been ideal during the past hundred years, and are far from ideal in any country in the world. Briefly, there is a gross insufficiency of people of the right temperament and calibre entering the profession of residential child care and *remaining in it*. Therefore for the child placed in residential care the group may be too big; it may be under-staffed; identification with the permanent members of staff may be difficult to achieve; and because of staff turnover the relationships the child is able to make may be constantly interruped. However, we know that there are children who are better placed in residential establishments because placement in foster homes can only add to their problems. It is no use to foster children whose parents are unable to accept the fostering at any level, and who may be able to resume care of them at a later date; for example, two toddlers were received into care because of their mother's mental condition. They would have benefited from fostering, particularly in view of their age, but this mother could not tolerate the idea and it was decided that the matron of the nursery where they were should help her to retain her relationship with the children. After 3 years the mother's mental condition improved and she resumed complete care over them. She had been able to use the help of the matron constructively, but would have been too threatened by foster parents, and the resulting conflict of loyalties would have been intolerable to the children. Sometimes older children, especially those in pubescence or in adolescence, seem to make far better use of residential placement. This would apply particularly to children who have been so hurt by other people that they cannot at any rate for a time make any close relationships, and therefore feel safer in a more institutionalized setting where less is demanded of them. Clare, whose mother had deserted her and whose father had committed suicide, was only able for a very long time to make a series of superficial contacts. Charlotte, who lost both parents at the age of 12, said that she did not want to go to a foster home, meaning that she would feel disloyal to replace her parents, when she was in a state of mourning. In fact she settled extremely well in a children's home, but later, when she was ready, was fostered with former neighbours and married later from their home.

In the view of the writer, the principle established in section 13 of the Children Act 1948 is the right one. It is founded, after all, on the simple observations of generations of supervisors from the days of the Poor Law to those of social service, and its value is confirmed by modern psychological theory. The emotional growth of the child, and the strength of his ego, depend upon the relationships he forms with parents. When these growing and learning processes are harshly interrupted, as when the child loses his home, his growth is stunted and may remain at an immature level unless fresh relationships of intimacy can be provided. Fostering represents the richest opportunity for renewed growth; yet, paradoxically, the chances of further damage are increased, for almost by definition the foster home is more fragile and more vulnerable than the solidly based children's home. At the same time the very intimacy of the relationships the child enjoyed with his own parents may make him highly protective of them: he may well fear that his treasure will be plundered.

For any social worker in this field, then, the great art is to assess the situation before ever the placement is made. She needs to assess and educate her prospective foster parents; she needs to assess the life-experiences of the child, his needs, and his defences. If she is successful he will in due time grow to man's estate unharmed; if she is unsuccessful he may never do so. There would seem to be no greater responsibility in the whole field of social work.

CHAPTER 7

Residential Care

JOHN STROUD*

EDITOR'S INTRODUCTION

It is only comparatively recently that any large-scale diversion of resources to the preventive service has occurred, at least as far as the child care service is concerned. It cannot be said at this stage that that diversion was by any means systematic or that the full potential of social workers has yet been recognized. It seems clear that in spite of this increased attention to preventive work, and in spite of the development of a programme of fostering children in care described in the preceding chapter, there are a large number of children who still need to be accommodated in what has been the main form of provision for them over the past 100 hundred years: children's homes, schools, and hostels of various kinds and with varying regimes. Social workers in the child care field are therefore likely to find themselves working in close co-operation with their social work colleagues who are residential, that is to say, who are required by their conditions of service to reside within a community of children. As is pointed out in this contribution, social workers are apt to view residential establishments with very mixed feelings; but what seems obvious at this stage is that no matter with what degree of sympathy the social worker may view residential care, his association with it is inescapable. One of the challenges of the coming decade is likely to be the involvement of all social workers, whether they operate in a residential setting or outside it, in rethinking the whole concept and replanning the residential service to be much more efficacious, and with more clearly defined objectives.

* Assistant Director of Social Services, Hertfordshire County Council.

97

It is a curious fact that in the two decades since the war children's "comics"—or story-papers for children—have frequently, and sometimes simultaneously, published stories about orphans fleeing from a dreadful orphanage relentlessly pursued by a wicked old orphanage master. Most of these stories purport to be contemporary (though the latest, which is appearing as I write this, does have the grace to set its scene in war-time London).

Obviously there are several factors at work to make story-tellers choose this theme. The story itself is a classically simple one of pursuit, well-suited to episodic treatment. Children can presumably identify easily with the pursued waif, since most of the readers might well wish to be rid of such encumbrances as parents. The need to build up and retain a dramatic tension may force the teller of the tale to portray the orphanage master as a villainous figure. Yet it seems to be significant that such a figure should be selected as the villain. In children's literature, villains often have deep roots: their depth can be measured both historically (in terms of a long and consistent tradition) and psychologically (in terms of disturbing emotional experience). Thus "the wicked stepmother" appears in all sorts of guises in many fairy-stories, some of great antiquity; yet "the wicked stepfather" is very rare. Schoolteachers are rarely regarded as wicked, but often portrayed as buffoons: authority and pomposity slipping on a banana-skin. Yet I have never seen an orphanage master portrayed as a buffoon; and perhaps it will be a healthy sign when he is. Why is there that difference between the schoolteacher and the master?

It seems that there must be some element of dread at work here; and the interesting thing is that orphanages, or children's homes, or children's communities, or whatever they may be called, are a comparatively recent innovation in England. The mid nineteenth century saw the beginning of a great flowering of this sort of establishment. It seems as though within four generations the homes have created an ambience of uneasiness; and what appears so often in children's literature has, less often but increasingly, been echoed in books written for adults. In these books, children's homes have usually been portrayed not as wicked but as harsh, unimaginative, sterile, and stultifying. And yet the homes have all been founded with the "best" of motives, and the founders of them and workers in them have always believed they were providing child-centred establishments. They believed that the needs of the children were being put first.

But the literature would suggest that the children's needs were being put last, if anywhere. There have been very few sympathetic studies of the work of residential staff. I tried to do it in a book called *Labour of Love*, but I do not think I succeeded, and I was aware while I was writing it that I was myself conflicted in my feelings.

We are, therefore, here beginning an exploration of a confused subject. Public opinion itself seems ambivalent: people are quick to seize on and believe stories about ill treatment in homes, and yet other people can express an interest in the homes which is quite sentimental. The staff of the homes often express uncertainty about their own aims and purposes; sometimes, in the variable climate of public opinion, they oscillate between trying to satisfy the needs of the children and trying to placate society at large. To add to the confusion, the homes themselves vary enormously in size, location, regime, and clientele. Some of these variations arise for historical reasons, and it may be helpful to try and trace these elements.

Care and concern for the orphan child extends, of course, back into the mists of antiquity; and so long as society in this country was organized on a rural basis, such children were normally absorbed into the village community by neighbours or kinsmen. The illegitimate child was not always so lucky: and the destitute child—i.e. the child who had parents living but who had somehow lost them or been abandoned by them or was being ill treated or neglected—probably fared worst of all. But destitute children did not appear in any great numbers until the process of urbanization began to accelerate. As their numbers increased, so did the number of institutions, and the trend seems to have kept pace with the trend towards town dwelling.

Thus in medieval times we begin to see some sort of provision for children made by the religious communities, notably the monasteries, and by certain urban organizations such as guilds and corporations. Most of the provision then was in terms of education or training: thus there were seminaries, or the very early forms of grammar schools.

The economic dislocations of the sixteenth and seventeenth centuries, and in particular the dislocation of rural life under the Tudors, produced swarms of destitute people of all ages and a great increase in the number of children to be dealt with. By this time the monasteries had disappeared and the grammar schools were going over to the education of the sons of the middle classes. The social response to this situation was the establishment of the Poor Law; and, under that Law, the establishment of poor houses. In these houses destitute children were accommodated with vagrants, madmen, old people, unemployed people, and the sick. As far as the children were concerned, the object of the house was to train them to be industrious—to train them to be independent and not to be a burden on the state.

This philosophy was written into the statutes for the best part of three-and-a-half centuries, when the objective of administrators was clearly seen as the apprenticeship of children, teaching them a trade, or having them absorbed into a trade. "Independence of the state" was seen in economic terms, and in the eighteenth century the philosophy found expression in the establishment of houses of industry, where the preparation of youngsters for a laborious life was made more vigorous. By this time the industrial revolution had begun, and the new mills and mines and manufactories had an insatiable thirst for cheap and unskilled labour. Convoys of destitute children were moved from the houses of industry to the factories of the north and were there absorbed—often cruelly—into gainful employment.

In 1834 the Poor Law was reformed, and the approach of its administrators to destitute persons was made more harsh and even negative. Parishes were amalgamated in larger administrative units and, with this pooling of financial resources, workhouses were built. Help—or "relief"—for destitute people was made conditional upon their entering the workhouse, where conditions were deliberately made comfortless. This approach was obviously aimed at "the able-bodied poor", often unemployed adults; and except that it dealt with the symptom rather than the cause of unemployment, it was at least successful in its avowed intention to reduce public expenditure on the relief of destitution.

Unfortunately, however, the new harsh workhouse regime bore most heavily upon the most vulnerable inmates—children and old people. Within a very few years it was noted that the children were so crushed and despondent that many were incapable of achieving independence. What was more, the workhouses themselves were bitterly hated as symbols of repression, while the inmates—those who had succumbed to the hated regime—were regarded with contempt. The children, shaven-headed in their ugly uniforms, were shouted at in the streets: the contemptuous cry of "Workus!" was flung at four generations of such children. In addition, the children were to some extent feared as they were regarded as carriers of "the workhouse disease"—probably typhus fever. Somewhere around this date may have been born the suspicion and mistrust of the custodians of children in care.

In terms of achieving the economic independence of the children—of somehow inculcating in them the habit of industriousness—the workhouse regime was soon seen to be failing. There came first a movement towards education and training, with the establishment of district schools, to which children from surrounding institutions were taken for a very primitive form of instruction. Soon afterwards came attempts to establish institutions specifically for children. Such a one was Banstead, in Surrey, in which hundreds and hundreds of London children were accommodated, for whom in the 1870s enormous compassion was shown. They did not live in a "home" in any sense of the word; they had merely been segregated.

Meanwhile there was a parallel development in the related field of juvenile delinquency. In the first half of the nineteenth century children who broke the law—and there were many—were regarded as diminutive adults, and therefore to be subject to the same punishments as were applied to adults—transportation, hanging, imprisonment. But imprisonment, in the unreformed gaols of the time, where prisoners of all ages and degrees of desperation were mixed up together, was gradually seen to be as unconstructive and even as harmful to the children as the workhouse regimes. A movement led by a vigorous lady named Mary Carpenter produced, by the 1860s, a system of reformatory schools to which were sent children convicted of crimes.

It seems likely that the Victorians were guided by two principles. The first was summarized in the saying that "Satan finds work for idle hands to do". As far as could be seen, an idle or unemployed or unskilled child was highly likely to commit crimes. The second principle was that children were obviously influenced by the adults about them, and if they were constantly in the company of "hardened criminals" they would themselves become hardened. Therefore they should be segregated.

The Poor Law administrators felt themselves to be confronted by similar problems with their older children, who seemed to be developing idle habits and falling under evil influences; and therefore there slowly developed a system of industrial schools.

In the fullness of time—in fact in 1933—these two similar systems were amalgamated and the schools became known as approved schools. Children who were in need of care and protection; children who had become beyond the control of the local authority; and, most of all, children who had committed offences which in the case of adults would be punished by imprisonment, were sent to these schools. Some of the schools were managed by local authorities, more by voluntary bodies of various kinds, and all concentrated on a regime of fairly vigorous activity, education, trade training, and physical fitness.

The second half of the nineteenth century was a period of considerable activity in the field of child care. As we have seen in a previous chapter, systems of boarding out developed in this half-century. Following the principle of segregating children from pernicious workhouse influences, some local authorities, notably in the big cities, built what were virtually children's villages—a series of "homes", or "villas", each accommodating twenty or thirty children, built usually around a "village green", with a school, a chapel, a laundry, a bakery, and other workshops on the same site. A few local authorities preferred to build or acquire small homes scattered across the residential parts of their areas, trying to see that the children were more integrated in the community, trying to protect them from the old cry of "Workus!"

Nevertheless, large numbers of children continued to live either in children's barracks, such as those which surrounded London, or in the workhouses themselves.

Meanwhile, from the year 1869 onwards, there was a new development, and one which expanded at a phenomenal rate: the work of the voluntary, or charitable, societies. There had been earlier attempts, usually by individuals, to establish homes for children: one remembers Thomas Coram, who founded the Foundling Hospital in the mid eighteenth century; Andrew Reed, who built his Infant Orphans' Asylum some 50 years later; and a man named Mueller, who founded his Orphan Homes in Bristol in the 1830s; and there were many small charity schools or charity homes founded by provincial squires and landowners' ladies.

But in 1869 both Dr. Barnardo and Dr. Stephenson (who founded the

National Children's Homes) began their operations, and the following decades saw the establishment of many societies: the Church of England Waifs and Strays Society, the Catholic Crusade of Rescue, Mr. Fegan's Homes, Mr. Spurgeon's Homes, Mr. Quarrier's Homes (in Scotland), the Salvation Army, the Church Army, and so on. All these new societies grew, sometimes with phenomenal rapidity, into national organizations with numerous local branches and affiliations and, in due couse, a network of homes and foster homes.

These pioneers looked first to the city streets—many of them started life as "missionaries to darkest London". In the streets they found thousands of destitute children. Both Barnardo and Charles Booth, an early demographer, estimated that there were 30,000 such children in London alone. It was perfectly clear to them that the Poor Law services, which were still based on too small a unit of administration, had been overwhelmed by the problems of massive urbanization. The philosophy of the Poor Law administrators was in any case that help should be grudging and hard to obtain, and the loathing with which poor people regarded the administrators made them reluctant to seek help from that quarter.

The workers of the societies "sought out" the children who were adrift in the streets, an approach not used by the statutory service. In seeking out, the voluntary workers seem to have been inspired, at least at the beginning, by a rescue motive. They were, on the one hand, shocked by the conditions in which children lived; juvenile prostitution was, for instance, widespread in London. There is a sense of moral outrage in the early reports. On the other hand, almost all these workers were closely associated with religious organizations and themselves ardent Christians. They believed that children should be brought within sound moral influences. They detested what they saw of the Poor Law barracks for children, partly because of the obvious ugliness and inhumanity of the regime but more because there was no discernible Christian influence within the institutions.

From the beginning the societies went for foster homes and for small homes. Some of the homes established in the early days, for instance by the Church of England Society, were very small indeed, each containing four or six children. Later, rather larger homes developed, though they rarely accommodated more than thirty children each. There were a few examples, notably Barnardo's "Children's Village" at Woodford Bridge and the

National Children's Home Branch at Harpenden, of establishments accommodating some hundreds of children, but they were always subdivided into smaller units, a typical layout consisting of a number of "villas" grouped around a "village green".

The societies gave (on the whole) much more care to the selection of staff than did the Poor Law authorities: and, indeed, by offering a type of missionary work they seemed able to recruit more intelligent and better educated people. They nearly always insisted that staff were confirmed or communicant members of the appropriate church. They tended, nevertheless, to select somewhat austere, highly moral persons, the factor of "sound moral influence" being of overriding importance.

As we have seen, the growth of the societies in the late nineteenth century was phenomenal. The Church of England Society, for example, which started operations in 1881, acquired, furnished, staffed, and filled seventy homes in 15 years, and had found foster homes for a further 600 children. The growth of Dr. Barnardo's organization was even faster. The rate of growth slowed after 1900, and after the First World War it levelled off. There were changes in the patterns of residential care; individual homes were closed and opened, but the total voluntary resources altered little between 1914 and about 1960.

We have now identified the three main roots from which sprang the complicated tree of residential care. There was first the Poor Law service which in 1930 passed to public assistance departments with larger administrative units, and in turn passed to children's departments in 1948 and to social services departments in 1971, the size of the administrative unit remaining unchanged. Broadly speaking, within this "public sector", as it might be called, there was a very slow trend between 1850 and 1950 to create establishments of many different kinds and shapes and sizes, but designed specifically for children and set apart from the workhouses. The movement away from workhouses was all but complete by 1950.

The second root was the voluntary movement, or what might be called the "private sector", which, as we have seen, had established by 1900 its basic pattern of medium-sized homes but which continued to experiment with new kinds of care, often for children with specific types of handicap: one might instance hostels for diabetic children and training homes for dull girls.

The third growing point was the mixture of voluntary and local authority efforts to treat the delinquent child, the various establishments coming together in 1933 in the approved school system which was massively supported by grants-in-aid from central government funds.

There is space here only to mention certain other developments which further complicate the contemporary picture. From 1902 onwards there was a slow movement to provide boarding schools for handicapped children, often linked closely with homes or hostels. While those for blind or deaf children have perhaps a distinctive educational role, those for maladjusted children often seem to be dealing more with behavioural or social problems than with classroom problems, and their work closely resembles that carried on in some junior approved schools. Then, from 1908 onwards, there came a development in remand homes, established to provide for the observation and assessment of children found guilty of offences in order to make recommendations to juvenile courts as to the appropriate treatment of them. After 1933 these homes were also used for the short-term detention of young offenders. The economic depression in the early 1930s created heavy unemployment amongst teenagers and there was a corresponding burst of activity in the "private sector" where societies were formed to provide hostels and sometimes training schools for these youngsters. Finally, between the wars there was the limited development of probation homes and probation hostels designed to provide short-term training—usually for 6 months, never for more than 12—for children who were on probation for offences and whose home conditions were unsatisfactory.

After this necessarily oversimplified review of historical development, we must turn to the scene in the 1970s; and it will come as no surprise to learn that that scene is a confused one. All over the country there are residential establishments of different kinds, administered by different agencies, sometimes with clearly defined roles and objectives but more often with an uncertain role or, perhaps more truly, a mixture of different roles. In the following chapter practitioners in various kinds of establishments will examine their role as they see it. Here we must attempt to explore the mainstream of residential care, those middle-sized homes where the majority of the children live; and the majority live in local authority homes.

Let us now turn to look at the children themselves. The first question obviously is: how many are there to form this majority? The figures shown in Table 1 give some indication of trends in residential care over the last 15 years. They are taken from the annual statistics published by the Home Office and made up of returns submitted by local authority children's departments.

It will be noted that the number of children accommodated in small homes has steadily risen—absolutely and as a proportion of the total. It will

TABLE 1

Date of census	No. of children in		
	All types of local authority home (a)	Homes for not more than 12 children (b)	Larger homes (c)
November 1955	21,941	3,924	12,301
March 1960	19,732	5,064	9,539
March 1965	19,712	6,591	8,223
March 1970	20,720	8,557	7,276

Note: columns (b) and (c) do not together equal the total shown in column (a) as certain kinds of homes, such as reception homes, residential nurseries, and hostels have not been included in the table.

also be noticed that the total number of children in residential care has fluctuated very little over the years in spite of the encouragement given first to fostering schemes and secondly to "preventive" social work and the support of children in their own homes, which will be discussed a little later.

There is another factor of which we should take note, and that is that the average age of children in residential care is rising. This is unfortunately not so easily demonstrated by statistics because the Home Office returns only give the age groups of children "in care", not "in residential care". However we can make deductions from two other sets of figures. We have already seen that the total number in residential care remained fairly constant over the 15 years. However, the number in residential nurseries, i.e. those aged 5 and under, declined from 4622 in November 1955 to 2521 in March 1970.

Of the children coming into care, those of school age—i.e. between 5 and 15—accounted for 43 per cent of the total in 1959–60 and 47 per cent in 1969–70. Since the total number in residential care remained fairly constant, we can see that the average age must have crept up. This is in part due to the fact that local authority schemes of "preventative" work have been concentrated on the youngest children (on whom separation from parents might

TABLE 2

No parent or guardian	257
Abandoned or lost	728
Death of mother	750
Desertion by mother	5,241
Confinement of mother	5,798
Short-term illness	17,047
Long-term illness	1,458
Tuberculosis contact	54
Illegitimate child	2,709
Parent in prison	767
Homelessness	2,693
Unsatisfactory home conditions	3,074
Care orders: Offenders	1,641
Non-offenders	3,357
Other reasons (including committal orders under Matrimonial Proceedings Act)	5,968
Total	51,542

have the most serious effects); and in part due to the fact that fostering seems easier to arrange for younger children.

Our next question must be: For what reasons did these children arrive in the homes?

Again the available statistics do not give us accurate information, but useful deductions can be made from them. Turning to those last available, relating to the year ending 31 March 1970, Table 2 shows "reasons for children coming into care" and the numbers involved.

A closer analysis of these figures will be found elsewhere in this book, but the point which is immediately obvious is that a very small proportion indeed of these children have no parent or guardian anywhere on this planet.

References in the "comics" and the popular press to "orphans" and "orphanages" are wildly misleading. A study of the available case-papers over the last 100 years indicates that such terms have for long been misleading. For the majority of children in care—and therefore, I am convinced, for the majority of children in residential care—what might be called a "man-made separation" from home and parents has taken place. This may have been by order of the court; it may have been through a failure in parental or marital responsibility; it may have been through a failure of society—in, for example, the inability of society to make proper provision for homeless families.

It is difficult to avoid the conclusion that around this whole subject of the residential care of children there hangs a cloud of guilt—guilt that such care needs to exist at all. Its existence seems to symbolize a failure in some degree: the failure of parents to maintain a home; the failure of social workers to help the parents effectively; the failure perhaps of society itself to control those forces which tend to disrupt the less able families. Some placements in residential care (though by no means all) arise from a failure to provide adequate fostering resources or day-care facilities (i.e. non-residential placements such as day nurseries). Children's homes represent, in a visible and tangible form, the tendency in social work to treat the casualty and not the cause of the illness.

There is in social work generally a very strong movement towards treating the cause of the illness—towards attempting to dilute the destructive forces in society and strengthen the resources of family and community. The Children and Young Persons Act of 1963 was a very important signpost on the new path of development. What seems clear so far is that such efforts take a long time to "pay off", and that meanwhile the casualty service is still at full stretch. Children's homes have perforce still to provide what might be called a hospital service. Their task might be said to be to restore their patients to full social health.

In the fulfilment of this task there are certain elements which are basic and obvious. The growing child needs food, clothing, and shelter. The earliest homes provided these and nothing else. Soon, during the nineteenth century, it was recognized that the child also needed education if in due course he was to hold his place in society even if that education was in the first place only the attainment of simple literacy. It was rarely in the early years that the home itself provided that education, but it was the duty of those in charge to see that education was available and that the child attended the place of instruction. This is still their duty.

To these elements were added, mainly by or through the influence of the voluntary societies, what might be called "moral training". At first this was rather heavy handed and negative: the enjoining of such precepts as: "Thou shalt not steal. Thou shalt not masturbate. Thou shalt not wet the bed", the precept being backed by pretty ferocious punishments. There has been a distinct shift in the approach to such problems—an approach based more on example than on precept, more on understanding the causes than punishing the effects—but nevertheless it is still expected of residential social workers that they will try to teach the Ten Commandments.

For all the changes in technique that time has brought, these five elements —the provision of food, clothing, shelter, education, and moral training— remain the responsibility of the homes. What has been added to them, surprisingly recently, has been the task of trying to deal with the children's emotions.

It is surprising how recent has been the recognition that children have emotions at all; it is not certain how widespread that recognition is even now, and it is unlikely that even a majority of the population today recognize that babies have emotions. It is intriguing when one remembers that as long ago as the eighteenth century the behaviour of children in institutional settings was described, and described again with suitable expressions of alarm by the Poor Law authorities in 1836. It was not really until the development of the child guidance service in the 1920s, the study of children in establishments during the Second World War, and, finally, the classic work by Dr. John Bowlby (*Maternal Care and Mental Health,* 1952) that the two elements in the emotional life of children which are particularly important in the present context were identified. These were, briefly, the emotional disturbance produced by separation from parents, and the emotional stunting produced by prolonged residence in arid institutions.

It would be wrong to give the impression that all children's homes before, say, 1950 were arid, or that their staffs were unfeeling. Many of the over-worked staff were devoted to their charges. The difficulty was that the homes had developed in such a way and with so much emphasis on order, cleanliness, and the five basic elements, that personal relationships, affection, fondling, and intimacy, were all very difficult to develop even if not actively discouraged.

But the recognition that the nurture of the child's emotional well being is the "sixth element" of residential care has undoubtedly led to a revolution since 1950 (which, like other revolutions, has been painful) and has made the task of the residential worker more skilful, more demanding, and less easy to define.

The development can perhaps be described in these terms. In the early 1950s there were emerging from the old-type homes children who had been fed, clothed, sheltered, educated, and morally trained, and who could be described as "affectionless". They had, nowhere along the line, been able to form loving and trusting relationships with an adult, and they seemed unable to form relationships with foster parents, with employers, with friends, or, later on, with spouses or with their own children.

The children's committees tackled this problem of the "affectionless" or "institutionalized" child in various ways. There was a move away from single-sex homes in which girls saw nobody but other girls or women staff. "Mixed" homes with married couples in charge were set up as soon as possible. Large homes were subdivided into "family" units so that children could form closer relationships with adults; and more staff were moved in. Staff were selected differently: previously the head of a home was often selected for his disciplinary or organizing powers, but now selectors looked for warmth, richness of personality, an "outgoing" temperament. Opportunities were consciously created for staff and children to share in activitities —there was a growth in hobbies, craftwork, adventure holidays, and so on. There were other innovations: pets were much more often to be seen in the newer homes; cuddly toys found their way into the children's beds.

The movement from aridity towards richness has taken a long time and is still far from complete. The majority of children's homes are still rather too orderly, rather too clean, rather too organized, perhaps even rather too middle class; but the change in 20 years has been most impressive.

The staff have obviously become more exposed to the children's demands, and as the move away from the old autocratic regime has proceeded, so it has become apparent that the children have emotional problems over and above those induced by institutional living. Their emotional disturbance is due not only to the traumatic experience of "losing their homes" but to their whole life experience prior to that. If, for example, we turn back to Table 2 we see that more than 5000 children came into care because of desertion by their mothers. It is likely that many of those desertions came as the culmination of long years of marital disharmony. The parents' rows, the unhappiness and insecurity of home life, the continuous fears of "the big bang", can not only produce emotional disturbance in the children but can prepare them very badly to cope with the final loss of home and the adaptation to community living.

One has to beware of generalizations in this field. There have been children who have come into care almost with a sigh of relief, and who have welcomed the undemanding asylum of residential care. There are children, especially those who have been committed by the courts, who regard their period in residential care as their "stretch" of prison life, to be served as indifferently as possible. But the majority of children who come into residential care come as emotional casualties in need of therapy.

Some indication of what is meant by this may be obtained from the following. This is a list of children living in one particular local authority children's home at one particular point in time at the end of 1971. This is not a selected list: it is a list of all the residents without exception:

Boy aged 13 and his sister 15—parents had separated, the mother had died suddenly; the father having been out of touch for many years had reappeared on the scene. The girl was aggressive and delinquent.

Boy of 8 and his sister 5—mother had deserted, father unable to cope; he was himself brought up in care and was inadequate and a petty criminal.

Girl of 14—mother dead, no relatives traced; she was herself educationally subnormal.

Girl of 16—mother mentally ill, father deserted; she was herself so retarded as to be only just able to cope with a school for educationally sub-normal children.

Girl of 14 and her sister 11—children had experienced three broken marriages before their mentally unstable mother committed suicide. The elder sister has a mild degree of spina bifida.

Girl 16—rejected by both parents; had lived with a succession of relatives from the age of 3 months; had become seriously disturbed while living with a half-sister who was herself cohabiting.

Girl 12 and her sisters 11 and 8—mother, who was mentally ill, had finally deserted; father a long-distance lorry driver unable to keep the home going.

Boy 15—illegitimate and at odds with his stepfather, committed to care having been found guilty of fourteen offences.

Boy 13 and his brother 12—members of a large poverty-stricken family from which the father had deserted. The boys became beyond the control of their depressed mother.

Boy 16—eldest of a family of eight; committed to care after having been found guilty of stealing women's underwear; thought to be in the early stages of schizophrenia.

Boy 15—educationally sub-normal and emotionally disturbed; in care all his life; has broken down in a foster home placement.

Girl 14 and her brothers 16, 13, and 12—father deserted, mother mentally ill; children had grown out of her control.

Boy 10 and his brother 8—mother deserted, father at sea; both boys in care since infancy.

The majority of these children had been in care for the greater part of their lives and in this particular home for 4 years. I have no reason to suppose that this group of children is untypical of a group in residential care except that possibly the average age of this group is higher than the norm. It could be said with justification that every one of these children needs individual care and attention, and that it doubles or trebles the demand on the residential workers to congregate such children together in such numbers. Nevertheless, this is the sort of situation in which most residential workers find themselves living today. One of the problems of a local authority child care service is that it cannot be selective, as some boarding schools and some voluntary establishments can be: if a child needs care, then care has to be provided, irrespective of the child's intelligence, behaviour, deviancy, or imbalance.

How can residential workers cope with such tasks as this, armed as they are only with their own personalities and skills?

It is on that particular "how" that most of today's debates focus. Some workers advocate a completely "free" or permissive regime within which children may play out or act out their emotional conflicts. Some, on the other hand, say that disturbed children need a reliable and supportive structure—that the children are, after their disturbing experiences, frightened of freedom. Some say that the regime does not matter much so long as it is consistent and that the adults are continually "there". Some advocate that within a not too rigid structure there should be conscious and imaginative efforts made to involve the children in therapeutic activities such as art therapy, drama play, group discussion, and so on. There is almost certainly a place for each of these approaches in a comprehensive system of children's homes. Unfortunately, what may be the ideal regime theoretically is often upset in practice, either by staffing or by the expectations of the neighbourhood. A "free" regime puts great demands upon staff, and there is a scarcity of mature and well-balanced workers able to tolerate the demands year after year after year. Again, a local authority in England is, broadly speaking, expected to be beyond reproach, and if the children in its care seem to the neighbourhood to be "running wild" then there is often hostility and fury. On the whole, local authority workers are manoeuvred into a somewhat conservative position, as one of the criticisms which seems to his employers to be damaging is that the head of a home is not "in control" of his situation.

My own opinion is that the regime should be that in which the adults feel most comfortable, and that it should make sense to the children themselves. The published reminiscences of people who as children were in care seem to suggest that they appreciated firmness if it was honest. They were easily bewildered, often by such events as being parted from brothers and sisters, often because no adult ever spared the time to sit down and explain what had happened and what was happening. They disliked degradation. They were, on the whole, rather afraid of freedom.

Is it possible, then, to justify the continuing existence of children's homes? And, if so, is it possible to establish the objectives that might be attained in them?

In academic terms it is as hard to justify them as it is to justify the existence of hospitals or of nursing homes. Each of these represents the failure of the family or of the community or of the professional services to contain and treat a problem *in situ*. We do not, however, live in an academic world; and the complexity of the real world, the fragmentation of communities and, indeed, of families, the comparative shortage of professional resources, mean that the individual person "at risk" cannot be sustained. The mentally ill person, the very old and feeble person, and the young child deprived of a normal family life are the least able to deal with the bewildering and at times cruel community wherein they dwell. In these circumstances asylum becomes essential.

So the first objective of the children's home becomes to provide asylum. This is not so easy as it sounds, for it must be an asylum which the child himself recognizes as such, and many of the children who have been through bad times become suspicious, rebellious, angry, or emotionally inert. It is probable that not enough is done prior to admission to help children to recognize and accept their own need for asylum. Often parents, themselves in the throes of guilt and anger, use the word "home" as a threat: "You will be sent to a home if you don't obey me." Similar phrases are sometimes used in the juvenile court when children appear as offenders. Yet it is also probable that little that can be said or demonstrated can really help a child who is passing through a severely disturbing and even traumatic experience.

To provide asylum is therefore a first objective, and for the residential social worker it may remain the only objective. In some cases the important objective is to mend or re-establish the child's home, and the caseworker's task is, for example, to trace the missing spouse and to try to bring about a matrimonial reconciliation. The residential worker has, however, an important part to play; for amongst the parents' confused feelings there are often strong elements of guilt and dread about the child being in a home at all. There have been many parents who have loved their children yet have been unable to face the sight of them living in a residential setting: and so they have not visited, relationships have failed, and the children themselves have grown rejective and bitter. While, therefore, the home must be acceptable by the child, it must also be acceptable by the parent, and this—in the current climate of dread and suspicion—is the more difficult objective to attain, and requires the greater skill.

In the majority of cases the ultimate return of the child to his—possibly restructured—home is the objective; and that this statement can be made is indicative of the change in thought that has occurred since approximately 1950. Prior to that date, the home was regarded more or less as an end in itself, its aim being to secure the upbringing of the child during the period of his dependence; now the home is regarded much more in terms of rehabilitative treatment. Acceptance of this notion has been painful for many residential workers. Yet, when the notion is accepted, the attainment of the objective remains very difficult.

Another glance at the circumstances of the children listed above will perhaps provide the best illustration of this point. In how many of those cases is it realistic to expect the home to be re-established? Can this father change his whole pattern of living? Can that mother be "cured" of mental illness? In the children themselves can the damage that has evidently been done to their personalities effectively be repaired? Even if the parents and the children can change, is it possible that, independently of each other, they can change so that they knit together as splintered bones may knit? Some of the case histories look almost as if some demented chimpanzee had dotted down notes at random on a musical manuscript; the worker's task is to bring the dots into harmonious orchestration.

In spite of all the difficulties, this type of orchestration can be done and very often has been done. What has emerged has been the need for a variety of different techniques to be used. Sometimes, for example, a well-structured establishment with firm external controls applied to a bewildered adolescent has helped the boy to internalize those controls so that he becomes less impulsive, more thoughtful. The sticking-plaster of control may be thin and its adhesiveness may be in doubt, but its existence has given new confidence to the child's parent and some sort of rapport has sprung from increasing hope and confidence. In other cases, however, often with younger children, it is necessary for the child to regress emotionally and re-live difficult phases of development; and to permit this regression the regime has to be flexible. Sometimes the child's personality is disrupted by powerful suppressed feelings, and any progress in any direction depends upon the controlled release of those feelings. Sometimes this release is achieved within an adult/child relationship, and sometimes the child needs less intense or intimate treatment and finds it within group activity. Sometimes a child needs a powerful maternal influence; sometimes he needs a relationship with a genial giant of a father figure.

What is being recognized here is that the child needs to achieve a sense of personal identity—even though in many cases it may be thought that a rather crude identikit version of a personality may be the best that can be achieved. Often, then, the objective becomes to help the child to make sense of himself and of his world. Often this making sense is not "with a view to" anything at all—not to reunion, not to fostering, not to conformity with the rules of society. Some balance of personality, some happiness in highly individualistic terms, some basis from which the child can work out his own destiny, is what is aimed at.

Thus there has been a shift over the last 20 years away from the idea of a home as an all-embracing asylum towards the idea of an establishment within which a child may find himself. Future generations will undoubtedly judge that the movement was slow and the methods used were crude. Already, however, it is clear that the movement has produced important developments.

The first of these is in the matter of staffing. From its beginning, the residential child care service has been plagued by staff shortage. The shortage could often be measured in terms of quality as much as of quantity. There must have been many reasons for this, but one undoubtedly was that employers did not recognize that the care of children was a skilled job. Too often in the past, and far too often in the present, it was held and is held by appointing committees that "anybody who has brought up her own children can bring up somebody else's". The only qualification looked for seemed to be that of a reasonably competent housewife. In the course of one generation, however, there has been a profound change in attitude. Employers have looked for far more than personality factors: they have looked for skill, insight, and training. Training courses have multiplied; salaries have been pushed up; graduates of universities have begun to seek careers in residential care. Staff who at one stage were given no private living quarters at all are now provided with houses and flats, a visible sign of an increased status. A very great deal remains to be done: staff shortages still bedevil the service; there is a high wastage rate; much research is still needed into job satisfaction and motivation. Nevertheless, any observer who can compare, say, a staff photograph taken in 1950 with one taken in 1970 will be greatly impressed by the change—in vivacity alone—which has already taken place.

The second development which is significant has been in the field of assessment. It was in the late 1940s that the first assessment centres were set up, the first two both being run by voluntary societies as pioneer or experimental ventures. The idea was to attempt to assess the child's needs and to predict the type of establishment in which those needs could best be met. A network of reception and assessment centres was set up by local authorities during the 1950s, and in the same period classifying schools were set up within what was then the approved school system.

Progress was slow and at times disheartening. There was an unfortunate tendency to assess a child over a short period of time and then "label" him, as luggage is labelled, so that he continued on his journey with the label round his neck. Even within that system, recommendations might be made which could not be carried out because of an overall shortage of resources or because of an inflexibility in all the supporting services. Some assessment centres were overwhelmed because they were regarded as places of containment—all the most difficult children were sent to them because nobody could think what else to do. Nevertheless, the first crude attempts at assessment were successful enough to lead to further and further refinements of technique, and this process of refinement continues.

Arising both from the findings of the assessment centres and from the changing attitudes to children's needs, it came to be recognized that what had developed as frankly a hotch-potch of statutory and voluntary homes, often duplicating the work of each other, had in fact a great potential of flexibility. Because children's needs were recognized as varying so widely, it became clear that no one home could successfully deal with all the needs. Because of their historical roots, some homes were rigid and some were flexible; some could be highly selective in staff appointments; some were isolated and under-staffed. Speaking generally, all had attempted to do too much—all had taken too wide a spread of problems. Some movement towards specialization seemed desirable, and the very variety of establishments made specialism feasible.

Progress towards specialization was very slow and very haphazard. No employer seeking to fill a new residential post ever sat down (as far as I know) and thought: here we need a very firm, very strong father figure; or, analysis of the needs of children coming into care shows that a dominantly female home is needed. Employers tended to proceed empirically, appointing staff first then finding out what they were good at and then sending them children who seemed to fit in. The head of a home who proved herself "good with adolescent girls" might find herself overwhelmed with adolescent girls. The demand for residential care, which has been insistent and unrelenting since 1960, often forced unsuitable placements. Some local authorities were too small to be able to provide a reasonably wide range of residential care.

It was, perhaps, the last point which led to the establishment, under the Children and Young Persons Act of 1969, of Regional Planning Committees. These committees consist of representatives of a number of neighbouring authorities, and twelve have been established in England and Wales. The first task of each committee is to ascertain, as best it can, the actual and foreseeable needs of children in the region and to plan the most comprehensive and flexible system of residential establishments to meet those needs. Voluntary societies co-operate with the local authorities in the planning process. The process is, at the time of writing, in its earliest stages, and no doubt the first plans will be crude: but this part of this Act does represent the conscious attempt to formalize the changed attitudes to the needs of the individual child. It is interesting to note that other parts of the same Act reflect the same movement towards flexibility and choice. The approved school system, for example, which was a separated system with its own administration and rules and orders and assessment process, is to become integrated with other types of residential care. Children whose needs have changed may be moved from one type of establishment to another without administrative obstruction.

As, then, we near the end of this necessarily brief survey of the mainstream of residential care, we see that the currents are flowing strongly. There are innumerable eddies and whirlpools and there is the white foam of conflict, but these are far from being stagnant waters. There are all sorts of movements going on which seem exciting for the future. Traditionally, for example, homes were put in the charge of married couples who might be known as superintendent and matron and who tried to act as father and mother to what has been called their "parliamentary family" (a family created by statute, not by kinship); now there is a move to a more professional mode of grouped staff working. Traditionally, homes were for children only; now there is a conscious move towards involving the parents much more and in some cases encouraging them to reside in the homes for short periods. Traditionally, homes were somewhat isolated from their neighbourhoods and their notice-boards proclaimed that "unauthorized persons were prohibited"; now unauthorized persons (usually the children's friends) troop merrily in and out. Traditionally, children lived continuously in the homes; now many of them go to their own homes every week-end and the homes have become boarding hostels. Traditionally, there was a sharp dividing line: either a child was in his own home or he was in a residential establishment. Now there is a strong movement towards day care, day treatment, or day assessment. And in the near future there undoubtedly lies a movement to bring the homes into even closer involvement with the community. Traditionally, people in need of help have gone first to a social work office to be interviewed by a social worker who sits at a desk. Thence a request would go for a placement in a home. Now there is growing the concept of "the bed-backed consultancy": the arrangement whereby the social worker sits in the home, sees the client there, if necessary arranges for his admission there, works with him there, and maintains every possible link with his family.

And yet traditions die hard—in staff, in their employing authorities, in the children and their parents, and in society as a whole. There are staff who believe in taking a child into "total" care, cutting off his parents and old associates, bringing him up in accordance with firm tenets of philosophy. Such members of staff find more fluid ways of working disturbing and threatening: they like their objectives to be clear and sharp, and in the confused world of the 1970s they are not alone in their yearning for firmness and clarity. There are employers who believe that residential social workers should be "home-makers", and in their recruitment they look for competence in domestic service; they may look for some idealized qualities which "a good parent" ought to have. Parents and children often look upon the homes as the visible and tangible symbol of their own failures. They find it extraordinarily difficult, for example, to tell their next-door neighbour over the fence that "my child has gone into a home". They can say: "My child is at boarding school" even when the child has gone to what is unequivocally a penal establishment; but a Home, with a capital H, is not something they can admit to.

And in the end, do not all the people involved in a residential service reflect, and become affected by, the attitude of society as a whole? Does not society see any home as "the last refuge"—a place to be used only when everything else has failed, a place which by its very presence betrays the fact that people have not been loving enough, or clever enough, or competent enough, to deal with problems in an altogether more civilized way? And so long as that climate of opinion exists, is it not likely that the homes will not be given the money they should have or the staff they should have or the status they should have?

And is it not possible that the story-papers and the children's comics reflect truly the guilty feelings of society itself? In the grudging support that is given, in the attitude that homes for children are no more than a necessary evil, is not society expressing its fear of something it feels is bad? Something that has to be personified by a wicked old orphanage master?

CHAPTER 8

Residential Establishments

EDITOR'S INTRODUCTION

As has been made clear in the preceding chapter, residential establishments in Britain are extraordinarily varied in size, regime, clientele, and—perhaps above all—in the attitudes and philosophies of those social workers who live and work in them. It is very difficult to give a complete and satisfying picture of current residential provision; but the aim of this chapter is the very modest one of providing for the student, the lay reader, or for the overseas reader a little more insight into the complexity of the subject. This has been attempted by inviting four residential social workers who operate in different kinds of establishment to describe those establishments as they see them. It would have been easy, however, to obtain information on a hundred different establishments or fifty different viewpoints on just one type of establishment.

At present it might well be said that the role and effectiveness of an establishment depend upon the personality of the principal and his ability to communicate his thinking to the other members of his community. The freedom given to the individual to set his own style, or "do his own thing", might well be criticized, perhaps in the terms that is it not professional enough, or orderly enough, or even sufficiently self-aware. There has, however, been a long tradition in Britain of individualistic ways of working. Lip-service is nowadays paid to the notion that "the gifted amateur" is an out-dated person; but this is not really true—not in industry nor in the civil service; nor in sport nor in social work. The tradition of the amateur—the person in love with his work, who is deeply committed to it, and who therefore deals with it in the way that satisfies him most—is very strong in Britain, and has, perhaps, been one of those factors which

makes for commitment bordering on insularity, for creativity bordering on eccentricity, for sensitivity bordering on chaos. Nowhere,
perhaps, are these qualities of a proper amateurism more valuable than
in the field of children's communities. Here, it may be hopefully
claimed, the inflexible standard will never be set and the last word will
never be spoken.

Remand Homes and Special Reception Centres

Victor Hey, b sc*

Remand homes and special reception centres are short-term residential
establishments for children and young persons. They were created at
different points of time to meet the local authority's responsibility to
provide safe custody and primary steps in rescue, care, and comfort.

Individual remand homes cater for either boys or girls; only rarely are
they for both. Their child population is mainly delinquent, comprising
children awaiting forms of supervision, a court reappearance, or placements
in long-term residential establishments of various kinds. The Acts dating
from 1906 covering the setting up and functioning of remand homes first
placed responsibility with local education authorities. Later, with increased
awareness of the importance of social and emotional factors, responsibility
was placed with children's departments of local authorities acting either
singly or jointly. Gradually remand homes came to be regarded as associated more with the rescue of those needing care and protection and with
the commencement of their treatment than as punitive instruments of
juvenile courts.

Statutory remand homes rules apply to the conduct of remand homes.
Those rules which emphasize the importance of custody and of secure
control over wayward children have led to some degree of social insularity
and have made it difficult for many establishments to progress from

* Superintendent, Boyles Court Remand Home, Essex.

traditionally regimented ways of functioning to more integrated and socially acceptable forms involving the family, school, neighbourhood, and community.

Special reception centres, a post-war development, resulted from concern over the sort of care given to children when they were received into care. They were not asked initially to deal with children specifically identified as delinquent. Most centres provide for the needs of an individual authority and cater for boys of 2 to 12 years of age and girls from 2 to 16 years: rarely are they single sex.

The features of observation and assessment of individuals by professional and lay staff, common to remand homes and reception centres, are made within the context of the available resources in terms of care, work, education, social recreation, and medical facilities—particularly psychiatric services. An informed study and report of each individual is made with a view to determining needs and then planning placement and treatment as far as possible within reasonable distance of the child's own home.

Both types of establishment represent a most intensive and vital social cross-roads for the children involved. For many, removal from home and from what they like and know to such an alien and structured way of living is a traumatic experience; for the majority, of course, this is their first contact with "the authority" and with communal living. Control and integration are made more difficult by the children's reactions to their own fears and frustrations. These reactions may range from malicious aggression to despondency and withdrawal. Beneath these presenting problems or symptoms lies the basic personality of the child; and that personality is, within this group, almost by definition a disordered one. The range of disorder is immense as are the needs which are revealed. Some idea of the range of problems encountered may be gained from the realization that from one contemporary group of children individuals may proceed to their own homes, to children's homes or hostels, for treatment at child guidance clinics or in adolescent units in hospitals, to schools for the educationally subnormal or the maladjusted, to approved schools, open-air schools, attendance centres, detention centres, or for Borstal training.

Thus staff face problems of stamina if they are to maintain flexibility to accept and sensitively support the children and their parents, and communicate, manage, observe, and investigate a wide range of group and individual behaviour. They invariably require some in-service training within their particular establishments. Remuneration, promotion structure, accommodation, and the opportunity to lead a balanced satisfying life in and away from work are inconsistent at present and are generally lower than one would associate with the job expectancy. The opportunities to become skilled in intensive ways of working are excellent provided there is co-operative effort and loyalty. Staff wastage and shortage create inconsistencies in specific and general functioning which militate against healthy structures and goal achievement.

Regimes vary and are influenced by aims and usages, the interpretation of remand home rules and the leadership and degree of democratization possible. Flexible establishments involve young people, their families, friends, and relations in ways which encourage communication and the building of relationships and provide the opportunity for young people to exercise their rights of self-determination. Some are still traditionally regimented.

Generally speaking, the use of these establishments is becoming more flexible. Where it is difficult to find placements; or where a more protracted period of stabilization or transition to home, work, or school are required; or when further failure necessitates a readmission for reappraisal to a remand home or reception centre; or when temporary respite from home is required, a young person can remain on the establishment roll for several months.

Over the years, the overlap of function of remand homes and special reception centres has increased and delinquent and non-delinquent children are found in both establishments. The overall picture is of growth towards the sort of facilities of observation and assessment envisaged in the Children Act 1948, and new legislation is helping to promote effective development and broader function.

Under the Children Act of 1969 most remand homes, special reception centres, and approved schools are to become component parts of a comprehensive community home system for the residential treatment of children received or committed to the care of the local authority. Some are to become assessment centres, the premiss being that the best decision-making process determining treatment is via effective diagnosis. This in turn infers an awareness of and use of all diagnostic and remedial resources available and a co-ordination of the various social disciplines involved. Logically, observation, assessment, and treatment must be a continuous process carried out in terms of treatment and "cure".

Present development plans indicate that assessment centres will become strategic focal points. The consultant and information facilities will help integration with the social services and improve relationships with health and education departments. Public regard and use will reflect upon the centres' roles in neighbourhoods and the importance attached to them by the social services department itself may improve the allocation of training and research resources.

One might expect assessment centres to cater for those children requiring a short respite from home or neighbourhood and increasingly to help families. Family, community, neighbourhood, social services, health, and educational involvements must be such that a high degree of flexibility, imagination, and improvisation will allow needs and commitments to be met. So far the full potential of total interdepartmental co-operation has not been realized.

One would expect to find single-sex and mixed establishments offering temporary accommodation and intensive care for particular cases, with opportunities for fuller family participation. For example, in some cases accommodation could be provided for parents to "live in" and share in the treatment plan; and there will certainly be a considerable extension of day care or non-residential assessment.

As each person must be dealt with according to his or her needs, greater use will be made of outside services, with opportunities for day attendance and for experimentation in school and work situations. It is difficult to predict peripheral roles, but these could considerably increase the complexity of what is already an intense working situation.

In conclusion, successfully to implement the requirements of care and assessment against such a broad background, creatively and imaginatively, requires committed professional staff, duly recognized for their wide experience and specific skills.

Residential Nurseries

ROSEMARY ILOTT, MBE*

Why residential nurseries? It is pertinent to ask this question in the light of the contributions of John Bowlby and others on the deprivation of the young child, and the increasing awareness that a one-to-one relationship is necessary in infancy if the child is to grow into an emotionally adequate adult.

Over the last 20 years controversy on the most satisfactory care for the deprived young child, unwanted by his mother from birth or with the mother unable to care for him, has waxed strong.

If the hypothesis of early maternal deprivation is accepted it is necessary to examine why alternative methods of giving such children individual attention have not been wholly successful and why, for so long, residential nurseries have flourished and places in them often been at a premium.

Much as it may be thought desirable to place children in foster homes, offer them for adoption, or even allow them to grow up in all-age-range homes, there are apparently insuperable problems, amongst the most relevant being:

(a) That in spite of a sustained policy of boarding-out by both local authorities and voluntary societies (who all subscribe to this being the best for a young child) there has proved to be, overall, an insufficient number of suitable foster homes. In some counties resources are good while in others offers are few and far between.

(b) There are many babies with questionable medical histories or poor backgrounds who need skilled care and observation. For them it is even harder to find foster parents with the necessary skills and experience.

(c) Finding foster homes for coloured children, for those of mixed race, and those with physical or mental handicaps is far from easy, and it is

* Homes Secretary, Church of England Children's Society.

probably true to say that a high proportion of nursery children fall into these categories at the present time.

(d) Foster mothers who are prepared for visits from the child's own mother must be exceptional people, and with the growing realization that it is all important to keep parental contact not only for the child's own sake but also in the hope of rehabilitation and reunion, care in the nursery often makes this more possible.

(e) With the best will in the world, children can have too many changes in foster care; and since changes in care are highly damaging, yet another fostering placement may be considered too great a risk.

(f) Some very damaged children appear to find it impossible to respond to the emotional demands of a foster mother.

In expressing doubts about the suitability of residential nursery care for the small child, the question must be kept in perspective and it is, therefore, necessary to consider as well the positive benefits of such care.

Mention has already been made of some of the categories of children who are cared for in residential nurseries. Of these one can perhaps pick out the following as benefiting most from such an environment:

(1) Children whose mothers maintain a close contact.

(2) Those who have had several foster homes in a comparatively short space of time.

(3) The physically or mentally handicapped.

(4) The very emotionally damaged child.

To these might be added children destined for fostering or adoption but for whom a period of assessment and preparation is necessary (so long as the time spent in the nursery is carefully controlled).

The mother who keeps a close interest in her child is probably looking forward to the time when she can care for him herself. She may be a teenager or older woman who cannot, at the time of admission, make a home for him, yet she visits the nursery frequently. For such a child nursery care has a positive advantage, for the child can relate to his mother as his mother; she can, during her visits, feed, bath, and play with him, thereby strengthening the links. She will also learn from the qualified staff the basic needs of caring for him as well as many of his future needs, physical and emotional, and is far more likely to accept "teaching" and advice from professionally qualified staff than from a foster mother whom she may regard as no more than an amateur as well as her rival in the affections of her child. This can also apply to the mother who is "wavering" about her child and who might, with a little judicious encouragement, take him "out of care".

The physically and mentally handicapped deserve the best medical treatment that can be obtained, and encouragement and stimulus in their day-to-day lives. This requires dedicated and understanding foster parents, and the child may well be better placed in a nursery (although not all schools of thought would agree with this) where the trained staff will understand his needs, co-operate fully with the medical profession, and encourage progress to the limits of the child's abilities.

Those children who have experienced several foster homes or are severely damaged emotionally, find greater security in a group where they can readjust at their own pace and learn again, under the guidance of those with professional "know-how", how to form ties with other people.

Certain children need a period of assessment before it is clear what type of foster or adoptive home will best meet their needs; others require careful preparation before they are ready to accept a substitute family home. For these a limited period in a nursery can be beneficial and allows time for a slow introductory period through days out and holidays with the prospective foster parents until it almost becomes the *child's* decision to accept the foster home.

For all these types, care in a residential nursery is possibly the most satisfactory alternative to his own home and nurseries should not, therefore, be written off as "second-class care" for the deprived child in his early years. However, great care should be taken to differentiate, so far as possible, between those children who will benefit from a period of residential care and those who will develop most naturally in a substitute family atmosphere.

It is now necessary to examine the difficulties, the strengths, and the weaknesses of residential nurseries and what can be done within the nursery setting to give the children the best possible substitute care.

It is no easy task to care for perhaps twenty to thirty children under the age of 5 and to meet the emotional and physical needs of such a heterogeneous group. Only good organization, sufficient staff, and imagination can hope to succeed.

Twenty years ago the pattern in the nursery was to care for the children according to their ages, i.e. in groups consisting of babies, tweenies, or toddlers. The stultifying effect on the children of living permanently with a dozen or even more children of approximately the same age can be imagined. So within the framework of the total, "family groups" evolved —small groups of six to eight children of mixed ages in charge of a qualified nursery nurse helped by two or three students or assistants. The improvement in the children's well-being and development was marked. The older ones enjoyed being the "big boys" and the smaller ones had someone to copy, to help them to stretch their developing faculties. The staff have more time to give to the individual child, and their interest is maintained by having a group of different stages of growth for which to care. On both sides "variety is the spice of life".

Although in some nurseries the family groups may include the very tiny babies as well, in most they are cared for in a separate group and move up to a "family" at about 9 or 10 months of age. Although it is unwise to generalize, this is probably the best arrangement for it reduces cross-infection, it enables the very young to live at their own pace and, should the child's medical history be poor, to enjoy the specialized care that he needs. Small babies in a family group can suffer from the constant turmoil of half a dozen others constantly milling round of being trodden on and fallen over. It can also be restricting for the older ones. The best nurseries introduce a baby gradually into his family group by arranging for him to join the group for part of the day before becoming an integrated member of it.

These small groups give more opportunity for a child to learn to "play", and over the years the therapeutic value of "play" has become more and more valued.

Morning play-groups, to which children from the neighbourhood come, help those of 3 years and over. The "play" is at a higher and more sustained level; they learn to mix with children with whom they are not living; their imagination is stimulated; and it becomes easier and more natural to help them sort out relationships (Who is my mummy? Where is my daddy?)— always a difficult task for the staff of any nursery.

All this provides an ordered life for the children with the security which this can bring. But what of the defects? The "sharing" that is inevitable, not only of adults but of "things"; the difficulties of staff shortages and the change of handling due to "time off" and the demands of training; the staff themselves, mostly young, who, in spite of their dedication to the children in their care and to the job of looking after them, leave to be married or seek change of occupation too frequently to provide proper continuity of care; the limited male influence and the demanding attitude this produces in the children when a man *does* go amongst them; the impossibility of giving the children the sort of trivial daily domestic experiences which are part of life in an ordinary household.

Those in charge do a magnificent job in trying to combat these difficulties but it is the system which is at fault, not the will to give the child all he needs.

Mention has been made of qualified nursery nurses and of students, and this review would be incomplete without some reference to their training and the part they play in the life of a nursery.

A two-year training of practical work in a nursery and theoretical study at a college of further education leads, after a final examination, to the National Nursery Examination Board Certificate. The course covers the physical, intellectual, emotional, and spiritual development and needs of children from birth to 7 years of age. As a part of the course English and the Creative Arts, Man and his Environment, and Home and Society are studied to widen and deepen the students' awareness and "encourage those qualities which make educated citizens and mature women". These young women, then, are given the tools of their trade and play a large and important part in the upbringing of the children.

What has been written above cannot be left without mention of a current change. There has, over the last year or so, been a sudden and pronounced drop in requests for the care of small children, particularly in the southern half of the country. A changed social attitude to the unmarried mother, legalized abortion, and the "pill" as well as a more positive attitude to family casework, have all played their part. Whether this trend will continue it is impossible to forecast. If it does, a radical rethinking will be necessary and residential nurseries as we know them at present may well have to reorientate themselves to meet new needs. Possibly a smaller group of resident children and a day nursery running side by side would achieve a better balance and at the same time provide for the resident children a less circumscribed existence than is possible under the present system. Another advance might be for there to be accommodation within the nursery for mothers for a short time prior to having their children home or, as one voluntary society at least is planning, a mixture of residential care for a small group, provision for a few unmarried mothers and their children, and a day nursery in which day care could be offered to "at risk" children in the neighbourhood as well as caring for the children of the unsupported mothers. When the latter are sufficiently stabilized to establish themselves in outside accommodation, the children could continue to attend the day nursery and the mothers receive casework support according to their needs.

Such a scheme could, in the long term, result in tremendous benefit to mother and child by ensuring continuance of the mother and child relationship while at the same time relieving the pressures on the mother that so often force her to abandon her child, offer him for adoption, or merely maintain a tenuous and unsatisfactory relationship.

Family Group Homes

JANET MONTGOMERIE*

Family group homes usually have between four and twelve children. The homes vary in the type of building, but this is usually one that fits into the surrounding neighbourhood, so that the group is helped to fit into the community. Sometimes converted or adapted houses are used; others are purpose-built.

There are family group homes known only by the immediate neighbours and local schools, while others appear to be known by everyone in the locality, which makes it more difficult for the children to lead their own private lives unnoticed. Neighbours can be very helpful and will often

* Residential Social Worker: this article was written while she was working as a Housemother.

voluntarily help out or are prepared to be called upon if necessary. Unfortunately, sometimes the neighbours always seem to be complaining about the children and the way they behave, or try to pry into their past history.

The children who come to live in family group homes have very different backgrounds and standards of living. They come at varying ages, for unknown lengths of time, and for many different reasons. It can be very difficult for a child to adjust when placed in an area totally different from his home environment, e.g. slum to modern estate. It takes time for children to learn to accept each other and to live together fairly harmoniously. The staff have to work very hard in an unobtrusive way to help each child to find his own niche within the group. When children live together in a small group over a long period they form very strong relationships with the staff and other children. I have seen an only child have a very deep brother/ sister relationship with another that affected both children for months after they had to be parted. The children are able to mix freely with other children in the vicinity, and it is no more awe inspiring for their friends to visit the home than to visit any large family, especially when the ages of the children could form a natural family. In many ways the children almost become like a large family when they live together over a number of years with little or no change in the group. The home is the core and each individual follows his own special interests, e.g. sport, music, youth clubs, etc., and yet takes a lively interest in the activities of the other members of the group. All join in and work together to create a happy atmosphere in the home.

At times, because of the deprivation and disturbance of the children in our care, we have some very anti-social and destructive and bizarre behaviour, and this can cause problems with the neighbours. We may have, for instance, the aggressive child who beats up the boy next door; the absconder or the delinquent who constantly attracts the police to the home. Often the children cause problems in school, and stand out as being different. We can help with outward appearance by dressing them in a similar way to the others, but they have often led an unsettled life with many changes and are behind educationally; consequently they behave in an anti-social way and become unpopular and have no friends.

Children's own relatives visiting and taking their children out create an unnatural situation that we have to learn to accept and live with. This causes stress in the home, especially where some children never have visitors, some only occasionally, and others regularly.

It is very important for the staff to be able to live and work in harmony together to create a happy and lively atmosphere for the children to grow up in. Many of our children have had few good experiences in living, and it is up to us to enrich their lives with good healthy experiences, at the same time helping them to see that we love and accept their own families as they are.

The residential worker in a family group home will find that she spends many hours on her own, e.g. when the children are at school, after they are in bed at night, and when fellow staff are on leave. These can be very lonely times unless one has an interest apart from work that can be followed when the work of the home is done. One can become so centred on the work and problems of caring for children, that in time one becomes unable to cope with the job. It can also be difficult to get away from the home during off-duty periods; it may be too far from one's own home; one has no friends near or they are working; it is too expensive continually to pay for entertainment, and so it means going out alone. We owe it to the children we care for to refresh ourselves. Without interests outside the work we become very dull people with little to offer to the children in our care.

The children often cause the staff to worry. When one lives closely together as in a family group home, it is very difficult to be objective and detached about the children. Staff are more personally affected if they are responsible for a child described as "the most difficult in the school", or an absconder who is away for days at a time, or a child continually shoplifting or always being complained about. In time these things can begin to wear down the staff's resistance, and it becomes more difficult to be detached from the situation; then come sleepless nights, lack of concentration, short tempers, and a feeling of not being able to get away. These are times when it is vital to keep up one's outside interests so that at least for a time one takes one's mind away from chores and children.

Relief staff or part-time workers can be very valuable to the running of a home. They often have their own families and a life in the local community and can bring into the home a part of the outside world. Often they stay for a number of years and give stability to the group. When they live near enough to the home for the children to visit them, it helps the children to see and to hold on to the reality of normal small family life. On the other hand, these workers may not be prepared to be flexible in the hours they work, and it is not always possible to find anyone really suited to working with deprived and disturbed children.

Often when people work with a small group of children they become very involved with the lives of other members of the group. One always has to remember that the children in our care belong to their own parens. We have to learn to back out of a child's life while at the same time helping the child to look forward and to adjust to returning to his own parents or to moving on to a foster home or hostel. Because of the physical care, the dressing and washing, and feeding, the preparing of meals, and looking after clothes and possessions, and the whole business of living in very close proximity to the children, they come to form a very important part in our lives. It can be very hard on the staff's feelings and emotions when a child leaves the group—especially when one is not entirely happy about the placement of the child.

The Junior Approved School

JOHN HOWELLS, BA, DIP. SOC. SCI. (LOND.), DIP. ED. (WALES)*

Before the implementation of the Children and Young Persons Act 1969, every approved school in the country fell within the jurisdiction of the Home Office and took boys from the juvenile courts on approved school orders. The legal difference between the intermediate and senior schools and the junior approved school was that the latter accepted boys and girls who were between the ages of 10 and 13 on admission, either for 3 years from the date of committal or until the attainment of the age of 15 years and 4 months. Consequently, a child in a junior approved school might be kept there for a period of up to 5 years, whilst the stay in other categories of approved schools was only up to 3 years from the date of committal.

* Warden of Turner's Court Training School, Oxfordshire.

From 1 January 1971, when the relevant section of the 1969 Act was brought into operation, juvenile courts could no longer make approved school orders. They could make care orders. Under such an order, a child was committed to the care of the local authority until he attained the age of 18; and it became the responsibility of the local authority to decide on the type of placement best suited to his needs and also the length of time for which he should be detained in that place. The schools themselves became the responsibility of the Department of Health and Social Services, and the first steps have now been taken to integrate the schools into a comprehensive system of residential treatment.

In spite of these administrative changes, important though they are, the existing schools have continued to deal with disturbed children along much the same lines as previously, and the difficulties and challenges of the work have remained largely unaltered. All the schools are single sex; and as there always have been more boys than girls made subject to committal orders, the great majority of schools are boys' schools, and these notes should be interpreted accordingly.

The children admitted to the schools have all appeared before the juvenile court. The variety of offences varies tremendously, and whether or not a child is made subject to a care order depends upon the court's assessment of information collected by social workers, the police, and the psychological and psychiatric services prior to the child's appearance before the magistrates. After the making of the order it is for the local authority to select a particular establishment; and this may be done by placing the child in a classifying school where a full assessment will be carried out. A recommendation is then made for the child to be sent to a particular school which will most suit his or her individual needs. In recent years emphasis has been placed on the need for continued contact between the child and his family. Consequently, children are placed in schools which serve a particular catchment area, and this facilitates close contact between the school, the "field" social worker, and the family, in the best interest of the child.

Whilst most of the other categories of what used to be called approved schools have their links with trade and vocational training, that offered in the junior school is based firmly upon the state educational system. This is necessary since these children must be in receipt of full-time education as they are under school-leaving age. Most of the children who come into the junior school have experienced learning difficulties. These have a variety of causes: an innate lack of ability, the inhibiting effects of long-standing deprivation, a lack of encouragement and support at home, and the conditions and teaching methods in state day schools which may be unsuited to the developmental needs of the difficult child. Factors such as these combine to produce children who will withdraw from participation in class activity and who have large gaps in the basic knowledge necessary for their adequate functioning in society. Such children are distinctly apathetic towards learning so that the basic task of a teacher in the junior school is to motivate the child to learn and then to sustain his interest once it has been aroused. Inventive teaching based on a knowledge of each child's stage of development and interest is all-important if the barrier against learning is to be removed.

An added problem is created by the resentful attitude of a child who has recently been removed from home, and whose antipathy towards those in authority militates against work at school. The first task, therefore, is to gain the confidence of the child and to provide him with security and the reassurance that his period of training can be constructive, and need not be looked upon as a period of detention. This can be achieved only if the ratio of staff to pupils can be reduced to proportions which will allow adequate opportunity for educational progress to be based upon the development of relationships between teacher and child, and to allow each child individual attention within the classroom setting. Because of the time spent in the classroom, and because they are often involved in the organization of leisure-time pursuits, teaching staff play an inordinately large part in the life of the child in the school.

Boredom weighs heavily on the young person who regards his 3 year committal as an intermediate period, and strenuous efforts are made to ensure that leisure time is adequately catered for in the programme of the school. This has become one of the more obvious characteristics of the junior school. Most schools capitalize on the fact that at this age children are particularly ready to participate in group activity and try to offer a balance between creative and physical activities. A marked danger of over-emphasis on the latter aspect is that it has tended to create a setting where aggressive behaviour has been increased rather than kept within reasonable proportions. Where this has happened the young delinquent has been in danger of emerging as a more sophisticated, aggressive person than when he was admitted, and consequently the chances of him becoming a recidivist are increased. Social activity must aim at channelling aggression, to allow freedom of choice, and ease the expression for a developing personality even if this appears to mean less rigidly organized leisure activity.

Many children in the schools have deep-seated emotional problems common amongst young people in all types of residential care, but the manifestation of them in the junior school is often specific to the age group. Whereas an older child may be capable of contemplating his period of training in terms of his eventual release and continued life in the community, younger adolescents are unable to visualize the future. Their actions, therefore, tend to be more impulsive with less consideration of consequences.

Problems of depression based on home involvement and internal relationships are common, the balance of which can be very finely set. Comparatively minor events (e.g. a cross word from a valued member of staff or lack of communication from home) can precipitate the child into irrational action such as absconding. Because children of this age seek group involvement, ejection by peers is painful. This increases the need for effective adult support and care upon which the child is extremely dependent. This specialist-caring function is undertaken by house parents with the advice of the consultant psychiatric services, but intensively developed and sensitive care must be implicit in all activities whether domestic, leisure time, or educational if the child is to benefit effectively by his stay in this type of establishment. Although the basis of the junior school is an educational one at present, this must be related effectively to the emotional and social life of the school since the three are interdependent in the best interest of the child's development and rehabilitation.

CHAPTER 9

The Disturbed Adolescent

EDITOR'S INTRODUCTION

One of the indices of the health of a society and one of the indicators of confused values at a time of flux may be the general attitude of society to the rearing of children. If this is true, it is truer of the way in which society regards its adolescents. Even within the microcosm of the family itself, the appearance of an adolescent is often the signal for a mass of confused reactions and feelings. The child who was dependent and vulnerable has now become much more powerful, more independent, and is beginning to absorb values from the outer world which are not necessarily those of the parents. Often parents feel worried by the monster they seem to have unleashed on the world and wonder where they went wrong. Just as these feelings are stirred up within the confines of the family circle, so they appear to be within society at large. When adolescents are intrusive by their music, or their style of dress, or by the hours they keep, society itself seems to wonder what monster it has created. It then questions its educational system, or its television programmes, or even baleful influences from overseas. Like the family, it wavers in its views, claiming at one point that more discipline is necessary, and at another that the situation is hopelessly out of control. Hands are alternately wrung and thrown up, and occasionally are doubled into fists. Very rarely are commercial values questioned or the structure of society itself. Still less rarely is there any discussion on the question of why there need be such a phase as adolescence; yet it remains a fact that in

* Warden of Turner's Court Training School, Oxfordshire.

primitive societies there is no long-drawn-out period during which the growing human being is neither child nor adult. Only in the more sophisticated societies is there, first, this long period of uncertainty, and, second, this disproportionate reaction to a group who are numerically very small.

Clearly there is much room for discussion as to why "an adolescent problem" exists at all and why social reactions are so curiously mixed and strong. Nevertheless, just as in the wider society a fairly small number of adolescents create anxiety, so in the smaller world of child care there are always a small number of extremely disturbed teenagers. Almost every social worker, sooner or later, finds himself involved in some desperate adventure with a girl or boy who seems to be extraordinarily upset and upsetting to those around him. In perhaps no other area of social work does the worker have to think more closely about his own ideas on authority or permissiveness and about the conflict between his responsibility to his adolescent client and that to the society which employs him. John Howells, who has had long experience in the world of the approved schools and is at present Warden of Turner's Court Training School in Oxfordshire, introduces this subject.

Even if they have been brought up by their natural parents in a stable and emotionally secure environment, adolescence can be a trying time for many children and those who have to deal with them. In adolescence physical and emotional development are often out of step, and the adolescent exhibits an uneasy awareness of physical potentialities the expression of which society is slow to accept. It is also a period when young people become conscious of their thinking in relation to that of others and attempt to justify their judgement in logical ways. Such developments inevitably cause periods of insecurity when adolescents find that they are at odds with themselves (when their judgements are confused) and with the society in which they live (when it rejects the judgements at which they have arrived). Such states of physical and emotional flux can be eased by the security of the base from which the teenager ventures into the outside world as a young adult. In a normal family such a base has been made secure over the preceding period of 15 years or so, during which the child's changing developmental needs have been met by his parents. When the family is called upon to withstand the pressures of adolescence it does so with understanding and fortitude, based on long experience of the child as an individual.

This is the situation in which most adolescents develop to adulthood, but for the minority the base is so insecure that the problems of normal adolescence are aggravated and stresses become more than can be managed internally. They erupt as crisis behaviour. Such symptoms are often disturbing to adults who witness them, but if we are to understand the problem of difficult adolescents we must examine the behaviour in the light of the circumstances in which it has developed.

If we take time to consider why some children are deprived of a stable base we realize that this does not always imply the absence of parents. Although some children are never cared for by their natural parents, or are removed from them at an early age, it is possible to provide them with adequate substitute care through the agency of the social services department. Such provisions are elaborated elsewhere in this text. Suffice it to say that this may mean placement in children's homes, foster homes, or adoptive homes, and through the affection and care which they receive children can develop into well-adjusted adults. Sometimes, however, through such factors as lack of thorough investigation of circumstances, and inadequate provision of support for the substitute parents, the agency fails to provide such a stable base. The misunderstanding and breakdown of relationships which may then occur in the substitute home produce an adolescent who has been exposed to further experience of failure and will probably show signs of stress. Occasionally the substitute home over-protects the child from the consequences of his own actions, and fails to instil in him a realization of the pressures of the society in which he lives. When he leaves such a home in late adolescence, the demands of adjustment to a normal working and living situation are too great, and breakdown ensues. Such children contribute to the disturbed minority of young people.

More often a child remains at home with his natural parents who may be unable or unwilling to cater for his needs. In such situations the imbalance may be on a physical or emotional plane. Perhaps father cannot or will not provide adequately for the family, so that mother must also work in order to maintain a reasonable standard of living, leaving the children to care for themselves too often. It may be that one parent has deserted the family, or has been hospitalized, or sent to prison for long periods, so that the remaining parent is overburdened by responsibility towards the children. Not uncommonly a parent may be neurotic or mentally ill, and makes unreasonable emotional demands on the rest of the family. Such factors occur in various intensities and in innumerable combinations, but whatever the circumstances the resultant distortion of relationships to which the child is exposed pertains over a long period of time. The effects of such living situations may be visible to the trained observer from an early age, and measures taken to alleviate the stress. Supportive care may be offered within the setting of the child's home, by the social services department, or psychological and psychiatric services. Such provisions, which have been discussed elsewhere, can be extremely effective, but if the situation at home is deemed to be too damaging, a child may be removed from it to establishments in which he may receive special help.

Where the home situation fails to meet the emotional needs of the adolescent it may be possible for a certain degree of stability to be obtained through his wider activities. Since he spends a great part of his life at school, symptoms of stress should be readily visible in this setting, and support and healthy substitute relationships made available to offset the inadequate home. Such a service could be provided by the implementation of effective school counselling. Often, however, a child's misbehaviour is not gross enough for him to be regarded as more than "odd" or "a sheer nuisance" by his teachers, and to be in receipt of inept or even punitive handling, which adds to his difficulties by enhancing his sense of failure and inadequacy. Children of this type are lacking in self-regard and either withdraw from social contact or attempt to find substitute relationships elsewhere. In an environment where there is little constructive attempt to make provision to meet their needs in a social and recreative setting, such young people attempt to find satisfaction in peer group activities which in adolescence can become violently anti-social.

The disturbed adolescent can therefore be seen as the product of failure, either of the adults concerned with him to diagnose the early warning signals and respond to them with appropriate measures, or of the failure of the measures which have been applied. Society then has to cope with violently expressed crisis behaviour, the variety of which is as great as the variety of circumstances which are its cause. We are well aware of some of its manifestations since our publicity media take pains to draw public attention to adolescent behaviour which threatens persons and property, e.g. taking and driving away vehicles, breaking and entering buildings, the abuse of drugs, sexual promiscuity. Less publicity, perhaps, is given to the incidence of neurotic behaviour, which although no less a sign of adolescent disturbance, may have no anti-social repercussion. For adolescents with neurotic disorders, treatment provision is sparse, and insufficient recognition of the neurotic element in anti-social acts militates even against adequate treatment being afforded to many young offenders.

The establishments which are available for residential treatment of disturbed 16 year olds, therefore, have to treat a great variety of behaviour problems which have complex origins. They have to attempt to reverse long-established patterns of behaviour in insecure young people, many of whom have been repeatedly exposed to failure in their relationships with adults and sometimes with their peers. Such complex tasks can hardly be expected to have simple solutions, and the system which has to deal with them should be flexible enough to provide treatment of individual needs within establishments catering for general types of problem.

By far the most difficult group to accommodate are the young people who require help in a psychiatrically orientated setting. Adolescent units within the hospital service catering for gross disturbance are few and far between. With the increased knowledge and confidence in psychiatric services demand has increased, and those places which exist are at a premium. It has become increasingly difficult to obtain for these young people a secure environment where they can receive the intensity of care and psychiatric help which they require. Everyone concerned with adolescents is aware of the ever-increasing need for providing more places to cope with the severely emotionally disturbed who will not respond to the more conventional methods of dealing with socially non-acceptable behaviour. For those who do not need such long-term or intensive care, a certain number of homes and hostels are available which will afford continued support whilst the disturbed adolescent adjusts to a working life. The responsibility for providing this facility is shared by local authorities and voluntary bodies. Most are comparatively small, offering personal contact and individual attention to those young people who have either lived in residential accommodation for a number of years or who have experienced difficulties in the transitional period between full-time education and work. A large number of these hostels and homes provide opportunity for the young person to follow full-time employment and yet to experience "home-type" life in a supportive community. The head of the hostel will invariably assist in finding employment for the youth through his regular contact with the employer or the youth employment service.

As far as possible, local authorities attempt to deal with youngsters who are disturbed and in need of help on what might be called "a voluntary basis". This is to say, in simple terms, that if a youngster is referred to the social services by the police, or by his parents, or if he comes himself because he is distressed or fearful, then help will be offered without any imposed sanction in the shape of a court order. Thus counselling may be offered instead of a probation order; the child may be received into care instead of being made the subject of a care order; psychiatric help may be made available without recourse to a hospital order. In short, the "contract" between the youngster and those trying to help him is entered into voluntarily. This is in keeping with the spirit of the Children and Young Persons Act 1969 which seeks to reduce the number of children appearing before the juvenile courts; and in certain circumstances court proceedings cannot begin until the local authority has agreed that the child cannot be helped without a court order of some sort.

Nevertheless, because of some of the circumstances outlined above—because the youngster's judgement is confused, or he is impulsive and lacks self-control, or is malevolently anti-social—there are many cases where it seems clear that a court order is necessary.

In respect of any youngsters appearing before them, the magistrates may, when the case is proved, take one of the following actions:

(a) an order requiring his parent or guardian to enter into a recognisance to take proper care of him and exercise proper control over him; *or*
(b) a supervision order; *or*
(c) a care order (other than an interim order); *or*
(d) a hospital order within the meaning of Part V of the Mental Health Act 1959; *or*
(e) a guardianship order within the meaning of that Act.

With fines, conditional discharges, and supervision orders we are not here concerned. We are concerned with those youngsters who seem to need help and training away from their own homes.

Hospital orders are infrequently used at present. They are used principally in respect of youngsters who are mentally handicapped to a severe degree or exhibiting signs of psychosis and who are so wayward or so violent as to need compulsory treatment and detention in mental hospitals.

Detention centres were set up in the 1950s and were described at the time as geared to give the delinquent boy a "short, sharp shock". The maximum time a boy can remain in a centre is 3 months; and during his stay there he will experience a rigorous discipline, a spartan regime, and tight security.

The majority of teenagers who are considered to be in need of training away from home are made the subjects of care orders—that is to say, they are ordered by the magistrates to be committed to the care of the local authority. If the youngster is over 16 when committed, the order lasts until his nineteenth birthday; otherwise it lasts until his eighteenth birthday. It is left to the local authority to decide upon the type of establishment best suited to his needs and the length of his detention therein (though it is always open to the youngster or to his parents to appeal against a care order or to apply to a court for its revocation).

Usually, the youngster will, prior to the making of such an order, have been remanded or made subject to an interim care order so that some assessment of him will have been made and the local authority will have made a tentative plan for him. It may well be that the most appropriate placement for him will be what used to be called a senior approved school and which, under the provisions of the Children and Young Persons Act 1969, is now known as a community school.

If training at a senior school has been decided upon, allocation will depend to a large extent on geographical location, although special provision may be made in the case of a young person who requires special care or tuition. There are certain differences in organization of establishments based on the sex of the offender, but in general the schools have their traditions firmly based on vocational training, and the provision of a specialized facility is the exception rather than the rule. The general object of training is to equip young people with certain skills in a given trade, to give them the opportunity to come to terms with their problem, and to develop a work habit which will prepare them for their release.

Many of the schools concerned with male offenders originally based their vocational programme on agricultural training, and quite a number of the senior schools had farms attached to them. In fact, a few still bear the "farm school" title. Although through the years other trades have been grafted on to this system, it was felt that a therapeutic effect was inherent in working with animals. It is doubtful, however, whether sufficient consideration was given to the fact that a large proportion of the population of an approved school came from urban areas and consequently, as a work experience, farming was largely irrelevant in the context of their rehabilitation in their home environment. This agricultural basis is not so prevalent at the present time, although a few establishments still have farms attached to them. Alternative provision has been made for the training of young people in building and engineering trades which are obviously more relevant to their future working life. Controversy nowadays seems to centre on whether vocational training should be pursued in a setting that is commercial, or whether it should be considered as part of the overall programme of helping the maturation process. Where it is of the former type, the trainee experiences quasi-industrial conditions, albeit in a protected environment, and it is felt therefore that he will be more likely to develop a work habit in keeping with the standards expected of him in industry. Such training is usually directed at short-term goals, the attainment of which entails financial reward and special privileges. It is argued, however, that any form of training given to disturbed adolescents will be only partly assimilated if their basic emotional and social problems are not also dealt with. Viewed in this light the former method would appear to cause great wastage of effort on the part of the instructing personnel. Where vocational training is viewed as part of an integrated therapeutic programme, it is felt that social and emotional support will allow the youth to make full use of his potential both during his period of training and in later life. This approach would seem to be more effective in terms of manpower, training, and long-term results.

So many young people in residential care have failed to respond to school that the level of their educational attainment at the age of 16 is very low. Many have great difficulty in reading and writing and, because of this, results of testing tend to indicate that many young offenders are educationally sub-normal. In fact, careful remedial teaching and encouragement can often help to alleviate this problem, originally caused in part by the inability of the child to respond to normal teaching methods. Even such common facets of day-to-day living as the filling of hire-purchase contracts, road-tax applications, and family allowance claims, make it advisable that citizens should be able to read "the small print". The tremendous handicap of the non-reading adult in modern society is obvious, yet, until recently, little constructive thought had been given to the relevance of expert tuition in this field in the senior school. If only in the practical sense, investment of time and effort in imaginative and creative teaching would be well worth while. When the emotional bonus of achievement for the adolescent, who has been a failure in his educational life, is added, it is difficult to understand why development in further education in these establishments has been so tardy.

In many of these schools routine and discipline is considered an important part of rehabilitation, together with the challenge offered through their vocational training. It could be argued on this basis that the senior school offers a model upon which the young person can organize his later life. In fact where routine becomes over-important, the establishment loses the ability to view independently the problems of individuals. Far from being able to come to terms with young people and help them to tackle their deep-seated difficulties, such over-organized establishments often refuse to acknowledge the existence of any problem other than that of discipline. Because of the rigid structure of many schools such an approach makes it more important that a youth keeps on the right side of authority so that he may gain his release in the earliest possible time than that he should act out his difficulties in the controlled situation. In effect these difficulties express themselves in under-cover activity and the formation of sub-cultural groups which may dominate the residential community.

One factor often overlooked is the young person's need to rebel—to act out his difficulties against those in authority, or even the adult whom he trusts. Unfortunately this creates problems of containment within the establishment which are often dealt with in a punitive or rejecting manner. Such problems can be so severe that they ensure that the adolescent will fail to respond to training. The containment of the persistent absconder is a problem which vexes the staff of residential establishments, and unless adequate provision is made for this group they will continue to constitute a large proportion of the failures of the community school system. Where there appears to be a compulsive desire to return to old haunts and pastimes, the "open" establishment is powerless to help. The lure of drug taking, car stealing, and high living is too great for some youths of this age, and in many cases there is a real need for physical restraint if the skills of the establishment are to be used—the client cannot be helped if he is never available. The secure units attached to some schools may contribute a solution, but unfortunately such provision is resorted to only when other forms of training have failed, and the young person has shown that he cannot respond to more permissive regimes. The need for secure intensive care supplied by highly skilled and trained personnel should be recognized much sooner and used within the context of the therapeutic community. This would prevent the problem becoming so acute that its resolution within a comparatively short period of time is impossible. The need for time to work through problems of behaviour, to experiment with relationships, and test out the reactions of adults with whom he comes into regular contact, is of high priority in the rehabilitation of the disturbed youth.

Because of the intensity of their disturbance, many adolescents in senior schools are found to be in need of psychiatric oversight, and, because of the lack of available places in adolescent units, some need psychiatric treatment on a long-term basis. Such facilities are usually provided by either a consultant psychiatrist or, in a few cases, by more than one, who visit the school on a part-time basis. Their approach will vary tremendously from one establishment to another. Some will treat individual cases, others view their role in terms of diagnosing the problems and consulting with staff who effect the treatment plan, and a few will now use group counselling methods to accelerate the process of rehabilitation. However, psychiatric oversight will only be effective in settings where the headmaster and staff will accept the methods used, and not discard the approach as unreliable.

Many adolescent problems are minor and transient but can be greatly aggravated in a setting which insists on communal living. Most senior establishments are large and only a few can offer the privacy which the adolescent needs from time to time, if only to sit alone and brood over his own problems. Recreative activities are approached from the point of view which accepts that "a sound body makes for a sound mind" and are therefore largely of a physical nature. Little diversity or choice in participation is offered, and most activities are determined for and not by the young people. Opportunities for contact with people outside the school on a social basis is greatly restricted and, although participation in the activities of the local community has been encouraged in recent years, there are often problems of acceptance by the general population. Even when such inter-mingling does occur, standards of conduct and dress are expected to conform to accepted social standards, and regression is not taken kindly.

The young offender in the senior school, therefore, finds that he has little freedom of choice. He is placed in this situation by teams of experts who think it appropriate for him, and he is expected to work at a trade for which his ability and aptitude are often minimal. The standards expected of him are set by adults who wish to provide a model which conforms to the norms of previous generations which the young offender either does not under-stand or has rejected. Regimented into group living away from the street-corner café society, girls, scooters, and perhaps illicit drugs, he considers his predicament to be both unnatural and degrading. Such a situation militates against his increasing in self-regard and developing as an individual; rather it tends to treat young offenders as being of one type, and encourages depression and the breakdown of personal standards. Many trainees at senior schools see their predicament as a deprivation of liberty, and consequently become even more resentful of the authority which is the instrument of their detention.

To emerge from such an inward-looking society which is so divorced from normal living conditions all too often leads to further breakdowns and reversion to the anti-social pattern which the residential setting should be attempting to remove. After a lengthy period in a controlled setting, much will depend on the relationship of the young person to the supportive agency which looks after his interests when he leaves the school. "After care" is undertaken by the social workers of the social services department. Finding a suitable job is only part of the problem; keeping in regular employment can be a trying task for the adolescent "on after-care", and he will need support for quite a long time. Unfortunately, in many cases social workers change, and it is sometimes possible for a youth to be discharged under the supervision of an officer he does not know. Prior to his release from the school much can be done to ease the stresses of this transition period by casework within the school and with the parents and by close co-operation between all concerned; but this is often more easily said than achieved. The adolescent is at an age when he should be encouraged to participate in decisions about his future, and where this happens the chances of the success of any plan made for him should be increased.

Because of the enormous problem which this age group presents in a residential setting, it is tempting either to use methods which simply control and discipline, or to allow the adolescent to work out his problems in a setting with minimum structure. Neither of these solutions is satisfactory.

In the first instance, the approach increases the youngster's rebellious outlook and introduces an overwhelming desire to thwart the people who are supposedly attempting to fashion his life. The second method is so lacking in control that it fails to offer boundaries within which the adolescent can develop and so imposes a strain on him which he cannot understand. The need for a carefully planned compromise between these extremes is essential, for this enables the youth to lean on adult support and yet feel that he is being given a chance to think out his future. In order to deal effectively with the problems of this or any group of difficult young people, in my view establishments should either be small or subdivided in such a way that young people are dealt with in manageable groups. This is relevant not only to the work situation but also in the living units and recreational setting where staff and young people can make ready contact. In dealing with the mid-adolescent group the emphasis should be therefore not on moulding and regimenting but on personal contact, encouragement, and a training programme geared to the needs of each individual. In recent years in all types of establishment dealing with young offenders, far more emphasis has been given to the role of the psychiatrist and other specialist consultant staff. Standards of care have improved and government legislation, coupled with recruitment and training of skilled staff, have made inroads, although perhaps in too piecemeal a fashion, into the long-established attitudes towards the handling of difficult young people. More constructive approaches are employed when the difficulties are dealt with at an early age, and obviously it is in this sector that a great deal of expertise needs to be invested if the effects of deprivation, which have such far-reaching effects on society, are to be reduced. Even with greatly improved provisions for family support and substitute care, however, it would be idealistic to imagine that adolescents in trouble would cease to need residential care. At present, if early treatment fails, or where difficulties do not become gross until adolescence, society adopts an increasingly punitive attitude which reflects itself in the regimes of residential establishments. Adolescence may be the last opportunity for the resolution of long-standing difficulties and the reversal of established behaviour patterns. If this is so then it is vital that concerted effort should also be made towards the adoption of a more constructive approach to the rehabilitation of the adolescent offender. Until this is achieved the minority of adolescents who find themselves in difficulties at the age of 16 will continue to present a major problem to society and to be a drain on the finances and manpower of our social services.

CHAPTER 10

Adoption

Alexina McWhinnie[*]

EDITOR'S INTRODUCTION

In the preceding chapters there has been considerable emphasis upon the links which exist between the child and his natural family and the efforts the social workers make first to preserve those links without breaking the family or subsequently (if the links do snap) to try to mend them and restore the child to his rightful place within his own family. When we now come to the subject of adoption, however, we are considering a situation where the return of the child to his natural family has been ruled out and his total settlement in a substitute family is considered to be in his best interests. As will be seen in Alexina McWhinnie's opening paragraphs, legalized adoption in this sense is of surprisingly recent origin in England and Wales. The involvement of social workers in this process, and in particular local authority social workers, is more recent still. In fact of the 20,000 or so adoptions legalized every year the majority are arranged by voluntary societies. Not all local authorities have undertaken adoption work by having themselves registered as adoption agencies; and even in those authorities which do arrange adoptions there is often a specialist adoptions officer who does this work and no other.

At first glance, therefore, it may seem that the social worker newly entered into local authority service may not be involved to any great degree in adoption work or with a great number of adoption cases. The question could then well be posed: Why devote considerable space to this particular subject when much of the earlier emphasis has been on the importance to the child of his need of his own family?

[*] Principal Social Services Officer, Berkshire County Council.

151

One answer must be that the consideration of adoption brings into the limelight all the social worker's thoughts about parenting, emotional well-being, the desirable qualities of adoptive parents, and the implications of any agency (statutory or voluntary) "playing God" and determining the future of a child by certain irrevocable decisions. In spite of the vogue for saying that adoption cases do not loom large in the average social worker's workload, no other subject (except possibly that of adolescence) produces so much debate and so much anxiety in social work circles. It may well be that this anxiety reflects a more general one about the value-systems of present-day society. Dr. McWhinnie has given a searching examination of the current process and focuses on some of the uncertainties about it and some of the implications of the work. Quite apart from the fact that it is a masterly survey of current thinking on this subject, this author's chapter presents the student social worker with a number of concepts which he would do well to examine thoroughly, both objectively and subjectively.

N.B.—After this chapter was written the Stockdale Committee reported on its inquiry into adoption law and practice. A summary of the committee's main recommendations is therefore included as an appendix (see p. 233).

Child adoption has been defined as follows: ". . . the essence of an adoption, whether legalised or *de facto*, seems to us to lie in the creation of an artificial family relationship analogous to that of parent and child, or sonship, which is accepted by all parties as permanent. The child is absorbed into the family of the adopters and is treated as if it were their own natural child."[1]

Such adoption of children has been practised for long in many cultures. This chapter looks at the practice as it has evolved within the United Kingdom. The question posed by adoption for every community is how far does the adopted child in fact and in feeling become a member of the new family and how far does he, or should he, remain tied to his blood family? This involves people's basic ideas and attitudes about family loyalties and identifications and their concept of the self. The law tends to

[1] *Report of the Departmental Committee on Adoption Societies and Agencies, 1937* (the Horsburgh Committee).

reflect each community's attitudes to these, and different countries have often widely differing laws about adoption.

Adoption was first made legal in England and Wales in 1926 and in Scotland in 1930. The figures of legalized adoptions since then reflect the public's attitude to adoption. These show a steady increase from 14,026 in the first 4 years of legal adoptions to 88,123 for the 5-year period 1946–50. Thereafter there was a decline, and between 1951 and 1958 the annual figures for England and Wales remained at between 13,000 and 14,000 legalized adoptions per year. There followed a further steady increase in the annual figures with the total rising to 24,855 in 1968. The figures for Scotland show a similar picture with a total of 2155 legalized adoptions in 1968.

Although exact figures were always difficult to obtain, it used to be estimated that for every child available for adoption there were approximately ten couples applying to adopt. During the 1960s there was a change with the number of babies available for adoption increasing more rapidly than the number of adoptive applicants. Since 1970, however, there has been a decline in the total number of adoptions, reflecting not a decline in its acceptance or popularity as far as adopters are concerned, but a decline in the number of young babies available or being offered for adoption. The Association of British Adoption Agencies reports an overall decline of 29 per cent in agency placements since 1967.[2] Whether this total figure will continue to decline will depend on many factors.

The present decline in the number of babies available for adoption arises from several causes: the wider use of contraceptives by those having sexual relationships outside marriage, the availability now of legal abortion following the Abortion Act 1968, and also the fact that more unmarried mothers are keeping their babies. The climate of opinion in the United Kingdom is certainly now much more accepting of the unmarried mother who keeps her child, although still not as accepting as in some Scandinavian countries, e.g. Denmark, where the majority of unmarried mothers keep their children.

Though these factors may result in a smaller number of babies being available for adoption, counterbalancing this is the trend for social workers

[2] See also L. Lambert, Adoption: the statistical picture, 1970, *Child Adoption*, vol. 63, No. 1, 1971.

to place in adoptive homes children who previously were considered "unadoptable" or unsuitable for adoption. In this group are the child past babyhood, perhaps cared for in a children's home, the child with a medical or psychological handicap, and the child of mixed racial origin.[3]

On the side of adoptive applicants the situation is also in a state of flux. Where previously adoption was seen as a way to parenthood for couples unable to have biological children, increasingly adoptions are being arranged into families where there are already biological children. There are now also adoptive applicants who, of deliberate choice, have felt they should not add to an already over-populated world by having further biological children. Instead they apply to adopt children. Advances, too, in the effectiveness of the medical treatment of infertility are also altering the pattern of who apply as adopters, and many who previously might have considered adoption will now seek continued medical treatment.

From this it will be clear that many factors influence the child adoption picture in any country at any one time, and that behind the annual figures available about legalized adoption lie many human influences and variations. The pattern, too, of how adoptions are arranged has changed over the years.

Prior to the first Adoption Act, children were placed informally, but permanently, in adoptive homes and they frequently used the name of the family adopting them. This change of name could be legalized in England by deed poll, while in Scotland such a change of name has always been legal by "custom and wont". Also, although it was not possible to legalize adoption until 1926, voluntary societies had been acting as adoption placement agencies from the 1890s. The real impetus, however, to adoption work in the United Kingdom came from the need for homes for many children orphaned or born out of wedlock during the First World War. This led to the setting up of two large national adoption societies in London. These early adoption workers believed fervently that it was better for a child to be brought up in an adoptive home than in an institution. Gradually other adoption societies sprang up throughout the country although there were still many social workers and administrators unsure about adoption and its outcome, seeing the preservation of the "blood tie" with the biological

[3] Figures are not available as to the number of children in any of these groups who might become available for adoption if adoptive homes were available for them.

parent as of paramount importance for the welfare of the child. This, too, was the attitude of the early departmental committees which looked at the possibility of introducing adoption legislation. As an indication of the community's attitude it is relevant to note that adoption in these early days was much more a phenomenon of the lower social economic groups rather than of the middle classes. Its acceptance and prevalence in the middle and upper classes have come gradually, coinciding with the greater social acceptance of adoption. How far this social acceptance is also an acceptance of the probable illegitimacy of the adopted child's birth is something which will be discussed later in this chapter.

There was a gradual growth of adoption work in the 1930s and a rapid expansion during the Second World War years with many of the large organizations which had been doing general social work with children becoming themselves registered adoption societies. This trend continued into the post-war years, with many of the "rescue" organizations, primarily set up to provide social work care for unmarried mothers and women having out-of-wedlock pregnancies, also becoming adoption placement agencies. In England and Wales there are now sixty-six registered adoption societies, whilst in Scotland the figure is nine.

The concept of a "registered" adoption society was introduced by the Horsburgh Committee report in 1937, the aim being thus to control the standards of practice of adoption societies by registering them with the local authority. The committee also recommended that adoption agencies should conform to certain forms of procedure; for example, that all placements should be legalized, that all applicants should be interviewed, their home visited, references obtained, that there should be a probationary period of 3–6 months between the placement of the child in a home and the legalization of the adoption, and that any monetary charges should relate to the ability of the adopter to pay and should be approved first by the court. These two controls, incorporated into the Adoption of Children (Regulation) Act 1939, which came into operation after the Second World War, helped towards ending some of the worst abuses of some of the agencies[4]

---

[4] Evidence had shown that although some adoption societies made thorough inquiries, others were very superficial, dispensing with a personal interview and failing to verify statements. The result was children being placed with elderly, deaf, blind, unreliable, mentally unstable people. Money, too, had been asked for from the

and have set the pattern for the procedural requirements in adoption to the present day.

Although standards of administrative policy improved through the introduction of these regulations, the control by registration of the society with the local authority has not been really effective as far as standards of day-to-day practice are concerned, and this is one of the aspects of the adoption services about which there may soon be suggested changes.[5]

The Horsburgh Committee also stated two principles which should be followed in adoption work and to which at least lip service is now given in adoption practice: first, that the interest of the child must come before those of the would-be adopter; secondly, that the decision to be made was not simply whether the child was suitable for adoption in general, but that "an attempt should be made as far as possible to place the right child in the right home".[6]

There was also comment on the complete lack of trained social workers in any of the large societies, and the idea was introduced of a case committee to which all applications should be submitted, the hope being that trained social workers could be recruited to these case committees. Gradually trained social workers have in fact been recruited into the fieldwork itself of voluntary societies, but many societies still use untrained or volunteer workers, either from choice or because of shortage of funds to pay qualified staff.

Adoption placements had also been made over the years by the public assistance departments of the local authorities. After the 1948 Children Act, which set up a special and separate children's department for each local authority, many, though not all, of such departments interpreted this Act as allowing them to arrange adoptions. The Adoption Act of 1958, however, gave them specific power to make and participate in adoption placements and since then an increasing number have become official placement agencies and an increasing amount of placement work has been undertaken by these local authority departments.

Throughout all this time, too, adoptions have been arranged by many

unmarried mothers, and supervision had not been provided to see that all placements were legalized.

[5] See *Adoption of Children*, working paper containing the provisional proposals of the Departmental Committe on the Adoption of Children, HMSO, 1970.

[6] *Ibid*, p. 14.

people in the community who come into contact with unmarried mothers, illegitimate children, and childless couples or others wishing to adopt children. Such intermediaries could be midwives, doctors, clergymen, or lawyers. This practice of "third-party placement" still continues, although now on a comparatively small scale. The need for this method of placement has decreased as the number of adoption agencies has increased, but gaps still remain in agency provisions. It is sometimes argued that the standards in third-party placements are so poor that such placements should be prohibited by law. Research evidence, however, as to the outcome of adoption placements made in different ways is inconclusive,[7] and although it is generally agreed that such third-party placements should be particularly carefully supervised, because of the increased possibility of thoughtless or unscrupulous intermediaries, there is divergence of opinion as to whether they should, or could, be prohibited.[8]

There is a fourth type of adoption placement. This is where no intermediary is involved at all and the mother places her child direct with someone who wishes to adopt her child. This type of placement is obviously open to potential abuse, with hasty decisions being sometimes made and later regretted. It also lacks the involvement of a social worker and has the hazard that the unmarried mother knows the name and whereabouts of her child with the possibility of later contact. Such tracing of the adopters by the biological parent is not possible in agency placements because of a policy of secrecy and because of the use of a serial number instead of the name of the adopters when the legal consent is signed by the biological mother.

It is relevant to ask how many children find their way into their new homes through each of these channels. A recent survey[9] gives figures for 1966–9 (Table 1).

From these figures it is clear that social work agencies were only responsible for making adoption placements in approximately 50 per cent of all adoptions and that of these voluntary societies were placing many

[7] M. L. Kellmer Pringle, *Adoption—Facts and Fallacies*, Longmans, London, 1967, pp. 14 and 15.
[8] Evidence submitted to Departmental Committee on the Adoption of Children which is currently studying the need for changes in adoption law. The Working Paper, *Adoption of Children,* prepared by this committee, suggested prohibition.
[9] See *Child Adoption,* vol. 62, No. 4, 1970, p. 14.

TABLE 1

	1966	1967	1968	1969
Total number of orders granted in England, Wales, and Scotland	24,832	24,942	26,986	25,976
Total placements by voluntary societies	9,614	9,863	9,265	7,907
Total placements by local authorities	3,626	4,060	4,151	3,925
Difference between total number of orders and placement made by voluntary societies and local authorities	11,592	11,019	13,570	14,144

more children than local authorities. A further survey[10] conducted by Government Social Survey and the Home Office showed a slightly higher proportion of agency and local authority placements, i.e. 58 per cent. It also showed that 30 per cent of all adoption applications were made by a natural parent, e.g. a natural mother and her husband, while 4 per cent were third-party placements and 8 per cent were placements direct by the natural parent.

The figures for agency placements are of adoptions where a child has been transferred from his biological family to an unrelated adoptive family, and so it has been implied that this is by deliberate choice. There are also, however, within these statistics, adoptions which have evolved out of fostering arrangements. Figures are not available to show how many adoptions are of this kind. There is, however, considerable concern about such arrangements, particularly the situations where children are in a foster family for many years, and where there then develops conflict between the natural and foster parents as to who should have permanent care of the child. The natural parents have the right to claim back the child. The foster parents have the right to apply to adopt the child but can do so only with the

[10] E. Gray and R. M. Blunden, *A Survey of Adoption in Great Britain,* HMSO, London, 1971.

consent of the natural parents unless there are legal grounds for dispensing with this consent.[11]

The departmental committee[12] at present studying adoption law is also looking at ways of making the role of the long-term foster parent more secure in relation to the possible adoption of children in their care while at the same time preserving the rights of the natural parents. The problem arises as to how to interpret what is in the best long-term interests of the child. This would appear to be a matter where ultimately the courts will have to exercise discretion and judgement; there is considerable controversy[13] as to how this dilemma can be resolved.

Many fostering arrangements do, however, become permanent adoptions without any conflict or dispute. These are frequently situations where a decision as to whether the baby or child should be placed for adoption had to be deferred on social or medical grounds. Until these uncertainties were resolved the child had been placed in a foster home and the biological mother may or may not have visited the foster home.

There is a final group of adoptions which are important, which constitute 30 per cent of the total, but where social workers are only involved peripherally, or at least usually after the decision to adopt has been taken. These are adoptions where the mother adopts her own child, either singly, or more frequently in a joint application with her husband, the child having been born before her present marriage and usually out of wedlock.[14] The decision to proceed to adoption is made by the parents themselves, and the court then asks for inquiries to be made by the representative of the court, i.e. the guardian or curator *ad litem*.

There are also adoptions by relatives—grandparents or aunts and uncles of the child. These presumably would appear in the survey as amongst those placed direct by the mother. Again there is controversy at the moment as to whether adoption by relatives is constructive for the child by offering it security within its biological family, or confusing in that it replaces a

---

[11] Adoption Act, 1958, para. 5(i).

[12] *Op. cit.* (see note 5).

[13] In evidence being presented to Departmental Committee on the Adoption of Children.

[14] Occasionally a child conceived extra-maritally will be adopted by the mother and her husband.

natural relationship, i.e. grandparent or uncle or aunt, with an artificial one, i.e. adoptive parent. It is suggested[15] that "guardianship" would be more appropriate than adoption in these situations. It is possible, however, that the needs of the individual children would best be served if both types of provisions were available, thus affording flexibility to meet different situations.

Many different adoption societies and children's departments are concerned in the 58 per cent of all adoptions shown as arranged by agencies. The adoption societies as such are all voluntary societies, not state-aided, and their adoption work has evolved in accordance with the aims and objects of the organization. Thus some of these organizations have definite religious and denominational affiliations, some are interdenominational, and one society was recently set up for those adopters who have no church affiliation or are agnostic. Some societies cover the whole country and some only particular areas, and some are also child care organizations with their own children's homes and also making fostering arrangements. Some have adequate finances, but more usually these societies are very short of money. Their standards of work vary considerably,[16] although they must all conform to the basic essential inquiries laid down in the Adoption Agency Regulations. They have sought over the years, however, to improve their work, and in 1950 the Standing Conference of Societies Registered for Adoption was formed. This Standing Conference became the mouthpiece for all voluntary adoption societies; it published a journal, *Child Adoption*, and held regular national conferences which were attended also by local authority representatives.

As more medical practitioners became involved in adoption work, the need was felt by them to have a separate group, and in 1963 the Medical Group of the Standing Conference of Societies Registered for Adoption was formed. It too holds annual conferences and has become an influential body. As children's departments have increasingly undertaken adoption work

---

[15] See Part V of *Adoption of Children*, HMSO, 1970.

[16] Iris Goodacre, *Adoption Policy and Practice*, Allen & Unwin, London, 1966.

A. M. McWhinnie, *Adopted Children. How They Grow Up*, Routledge and Kegan Paul, London, 1967.

J. P. Triseliotis, *Evaluation of Adoptive Policy and Practice*, Department of Social Administration, Edinburgh, 1970.

and provided a service alongside the voluntary adoption societies, it was clear that they too should become part of the national adoption organization and so in 1970 the Standing Conference of Societies Registered for Adoption became the Association of British Adoption Agencies. This organization can now represent both voluntary societies and local authority departments, and the Medical Group has also become affiliated to the new association.

Because of wide divergencies in casework practice and variable standards, the need was felt to establish guide lines for good adoption practice. The advisory councils on child care of England and Wales and of Scotland therefore in 1967 set up a Joint Committee to study how best to give such guidance. Their report, *A Guide to Adoption Practice, 1970*,[17] offers guidance on all casework aspects of adoption practice, basing this on available research evidence. It is therefore of interest to all studying adoption practice whatever may be the legal framework within which they operate. The guide also discusses and advises on the administration of an effective adoption service, staffing ratios, case loads, etc. It recognizes throughout the need for a team approach[18] to adoption work, and states clearly what can be the role of medical and other specialist consultants.

Although changes may soon be recommended in adoption law, the present procedure for adopting a child can be described. The statute under which all adoptions, no matter how arranged, are legalized, is the Adoption Act 1958.

Under this Act the court may grant an order for the adoption of a child provided the court is satisfied that all consents to this have been given, "that the order if made will be for the welfare of the infant",[19] and that no payment or reward in respect of the adoption has been made except with the sanction of the court.

Those who may apply for an adoption order must be domiciled in Great Britain and, if unrelated to the child, must be at least 25 years old. If a

[17] Published by HMSO, London, 1970.
[18] See also A. M. McWhinnie, *Adoption Assessments, A Team Approach based on Research and related to the Basic Needs of the Child*, Association of British Adoption Agencies, London. This describes one way of setting up such a team approach which has proved very effective.
[19] Adoption Act, para. 7.

married couple are the applicants, one must be 25 and the other at least 21 years old. If the applicant is the mother or father of the infant, there is no such age bar, and if the applicant is a relative he or she must be at least 21 years old.

An application to adopt may be lodged by a person singly but more usually is done jointly by married couples. Either the husband or the wife, however, may adopt singly provided they have the consent of their spouse. In fact most adoptions of children unrelated to the adopters are by married couples where the application is lodged jointly. The adoption of a girl or female infant by a sole male applicant is not permitted unless the court is satisfied that there are special circumstances which justify "this as an exceptional measure...".[20] Spinsters or widows may adopt, but courts are less sure of granting such orders than they used to be.

Prior to 1958 it was not possible for British people who were not resident in this country to adopt a child; neither could foreigners who were resident. Since 1959, however, both groups can adopt. Non-resident British couples have to satisfy some conditions of residence; one must stay in this country for 3 months with the child and the other spouse must stay for at least a month. Foreigners resident in this country can be granted a provisional adoption order on the understanding that they can and will adopt the child fully under the laws of their own country.

The law does not have an upper limit for the age of adopters although the courts would exercise their discretionary powers here. Adoption agencies, however, do set an upper limit. Usually they will not consider applications from adopters where the wife is much above 40, at least for a first child. Few agencies will consider at all a couple over 45 or where there is a wide difference in age between the husband and the wife. In practice, however, exceptions are made for exceptional couples or where couples will consider taking a child for whom, on medical or social grounds, it has been difficult to find an adoptive home. One might argue that a child with any such potential problems arising from his or her background should be placed with younger, more resilient couples rather than with those who are viewed as too old for the child without problems.

An adoption order will only be granted after the applicants have had the child continuously in their care for 3 months; and this "probationary

[20] Adoption Act, para. 2(3).

period", as it is called, cannot start until the child is at least 6 weeks old. At the beginning of this probationary period the applicants to adopt must notify the local authority of their intention to adopt, and under present law the local authority undertakes "welfare supervision" during this period. This is a statutory obligation and is separate from and as well as any visiting which may be done by the placement agency. When an application to adopt is presented to the court, the court then appoints a guardian *ad litem* or, in Scotland, a curator *ad litem*, to ascertain that all consents to this adoption have been freely given and that the adopters are suitable to adopt. Such a court representative is usually a social worker from a statutory department or a probation officer, although they need not be, and in some Scottish courts solicitors are appointed.

Although originally intended to safeguard the interests of the child, this arrangement whereby three different social workers can be visiting an adoptive home, each with an obligation to do so, can be confusing for adopters and can result in overlap, difficulty, and a diminution of responsibility as to who is ultimately responsible. Changes in these provisions are currently being considered[21] to avoid this overlap; for example, agencies might well be expected to do their own welfare supervision, and the appointment of a guardian *ad litem* might not be mandatory in all cases but at the discretion of the court. These proposals, however, can only be considered in the light of changes also being suggested in the future administration of the adoption services, and discussion of these is beyond the scope of this chapter.

The guardian *ad litem*'s present role is threefold: firstly, to check that consent to adoption has been given; secondly, that the order, if made, will be in the interests of the child; and, thirdly, that the applicants are suitable to adopt this child. On the question of consents there is again overlap, double checking, and current discussion about the need for changes in procedure. Under the present law the parent, in fact usually the mother, is asked three times to give her consent; firstly, when she asks an adoption agency to place her child for adoption, secondly, when the application is filed by the adopters when the mother signs legal consent formally before a justice of the peace, and, finally, she will be questioned by the guardian *ad litem* to ascertain that she really wishes the adoption to proceed. When she

[21] In working paper, *Adoption of Children*.

signs consent at the second stage she does not need to know the name of the adopters since they are given a serial number by the court. The mother may not sign legal consent to adoption until the child is at least 6 weeks old and she may withdraw her consent any time during the 3 months' probationary period and up until the adoption is finalized by the court. Where the child is legitimately born and being placed for adoption, both husband and wife must give consent. Where the child is illegitimate and the mother is married, under present law the mother's husband may also have to be informed and give consent even where the couple are and have been separated. Courts, however, differ in their practice here. The putative father can ask to be considered by the court as a suitable person to be given custody of his child[22] if he so wishes, but he has no legal status at the moment as far as giving his consent to adoption is concerned. This rests with the mother.

In Scotland the formal consent of the child being adopted is also required in the case of a boy of 14 or over and of a girl of 12 or over.

The court can dispense with consent if the person whose consent is to be dispensed with "has abandoned, neglected, or persistently ill-treated the infant; cannot be found, or is incapable of giving his consent, is withholding his consent unreasonably or has persistently failed without reasonable cause to discharge the obligations of a parent".[23]

These clauses can cover a wide range of situations. Differences of interpretation, however, arise as to what can be viewed by the courts as being "unreasonably withheld", and some of these judgements seem to favour the rights of biological parents and others the rights of those caring for the child, whether adopters or long-term foster parents, who, having cared for a child over a long period, wish to adopt him.

The role of the guardian *ad litem* is to represent the child's interests. He or she verifies all statements and documents and interviews all concerned. The court, through this representative, wants to ascertain that the adopters are suitable, that they are medically fit, a medical certificate being required, and that this placement is in the child's interest. What constitutes "suitability to adopt" is not a legal concept, and the court's representative is at a disadvantage in making his assessment of "suitability" in that the child is already in the home and has been there for at least 3 months. Many feel that

[22] Under Legitimacy Act, 1959.
[23] Adoption Act, 1958, para. 5(1) and (2).

the court should be brought in at an earlier stage if their representative is really to be able to assess the strengths and weaknesses of any adoptive home.

The actual legalization of adoptions can be carried through in the juvenile court, the county court, or the High Court in England, and in the three equivalent courts in Scotland. The actual court hearing is held privately and the natural mother need not attend. In Scotland court hearings are the exception rather than the rule, and usually only occur in cases of doubt and dispute. Otherwise the adoption order is ratified by the sheriff after he has studied the application and all the relevant documents.

The legal processes are the same in all adoptions no matter how the placement has been arranged, with the exception that it is only in the case of adoptions into unrelated families and where these are arranged by placement agencies that secrecy and anonymity are obtained or desired through the device already mentioned of a serial number.

The legal effects of an adoption order are that as far as custody, maintenance, and education are concerned, the adopters stand to the child in exactly the same relationship as they would to a child born to them in lawful marriage. Adopters and adopted child come within the same prohibited degrees of consanguinity; but adopted brothers and sisters in the same family are not thus prohibited from marrying each other.

Adopted children now inherit from their adoptive families in exactly the same way as naturally born children, and as a corollary they lose the right to inherit from their biological parents. The exceptions to this are that an adopted child cannot inherit a title or estates and entails accompanying a title from his adoptive parents, but he would inherit these from his biological parents. Of course, in practice nearly all adopted children lose all contact with their biological family, and their family becomes literally as well as legally the family which has adopted them.

The administrative and statutory provisions already described give the outward picture of how adoptions are arranged in the United Kingdom. It is important, too, to ask how adoption works out for individual children, their adoptive parents, and their natural parents. This is a much more difficult question to answer, for research is only beginning to study this "inner world" of adoption. It is frequently asked how many adoptions succeed and how many fail and whether adoption is a better solution than other types of substitute care. It is not possible to give a direct answer to these questions. Estimates of "successful" adoptions vary from 50 per cent to 90 per cent.[24] This wide divergence is explained because different samples have been used and different criteria employed to define "success". In fact it is almost certainly a fallacy to pose this question at all, it being more meaningful to ask what kinds of situations do adoptive families meet which biological families do not; what are the problems, if any, that they are likely to meet as adoptive families and how do they adjust to these. Figures show that a greater number of adopted than non-adopted children are referred to psychiatric services. The quoted incidence of these referrals range from 1·5 per cent to 2·9 per cent with an incidence of 8 per cent of adopted children in schools for maladjusted children. These figures, however, cannot be used as conclusive proof about the proportion of adopted children who show serious psychiatric disturbance, since there can be many factors influencing the parents in their decision to seek help; for example, a greater readiness to admit to behaviour difficulties if the child is adopted; a greater familiarity with using agencies because of their experience of acquiring their child through one; and so on.

Cumulative research, however, has now shown that for eventual outcome in adoption it is the personal qualities of the adoptive parents which are of paramount importance. These qualities relate, not just to the parents' competence and good adjustment as individuals, as a married couple or as members of their family or community, but also to their acceptance of all that is involved in bringing up someone else's child. This is the crux, and from it basically spring many of the difficulties of adoptive families and why adoptive parenthood is different in kind from biological parenthood. Kirk's studies in Canada[25] have shown how this difference has been often ignored by adopters and viewed frequently negatively by the community.

The fundamental attitudes behind this difference in kind in adoptive parenthood emerged in the writer's research study of the adult adjustment of adopted children. This research, *Adopted Children: How They Grow Up*, studied, through retrospective life histories, the adjustment of a representative group of fifty-eight adopted adults. From this point of view, i.e. that

---

[24] M. L. Kellmer Pringle, *Adoption—Facts and Fallacies*, Longmans, London, 1967. This book contains a detailed analysis of completed adoption research in the United States, Canada, and Great Britain between 1948 and 1965.

[25] D. H. Kirk, *Shared Fate*, The Free Press, New York, 1964.

of the person for whom the adoption arrangements are ultimately designed, it became possible to answer the following questions. How does adoption look to the child adopted? Does it give him or her a secure place in a family where he feels he really belongs, or does the adopted child always feel "different"? Does he long to find and keep in touch with his biological parents, or are the ties with his adoptive family stronger than those of this so-called "blood-tie"?

What emerged generally from this study was that a wide range of adjustment is possible in adulthood for adopted children. Where the adjustment is good in all areas and where there have been no major problems in growing up related to adoption as distinct from the normal processes of maturation, then adoption works out so well that the child, although he will want and need to know that he is adopted, forgets that he is adopted. He can identify so much with his adoptive family that when asked for a familial health record he can give that of his adoptive parents, only realizing later that this is not relevant. Many in this group commented that, having been told they were adopted, they found themselves surprised that it made no difference. In fact their experience was that they felt closer than ever to their adoptive parents.

At the other extreme there were cases of poor and abnormal adjustment in many areas of the adult's life situation where there had been acute unhappiness for years and where the relationships between the child and the adopters were very strained or where there had been a complete breakdown in relationships altogether. In these situations the children felt powerless and resentful, yet still acknowledging their adoptive parents as their parents. Because they were adopted they felt they should be grateful; yet because they had not been accepted and loved for themselves they could not feel gratitude—only resentment. There was an intermediate group between these two extremes who were found to be experiencing, or to have experienced, severe problems in their upbringing related in some way directly to the adoption situation.

The figures in each of these categories are not so important for adoption practice as what was revealed within the whole scale of possible adjustments and what the individual histories showed as the recurring patterns which led to good adjustment and the recurring patterns which led to poor or intermediate adjustment. From these patterns and histories a clear picture emerged of the kind of total family situation to choose when making an adoption placement. It also was clear that a great many factors[26] would influence the outcome of an adoption placement for any individual child and that these factors related to parental and familial attitudes rather than to the age of adoptive parents, length of marriage, education, financial resources, other children in the family, and even, within limits, the age of the child at placement in the adoptive home.

The attitude of the adoptive parents to initiating adoption and accepting the adopted child for himself and not for what he may or may not be able to do to satisfy some unmet need in the adopters' own lives, was obviously important. Adoption did not work out well where one partner was reluctant to adopt and only did so to please the other, nor did it work well where the marriage was unstable or where the parents were inconsistent in their attitude towards the child.

In those homes where the marriage has proved to be infertile or subfertile, how the husband and the wife each feels about this inability to achieve parenthood biologically or to add to their biological family, clearly influenced their genuine acceptance of the idea of adoption, and so their acceptance of the individual child himself as he develops his own personality. If they have unresolved problems themselves in this area the child will be a reminder to them of their problems and they will find it difficult to consider adoption from the child's point of view and all that this entails in terms of sharing with him not only that he or she is adopted but had other parents.

Relevant for the child's adjustment is in fact the attitude of the adoptive parents towards these other parents and towards unmarried parenthood and illegitimacy. It is important for the child that the parents bringing him up should not transfer on to him or her any feelings of criticism they may have towards girls who have illegitimate children, or any feelings of envy which they may have of a woman who, out of wedlock, could give birth to a child whereas they, married and desperately wanting children, had been unable to have any. It must be recognized that people are still prejudiced about illegitimacy and critical of unmarried mothers. They think many of them are irresponsible, and the fear that this kind of behaviour is inherited is far from dead. The adoptive mother who fears that her adopted

[26] For full analysis see A. M. McWhinnie, *Adopted Children. How They Grow Up*, Routledge and Kegan Paul, London, 1967.

adolescent daughter may be promiscuous or flighty with men, since her bio-logical mother was, will behave in such a mistrusting way that she will drive her daughter into behaving in just the way that she fears. "As my mother did not believe me when I said I had not been with boys, I felt I might as well do what she suspected I was doing." When in the research study the question was examined of how the adopted child had heard of his or her adopted status, it emerged that this was information which they felt should come to them on the initiative of their parents. Even when they had heard reference to it from outsiders, or some hint of it within the family, they would not believe it, and they would say to themselves: "Well, if there is anything in it my parents will tell me." Even when very curious, few of them could bring themselves to ask their parents. This very definite one-way communication about adoption details was very marked. It was the pattern, too, with regard to details about the biological parents. Al-though often curious for such factual information, they would never ask their parents questions. Even when their mothers started to give them information they would pretend not to be curious and would not ask questions although they might be very anxious to be told.

A similar pattern of communications was evident in the sub-group of long-term foster children included in the study.

Other children rather than adults are the people outside the family most likely to mention adoption to a child. The age when this most frequently happens is when children are about 9, a time when they are very interested in family relationships and when many children have fantasies about really being the son or daughter of a famous person or a princess. Nearly every adult interviewed had experienced some incident about this time of another child mentioning his adopted status to him. There were a few cases where the child would recall an incident as early as age 5.

The conclusions from this then are clear. To preserve good adoptive parent–child relationships, firstly, adoptive parents must take the initiative in telling a child about adoption—they must not wait until the child asks—and, secondly, to be sure of avoiding their child hearing of adoption from an outside child they must themselves tell the child before he is 5 and certainly before he is 9. It should be recognized, however, that adoptive parents often find it difficult to tell a child about adoption, although at the same time they know that they should and want to tell him. They fear telling him, however, fearing that he will love them less or will want to find his biological mother. Often they feel their relationship with the child is so perfect that they are afraid of spoiling it, or they think that it is hard to have to tell a child that his biological parents were not married.

The study showed, however, that if the parent talks about adoption in an easy and relaxed way, then the child does not think of it as all that important, or else they are struck that having been told, it really makes no difference. Linked with this is the fact that these adopted adults all said that the people they looked on as parents were the people who brought them up. Their attitude to their biological parents was, on the whole, a curiosity about them as people and why they had placed them for adoption, but not feeling for them as parents. This feeling of identification with the adoptive parents and family occurred where the adoption had been happy but equally where it had been unhappy. In only five cases out of the whole fifty-eight was the biological mother actively sought as a mother, and in all these five the adoption had been very unhappy for the child and the biological mother was viewed as someone who would understand them in a way that their adoptive mother did not. Even in these five cases the adoptive person felt some filial obligation to the adoptive parents. This relationship with the adoptive parents appears, in fact, to be particularly compelling one—either the child felt particularly that since these parents had adopted him he must do all he could for them or he felt particularly rebellious against them although still, interestingly enough, viewing them as his parents. This close identification and the fact that the biological parents are not looked upon as parents are very relevant for casework practice, both in adoption and long-term fostering.

The curiosity of adopted children about their biological parents is not acute but it needs to be satisfied, ideally from within the adoptive home. The children want to be given by their adoptive or foster parents a word picture of what their other parents were like as people, their age, occupation, appearance, interests, why they had placed them for adoption, and whether they were healthy, normal people. This curiosity may lie dormant for years and then may be reawakened in different ways and often in reaction to an outside happening, e.g. when asked for a family health record, when about to marry, and for women when they themselves are expecting a baby. Then there is curiosity about "the stock I came from".

Doubts and uncertainties about the basic facts of their birth background can lead to many problems in adolescence. J. B. McWhinnie writing about this[27] has stressed the need for adopted adolescents to feel secure about their own identity and to be able to communicate about this with their adoptive parents. He shows how the inability of many adopters to come to terms with the barriers within themselves to talking in a relaxed way about adoption to their children can become one of the foci of unresolved problems in disturbed adoptive families and in the psychiatric illnesses of the adolescents themselves.

With regard to the adopted person's attitude to open discussion about his adoption, this was shown to be something which he felt was for the intimate family. He wanted to be told about it by his parents and to be able to talk to them about it, but as far as the outside world was concerned he wanted to be viewed as the child of his adoptive parents. All interviewed were emphatic that they did not want to be called "our adopted son or adopted daughter" but "our son or our daughter".

The pendulum then has swung too far in our community attitude to this. Parents are often so anxious not to make a secret of adoption—to be proud of it—that they are referring to it too much in general conversation. They also may talk far too much to the child about it.

Relatives, too, have a part to play in the child's adjustment. If they are critical and unaccepting, this can severely affect the child's adjustment. Too often in adoption work the emphasis has been on selection only of the adoptive applicants, but from the child's point of view he acquires by adoption not only a mother and father but a whole family network. The attitude of the wider family becomes particularly important where the child is obviously different from the adoptive parents, e.g. when handicapped or of mixed racial origin. Relatives, too, can be critical where a couple already with biological children add to the family by adoption, and the relatives may show a preference for the children born into the family.[28]

---

[27] In J. B. McWhinnie, 'Psychotherapy with adopted children in adolescence', paper presented at the Seventh International Congress of Mental Health, London, 1968.

[28] For attitude of relatives, see A. M. McWhinnie, *Adopted Children. How They Grow Up*, Routledge and Kegan Paul, London, 1967, and A. M. McWhinnie, Group counselling with seventy-eight adoptive families, in *Social Work and Adoption* (edited by R. Tod), Longmans, London, 1971.

The attitude of neighbours, friends, and the community can also influence outcome by offering constructive support to the adopters or negative doubting of the advisability of adoption and of the adopter's ability to be good parents.[29]

Research studies have highlighted that many adopters find it more difficult to tell their children of adoption than had been realized. Even when advised to tell and though they intend to do this and even want to do it, there are emotional barriers. There is much less evidence about how best to resolve these problems. An experimental programme of group meetings for adoptive parents several years after legalization has shown the extent of this problem even with adopters who had preplacement counselling. The experimental programme showed, too, how group counselling can be used successfully to resolve some of these difficulties.[30]

Other experimental group programmes[31] have shown, too, the need for such group discussion as measured by the adoptive parents' eagerness to attend. There is a growing awareness among adopters themselves that they need and want to meet with others in the same situation when their children are young and perhaps particularly when adolescent. Adoptive parents are themselves forming their own groups.[32] The adoption services in this country are now beginning to consider what their responsibilities should be to provide a service after legalization, the point at which services up until now have ceased, and how far they can use group methods.

In a recent research project[33] for the adoption of non-white children in the United Kingdom, groups were used before and after placement as an integral part of the service and the study.

Since the adjustment of the adopters and the child are closely interdependent, a good outcome for any adoption placement depends on the attitudes and qualities of those who apply to adopt, and the role of adoption agencies is to select from amongst those who apply those couples who are most likely

[29] A. M. McWhinnie, *op. cit.*

[30] *Ibid.*

[31] G. Sandground, Group Counselling with adoptive families after legal adoption, in *Social Work and Adoption* (ed. R. Tod), Longmans, London, 1971. (See also reports of group discussion meeting in the journal *Child Adoption.*)

[32] The first world conference of adoptive parents was held in Milan in September, 1971.

[33] L. Raynor, *Adoption of Non-White Children,* Allen & Unwin, London, 1970.

to be "good risks" as adoptive parents. The agency has to attempt to assess how the applicants will respond, not just to the immediate care of a dependent infant, but how in future years they will care and support in the widest sense the child they have chosen to adopt, and how far they will be able to meet his or her individual needs. As already indicated, there is currently discussion about how adopters could best be helped with the question of telling their children of adoption as, too, about how group methods could be used in the selection and counselling of adopters both at the time of their application to adopt and after placement.

At the moment, however, most adoption agencies in the United Kingdom rely on a "home study method" based on individual interviews with applicants, although some agencies now supplement this with group meetings as a method of giving adopters preliminary information about the whole adoption process and thus an opportunity of considering whether or not to proceed with an application.

The number of interviews and the quality of interviewing vary from one agency to another, but it is usual for both applicants, husband and wife, to be seen together and separately, and their home to be visited. The areas which ought to be covered in these interviews have already been indicated. A full discussion of these, however, is beyond the scope of this chapter, and those who wish to study this further are referred to the chapter on services to adoptive parents in *A Guide to Adoption Practice*.[34] Much assessment work currently being done in the United Kingdom does not reach the standards recommended in the *Guide*, and interviewing is frequently superficial and its content even irrelevant.

To supplement the casework interviews, references are taken about the community standing and suitability of applicants. These references may be obtained through a written request, but some agencies prefer to visit referees to try to secure a more honest appraisal of the applicant.

An up-to-date medical report is obtained from the family doctor. This report can range from a simple statement of fitness to adopt to a more detailed report depending on the request from the agency. The Medical Group of the Association of British Adoption Agencies has devised detailed medical assessment forms which it is urging placement agencies to use. Medical reports are also usually obtained about the couple's inability to

[34] Published by HMSO, London, 1970. See Chapter 3.

have biological children if medical advice has been sought. Some agencies go so far as to insist on proof of infertility before acceptance.

There is, however, a change in emphasis here, and many agencies now consider placing children into homes where there were already children. Whether the decline in the number of babies available for adoption will alter this again remains to be seen. It certainly can be argued[35] that well-chosen homes where there are already biological children avoid some of the dangers and stresses of placements into homes already experiencing the potential tensions arising from the consequences of infertility.

How the medical and social information and assessments are integrated and used to complement each other varies as greatly as how much use is made of medical and specialist advice.[36] There is an increasing awareness that more thought must be given to an administrative structure which can facilitate such an interdisciplinary approach.[37]

Once all inquiries are completed, each application to a voluntary adoption society is presented to the case committee who ultimately take responsibility for accepting or rejecting the application. In local authority children's departments there may or there may not be such a case committee.

Adoption workers have on the whole not resolved satisfactorily how to handle the non-acceptance of applicants. Some agencies have a policy that they will never give a reason for rejection, but it would seem better whenever possible to share with applicants the reasons for this decision, since the agency's decision, though aimed to protect the interests of any child to be placed, can also be viewed ultimately as preventing an unhappy outcome for the applicants too.[38]

Once accepted by an agency, adopters may have a child placed with them after a few weeks or months, but more usually now, because of the decline

[35] A. M. McWhinnie, *The Attributes of the Well-adjusted Adoptive Parents*, Medical Group Papers II, Association of British Adoption Agencies.
[36] C. A. Cooper, *Medical Practice in Adoption Agencies*, 1967; *Child Adoption*, No. 53, 1968, pp. 42–50.
[37] See (a) *A Guide to Adoption Practice* for discussion of such administrative provisions and (b) *Adoption Agreements* by A. M. McWhinnie where there is a description of the effective working of a team approach initiated by the writer.
[38] For a further discussion of this see *A Guide to Adoption Practice*, HMSO, London, 1970.

in the number of babies being offered for adoption, they will have to wait one to two years or more.

When couples consider adoption they usually think of adopting a baby under 3 months old and this is usually the age of babies offered through adoption societies, although older babies, toddlers, and older children are also placed. The baby can be placed even before he is 6 weeks old, which is the earliest age for the giving of consent by the biological mother, if he is taken into the adoptive home as a foster child becoming a child placed with a view to adoption from the age of 6 weeks.

Although research has not produced conclusive proof about the optimal age of placement of the child,[39] there is a consensus of opinion as to the desirability of early placement—although this can range from the first few weeks to the first or second year. What may in fact be more important than the age at placement is the quality of the care that the child experiences before placement and how the adopters respond to an older child.

By law the child must be medically examined before the adoption is legalized. In practice most adoption societies arrange for a medical examination before the the child is placed in the adoptive home. This may be done by the hospital doctor where the baby was born or by the general practitioner of the foster home or nursery where the baby is being cared for or by a paediatrician or child specialist. The Medical Group of the Association of British Adoption Agencies now commends the practice whereby paediatricians or medical practitioners skilled in developmental paediatrics undertake these examinations, and this is further discussed in *A Guide to Adoption Practice*.[40] Where there is good understanding between the medical practitioner and the social worker who is helping the biological mother, many babies who would otherwise be viewed as medically at risk can be placed in adoptive homes.[41] Also, as fewer babies are becoming available

[39] For a discussion of this, see *Adoption—Facts and Fallacies*, by M. L. Kellmer Pringle, pp. 16 and 17. See also work done by A. Kadushin, *Adopting Older Children*, Columbia University Press, New York, 1970.

[40] Published by HMSO, London, 1970.

[41] J. O. Forfar, Worth and need in medico-social assessment: the adoption situation, *Child Adoption*, No. 2, 1969, pp. 25–33; and A. M. McWhinnie, *Adoption Assessments. A Team Approach based on Research and related to the Basic Needs of the Child*, Association of British Adoption Agencies, London.

for adoption, adoption workers are turning their attention more to finding homes for children whose medical problems are such that these would previously have precluded them from adoption. Paediatric predictions will be particularly important as an integral part of these placements.

Another group who previously would not have been considered for adoption are non-white children of mixed ethnic origin. Increasingly, such children are being found adoptive homes, and more white couples are applying to adopt these children. In order to facilitate such placements, an Adoption Resources Exchange was set up in 1968. Through this exchange, in which there are now thirty participating agencies, it is possible to pool all the resources of potential homes throughout the country and not simply rely on those homes known to the agency which is trying to place a particular child.[42] How these adoptions will work out in the long run and how far the children will remain integrated into the family and the community is still not known, for the experiment of doing this kind of adoption is a comparatively recent development.[43]

When a baby or child is placed in an adoptive home, the adopters do not usually meet the biological mother. The biological mother in turn does not know the adopters' identity, although she will, or ought to be, given information about the home into which her child is being placed. The only stipulation which she has by law a right to make about the adoptive home chosen for her child is the religious affiliation. There are some agencies which arrange meetings between biological mothers and adopters as policy, but this practice is viewed as controversial. In direct and third-party placements such meetings are, of course, more common.

The adopters, at the time of deciding whether to take a particular child into their home or not, will usually be given background information about the biological mother and father, but practice here varies considerably, and sometimes adopters ask not to be given information. From the child's point of view,[44] however, it is clear that adopters should be given a word picture of each parent, together with details of their health history so

[42] M. M. Carrihine, Working with the Adoption Resource Exchange,*ChildAdoption*, No. 3, 1970, pp. 45–9.

[43] L. Rayner, *Adoption of Non-White Children*, Allen & Unwin, London, 1970.

[44] A. M. McWhinnie, *Adopted Children. How They Grow Up*, Routledge and Kegan Paul, London, 1967, pp. 243–6.

that this can be passed on to the child as he or she grows to maturity. Health history as such has obvious relevance, too, for the upbringing of the child.

Once a child is placed in an adoptive home and the placement legalized, any further contact with the placement agency is voluntary. Some adopters choose to keep in touch while others prefer not to. It is increasingly felt that agencies should be more accessible for adopters to return with any problems that they may have, but how best to offer this service to adopters is currently under discussion. Adopters often experience particular anxiety about adoption when their child is an adolescent and the adopted child at this time will be asking particularly "Who am I?", and feeling the need to be secure in his own identity.[45] For the adopted adolescent this search obviously includes his need, whether openly expressed or not, to have a picture of his own genealogical background.

Ideally this information should have been given to the child by his adopters as he grew up. Where, however, this has not been done, sometimes the adopters and sometimes the adopted child will go to the placement agency and ask for this information. Not all adopted children will, of course, know the name of the agency which placed them, and this will be particularly so where the adoptive parents have not been able to discuss adoption with them. In such a situation an adopted person may, indeed, wonder where to obtain information about himself.

In Scotland an adopted child, on reaching the age of 17, can go to Register House in Edinburgh and see the record of his original birth entry, which will give some factual information[46] about his biological mother and his father if he registered the birth. In England an adopted person must seek the permission of the court before being allowed access to this original entry, and many courts would be reluctant to give this permission. Experience with adopted adults also suggests that such a formal procedure will deter many from making inquiries at all. Whether changes should be made in either the

[45] See J. B. McWhinnie, Psychotherapy with adopted children in adolescence, paper presented at the Seventh International Congress on Mental Health, London, 1968, and D. W. Winnicott, Adopted children in adolescence, chapter 3 in *Social Work in Adoption* (ed. R. Tod), Longmans, London, 1971.

[46] The original birth entry gives name, age, address and occupation of parent, and place and time of birth of the child.

English or Scottish provisions in this respect is currently under discussion.[47] The dilemma here is whether the community has a right to debar adopted persons from access to information about themselves, which all other members of the community have by right, while at the same time affording protection to those who entered into the original adoption contract, i.e. the biological parents and the adoptive parents. Again experience with adopted adults shows that they themselves are very aware of this problem and on the whole want to act very responsibly towards both sets of parents.[48]

Discussion of adoption outcome has so far concentrated on adoptions made into unrelated families. How do the children fare who are adopted by their own mother, or their mother and her husband, or by a relative? Social work agencies and psychiatric clinics meet those where problems have arisen, but we do not know the proportion of good adjustments where the child accepts his adoption and yet also knows what the actual biological relationships are. Serious problems can arise when children are not told the true situation; for example, when grandparents adopt but the child is led to believe they are his parents and that his biological mother is a sibling. There are cases where grandparents have adopted their daughter's illegitimate child to retain custody of this child and then regretted that this decision was made so final. For such situations it is being suggested that extended guardianship[49] arrangements would be more appropriate than adoption.

This chapter has aimed to describe the major trends in recent years in adoption services, practice, and policy in the United Kingdom. From adoption being viewed as suitable for the working classes it has become socially acceptable in all socio-economic groups. From an emphasis on the exclusive right of the biological parents the climate of public opinion moved to viewing adoption as a means of finding babies for childless couples. Now the emphasis is becoming that adoption legalization and policy must consider first and foremost the interests of the child, and adoption decisions should be in terms of finding the right home for each child.

---

[47] See *Adoption of Children*, Working Paper and evidence being submitted to the Departmental Committee on the Adoption of Children; and A. M. McWhinnie, *Who Am I?* (a paper describing provisions and discussing these in relation to research evidence and adopted person's needs), *Child Adoption*, vol. 62, No. 4, 1970, pp. 36–40.

[48] See research evidence in A. M. McWhinnie, *Adopted Children. How They Grow Up.*

[49] *Adoption of Children.*

From an emphasis on placing for adoption only babies with no health and developmental hazards, the energies of adoption workers are now being turned to an adoption service for the child "at risk", and the so-called "hard-to-place" child, i.e. the child with an established medical and social handicap and of mixed ethnic origin. This new emphasis is being accelerated by the recent dramatic decline in the number of babies being offered for adoption.

Assessment and interviewing skills in adoption work have gradually become seen as an area for skilled social work practice, and a willingness has emerged to base decisions on research findings and to try out new methods. From the view that the responsibilities of the adoption services can and should end once the adoption is legalized, it is now becoming apparent that services should also be made available after placement.

Whatever the methods used by adoption workers for the difficult task of selecting adoptive homes for any child, from the child's point of view he—whatever his background or problems—wants to be placed with comparatively young, healthy, happily married couples who love and value children for their own sake and not for what they may or may not do to satisfy the parents' own frustrations and needs. He wants parents who accept comfortably their own problems in relation to child bearing, who accept, too, unmarried parents and illegitimacy or whatever the background reasons are for the placement of the child for adoption, and who will tell him in an easy and relaxed way that he is adopted and had other parents.

Given this kind of total adoptive environment, adoption can work out so well for the artificially created family that, having acknowledged that it is artificially created and so different in kind from a biologically created family, the members of the family can and do forget about adoption. Where, however, such an environment is not provided, then adoption works badly, and the ensuing unhappiness is acute. The adoption services, then, in any community must be thoughtfully organized and adequately financed and staffed in order that they may be an effective social work service for children.

CHAPTER 11

Special Education

David Pritchard*

EDITOR'S INTRODUCTION

Hitherto we have examined the primary role and functions of what were the children's departments of local authorities; but as was stated in the introduction to Chapter 1, such a department (or a voluntary society equally devoted to the care of children) does not function in a vacuum and has very strong links with other agencies. In the care of children the links are particularly close with the special education service of the local education authority and the hospital services dealing with mental handicap. To these topics the next two chapters are devoted. The question might well be posed here as to why there is an apparently illogical split between agencies in this field. As we have seen earlier, social services departments are now responsible for running community schools, or what were once the approved schools, which set out to be educational establishments. Yet at the same time a large majority of children are not educated under the Social Services Department but under the Education Department—with the exception of another minority who are educated inside the hospital fence. No doubt considerable rationalization of the system is desirable, but for the time being suffice to say that the social worker dealing with child care problems will need some understanding of the resources available to him within the other two agencies.

To add to the complication, what often brings a child to the position of needing special education may not be his actual organic

---

* Professor of Education, University College of Swansea.

handicap, but what he feels about it, and what is happening to him because of it. In other words a strong, flexible, and united family can often contain and help a severely maladjusted child, whereas another family, poorly endowed with competence and stamina, may be brought to the point of breakdown by a comparatively mild handicap in one child.

Another aspect of the problem to be considered is the situation which arises when a child comes into care because of the family breakdown. As we have seen, such an experience is traumatic for the child and if, in addition, he has a degree of handicap, then he is very much in need of what might be called total remedial help. The totality of the help needed is difficult to achieve when the responsibility for one part of his problem rests with one department and the other part with another.

David Pritchard introduces this subject with a factual account of the current scene in educational circles in England and Wales. Student social workers are invited to build, upon the facts here presented, their own concepts of what the most effective and humane use of resources might be between the education and social work departments.

As with the other social services, the development of educational provision for handicapped children was haphazard. However, despite the lack of planning and central direction and control during most of the nineteenth century, the early special schools, be they for the blind, the deaf, the mentally or the physically handicapped, displayed a number of common characteristics. The most evident of these, and the most far reaching in its consequences, was the emphasis placed upon protecting the children from the dangers and difficulties of the outside world. Consequently the schools were, without exception, residential institutions in which the children lost contact with and were cut off from the community. The emphasis was almost entirely upon segregation as exemplified by a contemporary account of the first residential school for physically handicapped boys established in 1865 at Kensington, London. "Once a boy is admitted he is not allowed to leave during the whole of his stay. Apart from walking out with the matron for exercise, he never leaves the building. He can have a visitor once in three months. He can write a letter once a month. Otherwise he is excluded from the outside world."[1]

This concentration upon segregation in residential schools had the unfortunate effect of cutting special education off from the mainstream of education. Moreover, it also influenced the kind of education given in the schools, particularly as many of the schools were part of or associated with institutions for handicapped adults to which the children moved, at least in theory, when they left the schools. This was part of the concept of permanent care and had as its corollary the assumption that as the children would not have to live in society they would not require the tools of society. The educational effects of this were long lasting, so much so that Mary Dendy, an assiduous worker on behalf of mentally handicapped children, could state in 1920 that children in the residential special school for the feeble-minded which she established should not learn to write since "in at least one great institution, the knowledge of how to write has led to great difficulties in managing high-grade cases, the men and women communicating with each other by means of notes".[2]

The second characteristic was a concentration upon trade training. As part of the concept of permanent care, the institutions for handicapped adults would also be in effect sheltered workshops. It was therefore felt necessary for the children while still at school to be instructed in the trades which they would follow when they entered the adult institutions. However, as the adult institutions became fuller, fewer of the children leaving the special schools could enter them, but, nevertheless, they were still instructed in the traditional trades, basket making, mat making, mattress making, whiplash making, which it was presumed that they would follow in the sheltered workshops. The result was that many children left the schools unprepared to earn their living in the outside world since they had been trained in work which could be carried out economically only under sheltered conditions. Even, well on into the twentieth century, when the concept of permanent care was disappearing, many of the special schools, day as well as residential, continued trade training because it was felt that without it the children could not hope to compete for work in competition

[1] G. C. T. Bartley, *The Schools for the People*, Bell & Daldy, London, 1871, p. 365.
[2] C. P. Lapage, *Feeblemindedness in Children of School Age with an Appendix on Sandlebridge by Mary Dendy*, 2nd edn., Manchester University Press, Manchester, 1920, p. 231.

with the non-handicapped. However, as the schools were small in size they could not offer a large choice of trades. The usual ones were tailoring, boot and shoe making, and carpentry, and many children attempted, and failed in, work which was unsuitable for them.

The third characteristic common to the earlier special schools was a preoccupation with religion. This was exemplified at its most extreme in the time-table for Sundays in a school for the deaf in Doncaster in the nineteenth century. There even the youngest of the deaf children studied the Gospels from 6.30 to 8 in the morning, 3 to 5 in the afternoon, and 5.20 to 7.30 in the evening. In addition, they attended public worship from 10 to 11.30 a.m. and 11.40 a.m. to 1.[3] One wonders whether time-tables like this one were actually followed, or whether they were included in annual reports to please the subscribers to the schools, who, being ardent Christians themselves, would wish to believe that the children were being given adequate religious instruction. On the other hand, it is quite conceivable that they were followed on the principle that as the handicapped are unlikely to achieve much success in this world, let us ensure that they succeed in the next. If this were the case it would merely reflect the pessimistic attitude towards the handicapped and their potentialities which sometimes prevailed, and which was reflected in sheltered workshops and segregation from the community.

The final characteristic was the part played by voluntary effort. For the greater part of the nineteenth century the special schools received no assistance, financial or otherwise, from the state. The first investigation of their needs was not carried out until 1889[4] in the case of the blind and the deaf, and 1898[5] in the case of the mentally and the physically handicapped, and the first legislation was not enacted until 1893[6] in the case of the blind and the deaf, and 1899[7] in the case of the mentally and the physically handicapped. It was, therefore, left to philanthropically minded individuals to establish special schools and make provision for the education of handi-

[3] K. W. Hodgson, *The Deaf and their Problems,* Watts, London, 1953, p. 172.

[4] *Report on the Royal Commission on the Blind, the Deaf and Dumb and others of the United Kingdom,* 4 vols., HMSO, London, 1889.

[5] Education Department, *Report of the Departmental Committee on Defective and Epileptic Children,* 2 vols., HMSO, London, 1898.

[6] Elementary Education (Blind and Deaf Children) Act 1893.

[7] Elementary Education (Defective and Epileptic Children) Act 1899.

capped children. This characteristic, this tradition of voluntary effort on behalf of handicapped children, has continued to the present day, although the place of individuals has now been taken by corporate bodies. The state, of course, now plays a full part, and local education authorities (LEAs) provide most of the special schools. Nevertheless, there are still 113 special schools out of a total of 855 which are completely voluntary and independent of any LEA.[8] These schools are known as non-maintained special schools and are run either by bodies like the Invalid Children's Aid Association, the National Association for Mental Health, the Royal National Institute for the Blind, the Society for Autistic Children, and the Spastics Society, or by boards of governors who are the successors of the individual pioneers who founded the schools. The fees of the children attending them are paid by LEAs. They are fully recognized by the Department of Education and Science from whom they can and do receive grants towards capital expenditure, much of which is devoted to rebuilding and modernizing, as many of the schools are still in the nineteenth-century premises in which they were founded. There are other voluntary organizations which do not maintain schools but which, like those already mentioned, provide advice, information, encouragement, and welfare. These include the British Diabetic Association, the British Epileptic Association, the Deaf, Blind and Rubella Children's Association, the Haemophilia Society, the National Association for Spina Bifida and Hydrocephalus, the National Deaf Children's Society, the National Society for Mentally Handicapped Children, the Royal National Institute for the Deaf, and the Society for the Aid of Thalidomide Children. Voluntary effort therefore continues to play an important part in the education of handicapped children, and without it there is no doubt that some severely handicapped cerebral palsied, autistic, and epileptic children would be without education even today.

However, although the fourth characteristic has remained, the other three have disappeared. The emphasis now is upon integration. Special schools no longer give training in a limited number of trades but rather provide vocational preparation in order that their leavers may take their place in open industry. Finally, there is no more concentration on religion

[8] Department of Education and Science, *Statistics of Education,* Vol. 1, HMSO, London, 1971. Published annually.

in special schools than in any other kind of school, although there is a conscious attempt to develop socially desirable qualities such as honesty, loyalty, punctuality, truthfulness, tidiness, perseverance, and politeness which will help the children to compensate for any intellectual or physical deficiencies. These developments have occurred partly because of a change in the climate of opinion which has brought a more enlightened attitude towards handicapped children and partly because of the Education Act of 1944.

Prior to 1944, special schools had been outside the general educational framework, and the children attending them had been looked upon as a class apart. Moreover, a considerable stigma was attached to special schools especially as children attending the mentally defective schools had to be certified as being feeble-minded within the meaning of the Mental Deficiency Acts. However, the Act of 1944 made the provision of special educational treatment part of the general duty laid upon LEAs to ensure that children are educated in accordance with their ages, aptitudes, and abilities. Earlier legislation had dealt separately with the education of the handicapped. Either they had been covered by Acts of Parliament which dealt exclusively with them, or[9] they had been dealt with quite separately in statutes of a general educational nature. In the consolidating Act of 1921,[10] whereas Part III covered elementary education and Part VI higher education blind, deaf, defective, and epileptic children were treated as a distinct class in Part V. But in the 1944 Act, section 8, which called upon education authorities to provide primary and secondary schools, also required them to have regard "to the need for securing that provision is made for pupils who suffer from any disability of mind or body or providing either in special schools, or otherwise, special educational treatment".

The fact that handicapped children could be educated other than in special schools was also a new departure. Previously they could receive their education only in special schools or certified special classes. But section 33 of the 1944 Act instructed LEAs to "provide for the education

[9] That is, Elementary Education (Blind and Deaf Children) Act 1893; Elementary Education (Defective and Epileptic Children) Act 1899; Elementary Education (Defective and Epileptic Children) Amendment Act 1903; Elementary Education (Defective and Epileptic Children) Act 1914; and Education (Deaf Children) Act 1937.

[10] Education Act 1921.

of pupils in whose case the disability is serious in special schools appropriate for that category, but where that is impracticable, or where the disability is not serious, the arrangements may provide for the giving of such education in any school maintained by the LEA or any school not so maintained". The reference to "any school" means that not only can special education be given in schools other than special schools, but it need not necessarily be given even in a special class. This is in keeping with the modern thinking of social workers, psychologists, and educators that the handicapped require to be integrated into rather than segregated from society. This view is shared by the administrators of the Department of Education and Science. Special education, they emphasize, is "not a matter of segregating the seriously handicapped from their fellows but of providing in each case the special help or modification in regime or education suited to the needs of the individual child".[11] A similar point was made in the Ministry of Education Circular 276 of June 1954: "No handicapped pupil should be sent to special school who can satisfactorily be educated in an ordinary school", and Sir Edward Boyle, then Minister of Education, reinforced this in the House of Commons in 1963 when he said: "It is the Government's policy that whenever possible children with handicaps should receive their education in ordinary schools."

When considering what makes it possible for children with handicaps to receive their education in ordinary schools it is necessary to examine each category of handicap separately. Ten such categories are recognized by the Department of Education and Science. These are not mentioned in the Education Acts, rather the Secretary of State is empowered under section 33 of the 1944 Act to make regulations defining the "several categories of children requiring special educational treatment". This power illustrates a feature of modern legislation whereby Acts of Parliament express certain powers and duties in very general terms and leave matters of detail to be dealt with by regulations which have the force of law. Such delegated legislation, although criticized on the ground that it is open to abuse, is, nevertheless, recognized as an essential necessity if parliamentary time is not to be taken up with the minutiae of administration. Certainly the regulations laid before Parliament under section 33 have conformed with the

[11] Ministry of Education, *Education of the Handicapped Pupil, 1945–1955*, Pamphlet No. 30, HMSO, London, 1956, p. 1.

intention of the Act since the categories are defined in such a way as to avoid, as far as possible, the rigid separation of the handicapped from the normal.[12]

This is exemplified in the case of physically handicapped children who are defined as "pupils not suffering solely from a defect of sight or hearing who by reason of disease or crippling defect cannot, without detriment to their health or educational development, be satisfactorily educated under the normal regime of ordinary schools".[13] The important words here are "normal regime", for if this is changed then it is possible for the physically handicapped child to be educated in the ordinary school. The changes that might be involved could include the redesignation of classrooms in order that the child may remain on the ground floor, permission for him to enter or leave by a special door, the construction of ramps instead of steps, excusing him from participating in games and physical education, allowing him to have a period of rest at midday, and providing special equipment and apparatus as well as transport. But even with such changes no generalizations can be made as each badly handicapped child must be considered individually in the light of certain criteria. Since most handicapped children are, understandably, slightly emotionally disturbed, it must be asked whether such disturbance will be alleviated if the child attends an ordinary school and so feels that after all he is not so different from other children, or, on the other hand, will it be exacerbated because being the only handicapped child he might feel more different than if he were with other handicapped children. This, therefore, is a question of the child's attitude to his handicap and the extent to which he has learnt to live with it. Equally as important is the attitude of the parent to the child. Many parents of handicapped children fall into one of two extremes—either they over-protect their child or they reject him. In either event it may be necessary for the child to attend a special school in order that the ill effects of over-protection or rejection can be combated. In the same way the attitude of the teacher in the ordinary school must be considered. If the teacher is likely to be distressed by or feel repugnance at the appearance of a badly handicapped child, then the child will not be happy in his class. Similarly, although certain modifications can

[12] Statutory Instrument No. 365, The Handicapped Pupils and Special Schools Regulations 1959.
[13] *Ibid.*

be made in the ordinary school, if the building is unsuitable for a child in a wheelchair, then it is clearly not the right place. The extent to which the child has missed experience is also important. The special school makes a conscious attempt to compensate the children for their deprivation of experience, but the ordinary school is obviously not geared to do this. As the child has missed experience, so he may well have missed schooling due to the need for operative treatment and subsequent convalescence. If this is the case he will have fallen behind in his school work and may be very retarded. He will therefore require remedial education which the special school is in a position to give. In addition, he may have learning difficulties arising from the nature of his handicap. If he suffers from cerebral palsy he may well have difficulties in visual and aural perception as well as in handling the ordinary tools of the classroom, pencil, ruler, and scissors. Therefore, unless he is given very special teaching which may only be available in the special school, he may become progressively more and more backward.

There are 146 special schools for the physically handicapped attended by 8111 children; 29 of the schools are non-maintained and 64 schools admit delicate as well as physically handicapped children.

The criteria governing the education of physically handicapped children in ordinary schools will apply *mutatis mutandis* to some of the other categories of handicapped children. They will not, however, apply to blind children who are defined as those "who have no sight or whose sight is or is likely to become so defective that they require education by methods not involving the use of sight".[14] These methods, of course, include learning to read and write in Braille, and since teachers in ordinary schools are not conversant with Braille it follows that the blind must be educated in special schools. Since the schools have large catchment areas they are all residential. There are twenty of them, of which seventeen are non-maintained, and they include two grammar schools, two schools for children who are both blind and deaf, and two schools which also admit partially sighted children. They are attended by 1161 children.[15]

Partially sighted children are defined as those "who by reason of defective vision cannot follow the normal regime of ordinary schools without

[14] Statutory Instrument No. 365.
[15] Department of Education and Science, *op. cit.*

detriment to their sight or to their educational development, but can be educated by special methods involving the use of sight".[16] There are twenty special schools, of which four are non-maintained, catering for 1825 children. In addition there are 108 children in the two blind schools which also admit partially sighted children, and 104 in special units attached to ordinary schools.[17] The schools have special lighting and adjustable desks, which enable the children to avoid stooping over their work and thus prevent postural defects. Many of the children are very backward in reading, and the special methods involve the use of books with extra large print, thick pencils, and magnifying glasses.

Deaf children "who have no hearing or whose hearing is so defective that they require education by methods used for deaf pupils without naturally acquired speech or language" and partially hearing children "who have some naturally acquired speech or language but whose hearing is so defective that they require for their education special arrangements or facilities though not necessarily all the educational methods used for deaf pupils"[18] are frequently educated together. There are forty-nine special schools of which fourteen are non-maintained, which admit deaf and partially hearing children. Five schools cater only for partially hearing children and one school is a selective grammar school for deaf children. There are 2976 deaf children and 1865 partially hearing children in the special schools. There are also 1709 children in partially hearing units attached to ordinary schools.[19] In recent years the number of pupils classified as deaf has been diminishing. At the same time there has occurred an increase in the number of the partially hearing. The variations are not due to changes in degree of hearing defects. On the contrary, they are the results of advances in electronic engineering which have made available improved amplifying equipment in the form of group and individual hearing aids. Better aids and an earlier start to auditory training have therefore made it possible to upgrade to the category of partially hearing children who would previously have been rightly regarded as deaf.

There are six special schools, all residential, and four of which are non-

[16] Statutory Instrument No. 365.
[17] Department of Education and Science, *op. cit.*
[18] Statutory Instrument No. 365.
[19] Department of Education and Science, *op. cit.*

maintained, catering for 602 children[20] "who by reason of epilepsy cannot be educated under the normal regime of ordinary schools without detriment to themselves or other pupils".[21] The number of children in the special schools is gradually declining as, with a more enlightened attitude towards them and improved methods of sedation, more epileptic children are educated in ordinary schools.

Children suffering from speech defects, "who on account of defect or lack of speech not due to deafness require special educational treatment",[22] can attend one of two special schools both of which are non-maintained: eighty-five children do so.[23] However, the vast majority of children with speech defects do not need to go to a special school but are treated by a speech therapist either at their own school or at a speech clinic.

Delicate children are those who "by reason of impaired physical condition need a change of environment or cannot, without risk to their health or educational development, be educated under the normal regime of ordinary schools".[24] Apart from the sixty-four schools already mentioned which provide for delicate and physically handicapped children, there are a further seventy special schools for them of which nine are non-maintained. These schools are attended by 7897 delicate children. Until recently, the schools were known as open-air schools, and catered solely for children suffering from tuberculosis, respiratory diseases, and malnutrition. Today the open-air side is little emphasized, and the schools are much more enclosed as it is realized that fresh air in this country is often cold and wet air, and not conducive to the health of delicate children. Moreover, with the decline of tuberculosis and gross malnutrition, the schools have widened their intake. They cater now more for children with peripheral handicaps, those with minor defects of sight or hearing, mildly physically handicapped children, and children suffering from nervous debility.

Nervous debility is, of course, an euphemism for maladjustment. Maladjusted children form the ninth category of handicapped children and are

[20] Department of Education and Science, *op. cit.*
[21] Statutory Instrument No. 365.
[22] *Ibid.*
[23] Department of Education and Science, *op. cit.*
[24] Statutory Instrument No. 365.

defined as those "who show evidence of emotional instability or psychological disturbance and require special educational treatment in order to
effect their personal, social or educational readjustment".[25] This is the least
satisfactory of the official definitions since all children at one time or
another "show evidence of emotional instability". A better definition is
that contained in the Underwood report:[26] "A child may be regarded as
maladjusted who is developing in ways that have a bad effect upon himself
or his fellows and cannot without help be remedied by his parents, teachers
or other adults in ordinary contact with him." The important word is
"help", and for the vast majority of emotionally disturbed children this is
provided by child guidance clinics. Help for those whose maladjustment is
more severe can be provided by residential schools, day schools, special
classes or units associated with ordinary schools, or hostels from which the
children attend ordinary schools. There are sixty-three residential schools
of which eighteen are non-maintained, catering for 1495 children, while
1439 children are in thirty day schools. There are 1692 children in special
classes or units, and thirty-seven hostels contain 714 children.[27] Although
there has been a rapid increase in the provision for maladjusted children
during the last decade, it still falls far short of requirements, especially as far
as the provision of special classes and units attached to ordinary schools is
concerned.

There is also a shortage of provision for the last category of handicapped
children—the educationally sub-normal. Such children are defined as
those "who, by reason of limited ability or other conditions resulting in
educational retardation, require some specialized form of education wholly
or partly in substitution for the education normally given in ordinary
schools".[28] This concept of educational sub-normality includes not only
those children who, being of low intelligence, had prior to the Education
Act of 1944 been considered suitable for special education, but also children
who, for whatever reason, were markedly failing in their school work. The
extent of the failure is not specified, for the definition has been deliberately
kept broad. However, the Ministry of Education, as it then was, did in fact

[25] Statutory Instrument No. 365.
[26] Department of Education and Science, *op. cit.*
[27] Department of Education and Science, *op. cit.*
[28] Statutory Instrument No. 365.

suggest that any child whose school attainments were 20 per cent or more below the average attainments of children of the same age, might be considered to need special educational treatment.[29] Children of low basic intelligence, with intelligence quotients below 70 or 75, will obviously fall into this category, but in addition there will be a large number of children whose intelligence quotients might only be slightly below average but who are markedly backward. The backwardness might arise from one or more of a large number of causes, though these causes can be considered under three main groups. First come causes connected with the child's home. The child may receive no intellectual stimulus at home; there may be a dearth of reading material, conversation may be primitive, and the opportunity for enlarging his vocabulary slight; there may be no facilities for homework and he may receive no encouragement to succeed at school. The home can also be materially inadequate so that the child arrives at school undernourished, ill clad, and, because of insufficient sleep due to overcrowding and late hours, tired and sleepy. Apart from being intellectually and mentally inadequate, the home may also be emotionally inadequate, so that the child, although not himself emotionally disturbed, is constantly aware of and unhappy about the friction which exists between his parents.

The second group of causes concern the child himself. He may have a slight defect of vision which could easily be corrected by glasses. But even if he has glasses, he may have lost them, broken them, or prefers not to wear them. In the same way he may have a hearing difficulty of which the teacher is not aware, so that he is not put to sit in a position where he can hear what goes on in the classroom. But apart from physical defects of sight and hearing, the child may have difficulty in visual or auditory discrimination which presents major obstacles to the process of learning to read.

The last group of causes concern the school. The child may have been infrequent in his attendance at school because he is delicate or has had prolonged illness and hospitalization or has been a truant. Frequent changes of school can also have an adverse effect, as can dislike of the teacher, inappropriate methods of discipline, and over-large classes.

The describing of such a large and heterogeneous group of children as educationally sub-normal has led to some confusion. Obviously only a

[29] Ministry of Education, *Special Education Treatment*, Pamphlet No. 5, HMSO, London, 1946, p. 20.

small proportion of them need to go to a special school, and the term educationally sub-normal tends today to be applied only to this small proportion. The remainder are sometimes known as slow learners, and in 1964 the Department of Education and Science encouraged the use of this term and suggested that "educationally sub-normal should be associated with pronounced educational backwardness". But whatever these children are called, there are a very large number of them, at least 10 per cent of the school population, and they all require special help either in special schools or by means of special provision in the ordinary schools.

49,175 children attend 449 special schools for the educationally sub-normal, of which 16 are non-maintained.[30] The number of special classes and backward departments in ordinary schools is not known, but, as in the case of maladjusted children, it falls far short of the number required.

Section 34 of the 1944 Education Act lays upon LEAs the duty of ascertaining which children "suffering from any disability of mind or body" require special educational treatment. To this end they are empowered to require parents to present their child for examination by a medical officer who will advise the LEA whether the child should go to a special school. The Act makes it clear that the actual decision regarding the child's educational future is the province of the LEA and that before making its decision the LEA should consider reports and information "from teachers and other persons with respect to the ability and aptitude of the child". That such reports should be considered is highly desirable. If, as still sometimes happens, they are not, and the decision is made solely on the advice of the medical officer, then the latter is in fact making an educational judgement. Ideally recommendations concerning the admission of a child to a special school, especially to a school for educationally sub-normal children, should be made by a panel consisting of a school medical officer, an administrative officer of the LEA, an educational psychologist, and the head teacher of the present and/or proposed school.

Parents can appeal to the Secretary of State against the decision of the LEA on one of two grounds. Either they can dispute that their child has a disability sufficiently serious to warrant special educational treatment or, if this fails, they can admit the need for special educational treatment but ask that it can be given in an ordinary school and not in a special school.

[30] Department of Education and Science, *op. cit.*

Two groups of handicapped children are not covered by section 34. The first group is made up of children in hospital. The decision as to when a child in hospital should receive education rests with the medical superintendent and not the LEA. The second group consists of the severely subnormal, and they are dealt with in the next chapter.

CHAPTER 12

Services for Mentally Handicapped Children

PAUL WILLIAMS, BA*

EDITOR'S INTRODUCTION

It will be seen in the fourth paragraph of Paul Williams's contribution that the year 1971 not only marked a reorganization of the social services department but a transfer of mentally handicapped children previously dubbed ineducable to the local education department. This department was then empowered to provide such education as the severely handicapped child needed. This transfer was, of course, of major philosophical significance in social attitudes towards mental handicap. As yet, for obvious reasons, it is difficult to assess what the administrative change will mean, but already there are signs of great interest within the teaching and nursing professions in developing a system of education which will positively help children who in decades gone by would have been regarded as permanently and intractably handicapped.

As in the previous chapter, it is desirable for social workers to know of current thinking and the resources available to handicapped children, for they will come into contact with many in the course of their professional careers. Mr. Williams makes the point very forcibly that there is a vast field here for preventive work or family casework or community work in helping handicapped children live as normal lives as possible. It is almost certain that the social worker specializing in this aspect of child care will find in the care of the authority a number of children suffering to a greater or lesser degree from a mental impairment. It is vitally necessary in the interests of the

* Tutor-Organizer, Castle Priory College, Wallingford, Berks.

195

children that the three professions involved—those of medicine, education, and social work—act together in the closest possible spirit of co-operation. All will be involved and each has a distinctive contribution to make.

Introduction

The children who are the subject of this chapter are described differently in different countries, and often there are different legal, medical, and lay terms for them. In America they are generally described as "severely or profoundly retarded", in Britain as "severely sub-normal". I shall use the term "severely mentally handicapped". I shall restrict discussion to children, though the problems of providing services for most of these people extend throughout their adult life. Unfortunately, space precludes adequate coverage of all aspects of the services. In particular, education for the children and social work for the families are not discussed in detail.

The criterion I will use for defining the children is that they have an intelligence quotient of below 50. Although this definition is to a large extent arbitrary, and the intelligence quotient cannot be regarded as constant, nor can the outcome of a single intelligence test be said to be always reliable for an individual child, nevertheless generalizations can be made about the group of children defined in this way which distinguish them from the group of children with intelligent quotients above 50.

First, only a small minority of these children will be able, as adults, to live independent lives, to hold jobs in open industry, or to marry and support a family.[1] Secondly, these children, unlike those who are mildly sub-normal (IQs between 50 and 70) or the educationally sub-normal, are roughly equally distributed throughout the social classes.[2] Also, the majority of

---

[1] See A. Kushlick, Subnormality in Salford, in M. W. Susser and A. Kushlick, *A Report on the Mental Health Services for the City of Salford for the Year 1960*, Salford Health Corporation; A. Kushlick, Social problems of mental subnormality, in *Foundations of Child Psychiatry* (ed. E. Miller), Pergamon Press, Oxford, 1968; and J. Tizard, Longitudinal and follow-up studies, in *Mental Deficiency: The Changing Outlook*, 2nd edn. (eds. A. M. and A. D. B. Clarke), Methuen, London, 1965.

[2] A. Kushlick, Social problems of mental subnormality, *loc. cit.*, and Z. Stien and M. W. Susser, The social distribution of mental retardation, *Am. J. Ment. Defic.* **67**, 811–21.

these children have identifiable gross brain damage, at least on autopsy after death.[3]

Basic Services

Education. Until 1971 in Britain, severely mentally handicapped children of school age were usually excluded from schooling within the ordinary education services. They then became the responsibility of local authority health departments which provided special schools known as "Training Centres". Some local authorities provided special units for severely mentally handicapped children who were of pre-school age or who were so severely handicapped that they could not be considered suitable even for the training centre; these were called "Special Care Units" and were usually attached to the training centre. One or two local health authorities also employed peripatetic home teachers.

In 1971 responsibility for the education of severely mentally handicapped children in Britain was transferred from local health authorities to local education authorities who thus became responsible for the schooling of all children, no matter how handicapped they are.

Not all severely mentally handicapped children attend special schools for the mentally handicapped or special care units. Some survive throughout their school life within the ordinary education system. Others are so severely handicapped that they cannot be catered for at a special school and, particularly in areas without a special care unit, they may remain at home and receive no day care or training outside. Education authorities, however, now have a legal obligation to cater for these children and, as resources increase, will no doubt do so.

Residential Care. Some children may also be admitted to residential care because, for a variety of reasons, they cannot be looked after at home. The main form of such care is in a childen's ward or villa within a National Health Service mental sub-normality hospital. At the hospital they may attend a hospital special school or training centre, or, if they are very

[3] L. Crome, The brain and mental retardation, *Br. Med. J.* **1**, 897–904; L. Crome, chapters 3–6, in *Mental Deficiency* (eds. L. T. Hilliard and B. H. Kirman), Churchill, London, 1965; and A. Kushlick, Social problems of mental subnormality, *loc. cit.*

severely handicapped, they may received no schooling off the ward. Local education authorities are now responsible for these hospital schools, and, again, have a legal obligation to cater for all children which it is hoped they will meet.

Social Work. Most of the severely mentally handicapped children of school age within a local authority area will be known to the local authority social services department which will provide a social work service for the children's families. Each social worker will generally have a varied case load which includes some families with a mentally handicapped member. Some social workers may have specialist skills or training for work particularly with these families.

Prevalence

A survey carried out by Dr. Albert Kushlick and Miss Gillian Cox in 1963 studied in detail the prevalence of severe mental handicap in the area served by the Wessex Regional Hospital Board (roughly the whole of Hampshire and Dorset, part of Wiltshire, and the Isle of Wight, in southern England—a total population area of about 2 million people). The figures they obtained related to the "known administrative prevalence" of the condition, i.e. the prevalence of children known to the agencies from which they obtained their information. Not all severely mentally handicapped children were known to these agencies. In fact the known administrative prevalence did not reach a peak until the age range of 15–19 years. They have presented evidence[4] that this maximum known prevalence does in fact represent the true prevalence of the condition between these ages, and that this prevalence rate may be taken as the true prevalence rate among children of all ages. The rate is 3·65 severely mentally handicapped children per 1000 children of the same age. This figure may be used to calculate the expected number of severely mentally handicapped children in any population area.

[4] A. Kushlick, Subnormality in Salford, *loc. cit.*; and A. Kushlick and G. Cox, The ascertained prevalence of mental subnormality in the Wessex Region on 1st July, 1963, in *Proceedings of the First Congress of the International Association for the Scientific Study of Mental Deficiency* (ed. B. W. Richards), Michael Jackson, Reigate, 1967.

For example, if a town of 100,000 population has a stable birth rate of 18 births per year per 1000 of the population, then 1800 children will be born each year of whom $1.8 \times 3.65 (= 6.6)$ will be severely mentally handicapped (and will survive at least through childhood). The total number of those children aged under 16 will be $16 \times 6.6 (= 106)$. A good guide to the number of severely mentally handicapped children expected is 100 per 100,000 total population.

Kushlick and Cox found that only just over half these children were known to the agencies providing special services for the severely mentally handicapped, i.e. the local authority mental health department (at the time of the survey) or the mental sub-normality hospitals. The remaining expected children were either of pre-school age and not yet notified to a specialist agency, or they were surviving within the ordinary education system and the need for notification had not yet arisen. The evidence suggests that all these children will eventually be notified, either on reaching school age or on leaving school.

Residential Facilities

Of the 100 expected children per 100,000 population, only 20 were in residential care, i.e. 80 per cent were being cared for at home.

Of the 20 in residential care, almost all were in sub-normality hospitals. Local authorities were empowered by the 1959 Mental Health Act to set up small hostels for severely mentally handicapped children, and although quite a number of these have been set up they are at present catering for only a small proportion of children requiring residential care. Not all such hostels provide long-term care; they may be used for short-term care only, or in rural areas they may be attached to a training centre to provide 5–day residence during term-time for children who would otherwise have long distances to travel.

Kushlick and Cox found that among the 20 children in residential care per 100,000 total population, about 6 had severe walking difficulties, 4 had severe problems of behaviour (with or without incontinence in addition), 4 were incontinent only, and 6 were continent, ambulant with no behaviour problems (or had only mild difficulties in these areas). It is widely accepted that children without severe walking difficulty and without severe behaviour problems do not require the specialist services of a sub-normality hospital and would be suitable candidates for local authority hostels were sufficient available. About half the children in sub-normality hospitals at present come into this category, i.e. about 10 per 100,000 population, or 5000 in a population of 50 million (approximately that of Britain). A vast expansion of the local authority hostel service to replace, at least partly, the children's wards of sub-normality hospitals, will probably be a major development in the future.[5]

Although sub-normality hospitals can provide specialist medical and nursing services for the more severely handicapped children, they have some major disadvantages. For example, many sub-normality hospitals have catchment areas of up to a million people (generating about 200 severely mentally handicapped children requiring residential care). This often means that the parents of the children have very long and expensive distances to travel to retain contact with their children.

An Experiment in Residential Care

In the Wessex Region, again under the direction of Dr. Albert Kushlick, a research team is evaluating the feasibility of providing small locally based hostel-type units to cater for all severely mentally handicapped children requiring residential care from much smaller population areas. The first of these units, in Southampton, is already open. It serves a population area of

[5] Since this chapter was written the Government have published a White Paper, *Better Services for the Mentally Handicapped*, Cmnd. 4683, HMSO, 1971. This is an extremely important document, especially in relation to the future development of residential services. Its recommendations include:

(i)   Local authorities will in future be responsible for the residential care of the more able children and adults at present in hospital.

(ii) Hospitals will continue to be responsible for the less able children and adults but the form of provision and standards of accommodation need not be different from those provided by local authorities.

(iii) There should be a move away from provision of a large number of residential places on one site.

(iv) Any residential unit should be locally based, i.e. should serve a defined catchment area and should ideally be situated within that area. Hospitals should consider defining geographical catchment areas for individual wards.

100,000 people and is designed to cater for all twenty severely mentally handicapped children who need residential care from that area, regardless of how severely handicapped they are. It is designed as much as possible as an ordinary home, and because it is situated in the middle of the area it serves (unlike many subnormality hospitals), it can utilize many of the local services that would be available to the children if they lived at home. The unit is, however, managed and administered as part of the existing hospital service.[6]

If successful, this experiment may point the way to future development of the sub-normality hospital service, i.e. away from centralization and large hospital complexes towards small local comprehensive units.

Admission of Very Young Children

It is only in exceptional circumstances that very young children are placed in long-term residential care. Kushlick and Cox found in their 1963 survey of the Wessex Region that there were less than 2 children per 100,000 total population, who were aged under 5 and in residential care. This represents only between 5 and 6 per cent of the expected number of severely mentally handicapped children in this age group. Many of these children will have been taken into care because of death of the parents, illegitimacy, a need for constant nursing care, or very severe problems of management in the home.

Family Contact after Admission

Despite the distances that parents often have to travel to see their children, contact is maintained after admission by a large majority of families. Pauline Morris found that 21 per cent of children in the hospitals she studied had not been visited in the previous years.[7] This represents only 4 children per 100,000 total population. From Morris's data and also from the studies of children being carried out in the Wessex Region, it seems likely that about 1 of these 4 children has no parents or known relatives and another

---

[6] Further units of the same type are now open in Portsmouth and in Poole, Dorset.

[7] P. Morris, *Put Away: A Sociological Study of Institutions for the Mentally Retarded*, Routledge and Kegan Paul, London, 1969.

1 will have been admitted to residential care through a social services department at an early age because of illegitimacy or very severe parental problems, together with the difficulty of finding an adequate foster home or arranging adoption for a severely handicapped child.

Thus, only about 1 in 50 of all severely mentally handicapped children is placed in residential care and is not visited by parents or relatives who are alive and theoretically should be able to visit. One does not know what factors may be preventing these few families from visiting.

The Role of Social Service Departments (under the Children's Acts)

Following on from this it can be suggested (and data from the Wessex study seems to confirm this) that about 10 per cent of all severely mentally handicapped children in sub-normality hospitals—2 children per 100,000 total population—are likely to be, or to have been at some time, in the care of a local authority social services department under one or another of the Children's Acts. Possibly a further 10 per cent could with advantage be accepted into the care of department while remaining in sub-normality hospital. Social services departments are empowered, and, if the authority has assumed parental rights, are required (section 10, Mental Health Act 1959), to maintain a parental interest in these children after their admission to hospital.

In addition, severely mentally handicapped children are sometimes placed in children's homes or fostered. The numbers vary in different areas, but the Wessex study suggests that the average is about 1 child per 100,000 population in a children's home and a further 1 child in foster care. Although an individual social services department would have relatively few severely mentally handicapped children in its care under the Children's Acts, there must be a considerable number of such children throughout the whole country (perhaps as many as 500 in children's homes, 500 in foster care, and a further 1000 in sub-normality hospitals in whom social service departments are required or empowered to take an active interest).

Hospitals and their Problems

The standard of child care within sub-normality hospitals has been subject to much recent criticism.[8] The bringing about of improvements, such as the setting of specific aims of care, treatment, and education for individual children, and provision of sufficient equipment and staff to carry out these programmes, involves finding solutions to many complex problems.[9] Suggestions for change have included a reorientation of nurse training away from medical care towards child care, and greater managerial training for administrative and medical staff.[10]

However, much progress is made in the care, treatment, or education of mentally handicapped children; and in the training of staff in residential units the practice of new methods is likely to require certain minimum staffing levels.[11] The staff of the hospitals realize this, and to suggest to them the need for adoption of new methods of child care or training, or for themselves to receive new training, is likely to be an impertinence if the possibility of increases in staff numbers is not also given. Pauline Morris[12] found that the ratio of nurses to children, when the children's wards of the hospitals she studied were visited, ranged between 1 to 5 and 1 to 19. These ratios need care in interpretation.

The ratio of one nurse to five children does not mean that the children can be split into groups of five with one nurse organizing activities for each group. Almost invariably there will be children in the group who need

[8] For example in the Howe Report (*Report of the Committee of Inquiry into Allegations of Ill-treatment of Patients and other Irregularities at the Ely Hospital, Cardiff*), Cmnd. 3945, HMSO, London, 1969; and Morris, *op. cit.*

[9] *Op cit.* See A. Kushlick, Residential care for the mentally subnormal, *J. Royal Society of Health*, Sept.–Oct. 1970.

[10] In, for example, A. Kushlick, *Residential Care for the Mentally Retarded* (ed. E. Stephen), Institute for Research into Mental Retardation, Symposia Series No. 1, Pergamon Press, Oxford, 1970; J. Tizard, the role of social institutions in the causation, prevention and alleviation of mental retardation, a paper given at the Peabody NIMH Conference of Socio-cultural Aspects of Mental Retardation, and published in the *Conference Proceedings* in 1968; and P. Williams, Child care and mental handicap, *Develop. Med. Child. Neurol.* **11**, 512–15.

[11] Kushlick, *Residential Care*; and A. Kushlick and A. Anidsen, *Staff–Patient Ratio needed in Hospitals or Hostels for the Mentally Subnormal* (in press).

[12] Morris, *op. cit.*

individual attention at times because of their behaviour or incontinence, for example. In order for a nurse to be available to give this individual attention, there must be at least two nurses with each group. The minimum grouping of children will thus be ten, with two nurses looking after each group, and even then, when one child needs the individual attention of a nurse, the other nurse has to cope with the remaining nine.

Some children may leave the ward to attend school for part of the day, so the numbers of children requiring care on the ward may fluctuate at various times of the day; also, staff may themselves go off for meals or rest breaks, and shifts may overlap, so the numbers of staff may fluctuate. These fluctuations in the numbers of children and staff may work against each other.

For example, staff may go off for their breakfast at "peak" times when they are most needed, for giving the children their breakfast or preparing them for school. Arrangements such as this may not be easy to change. The nurses' own meal times may have been carefully negotiated as part of their conditions of service or to fit in with their own domestic arrangements and the children's meal times may be determined off the ward by the routine of the central kitchen, the need to get children to the school by a certain time, the time of the doctor's rounds, etc.

One possible solution might be for the nurses to eat with the children at the same tables on the ward. This would also enable them to teach the children better behaviour at meals, or to feed themselves, or allow the table to be laid in a more homelike way. However, this would entail adjustments in the hours of work of the nurses and negotiations on whether or not they should pay for meals eaten on the ward.

Similar administrative problems arise with many suggested improvements in the hospitals, e.g. in the provision of individual clothing for the children. Ideally each child would have his own set of clothes, individually chosen and bought for that child according to his needs and tastes, and they would be kept for use by that child alone. This implies adequate storage space, a laundry service that will not damage clothes, sufficient laundry, domestic, or other staff to sort the clothes for return to individual children, a sufficient supply of clothes for each child, taking into account incontinence and the time between sending clothes to the laundry and their return; it may require facilities and staff for at least some laundry to be done on the ward itself. The buying of clothes may have been determined in the past by systems of financing, ordering, and accounting (involving bulk purchase and putting the order out to tender) that would have to be changed through consultation with, for example, the hospital auditors. The changing of such systems and the solving of these administrative problems may require decisions at Hospital Management Committee, Regional Hospital Board, or even Department of Health levels.[13]

Families with a Child at Home

Working on the basis of 100 per 100,000 total population, there are about 50,000 severely mentally handicapped children under 16 in Britain of whom 40,000 are living at home with their families. About 17,000 of these are under school age.

Not all these children can be recognized when they are very young. They may be slow in development, but this may not be seen as a problem until the child is several years old. Some conditions such as Down's syndrome (mongolism) are recognizable at birth or soon after. Also, some of the children will have overt physical conditions that may be associated with mental handicap, such as spasticity or hydrocephalus, which will bring them to immediate notice. Such children will be placed under the care of a paediatrician and may enter hospital for short periods during early childhood for investigations or treatment. The children's hospital or the local authority may run special clinics to which the parents may bring the children for advice.

General practitioners will be familiar with the problems of individual children. However, the average general practitioner working singly in a practice will only have two or three such children on his list at any one time, and so will not be very familiar with the general problems of severe mental handicap. Health visitors also may visit the parents, but again the number of severely mentally handicapped children that the average health visitor has experience of is likely to be very small.

For a small proportion of severely mentally handicapped children, a genetic basis for the child's specific condition can be found and the parents

[13] For further discussion of these problems, see Kushlick, Residential care for the mentally subnormal, *loc. cit.,* 1940.

can be given genetic advice. For an even smaller proportion the degree of mental handicap can be alleviated by the institution of a special diet very early in the child's life. An example of such a condition is phenylketonuria (so named because it is characterized by the presence of certain chemicals, known as phenylketones, in the urine) for which most children in this country are now screened soon after birth. However, the incidence of phenylketonuria may be as low as 1 in 25,000 births; there may only be one such child born in a population of 100,000 people every 14 or 15 years.

If a child is born handicapped, then the problem of telling the parents, helping them to accept the facts, and informing them accurately of the position and the services available to help them, must, of course, be very sensitively handled, and it is probably unwise to lay down general rules. It has been found that, in general, parents prefer to be told the facts as early as possible after the birth of the child.[14]

Some special schools may admit pre-school age children, and some voluntary societies may run special play-groups, but often there is no form of day care or training at all available for severely mentally handicapped children until they reach the age of 5. They may then start at an ordinary school or be assessed by a local authority medical officer as in need of special education, in which case the local education authority will decide on the course of action to be taken, usually admission to a special school for the mentally handicapped.

Once a child has been notified to the local health authority social services department, a social worker will begin to visit the family to provide any social work that is necessary, possibly taking over from the health visitor if she is still visiting the family.

Other services for which there is undoubtedly a need, such as a special home help service, a special laundry service, help with transport difficulties, help in provision of a telephone in case of emergency, an organized service of trained baby-sitters, are almost non-existent. To relieve families there are sometimes holiday homes available to take children for a week or fortnight per year, and sub-normality hospitals and some local authority

[14] See J. Leeson, A study of six mentally handicapped children and their families, *The Medical Officer*, **104**, 311; and J. Tizard and J. C. Grad, *The Mentally Handicapped and their Families*, Oxford University Press, Oxford, 1961. Also Elizabeth Hall's unpublished survey mentioned later in this chapter confirms these findings.

hostels may use a few of their beds for short-term admissions of children for a few weeks to relieve the families.

Voluntary Societies

The National Society for Mentally Handicapped Children provides an advice service and has many affiliated local parents' groups which may run play-groups or clubs for the children and arrange meetings for parents. Special schools often have a parent–teacher group organizing regular meetings for parents. The National Association for Mental Health and the Spastics Society, as well as the National Society for Mentally Handicapped Children, provide an information service on severe mental handicap with publications and conferences.

Many parents belong to other societies depending on the child's particular condition, such as the local Spastics Society or Society for Autistic Children. However, it is probably rare that a local society attracts more than a minority of parents of these children,[15] and advice, information, and help in overcoming their detailed day-to-day problems are often not readily available to the families.

The Problems of Parents

The problems of parents in looking after a severely mentally handicapped child are often formidable, and one cannot but have the greatest admiration for parents who bring up their handicapped children so well with (as services are at present) so little help.

Firstly, any of the problems that may arise in any family are likely to be made more severe by the presence of a handicapped child: housing difficulties, marital problems, financial difficulties, poor health. It is difficult to ascertain, for an individual family, the extent to which these problems may have arisen as a result of the presence of a handicapped child or whether they would be present anyway. Where they are present they add substantially to the problems of caring for the child.

Many families with a handicapped child will also have other young children to care for. Problems may arise in the apportioning of the mother's

[15] Tizard and Grad, *op. cit.*

attention, time, and effort to the handicapped child or to the other children in the family, or, indeed, to her husband. Here again, whatever knowledge is available about caring for or teaching handicapped children in order to ensure their maximum progress, these will generally require effort and time that a mother will find difficult to spare. Any suggestion to mothers that they should attend clinics or be taught new ways of looking after or teaching their children, however much the mothers themselves would like this, must be accompanied by provisions to give practical help to the mothers in the day-to-day problems of looking after their children.

It is probably worth while to outline the sorts of problems that arise. Not all these problems arise in all families, of course, but there are very few families with a severely mentally handicapped child who have not experienced several severe problems of this kind, and may well still be experiencing them.

If the child presents problems of behaviour or incontinence at night, or has great difficulty getting to sleep, or wakes very early in the morning, this can in turn affect the sleep of the other members of the family. The father's work may be affected because he is over-tired; the mother has less energy to cope with the child and her housework during the day; the other children's schooling may suffer; the parents may be unable to relax in the evening; the other children may be unable to do their homework satis-factorily. In extreme cases one of the parents may have to sleep with the child or sit up late at night with the child until he goes to sleep, with consequent effect on the marriage relationship.

Even if the child's behaviour during the evening is not in itself a problem, many parents are unwilling to bring in a baby-sitter, or cannot find one who is prepared to look after a handicapped child. This is particularly the case when the child has epilepsy and may have a fit. Many parents thus have not had an evening out together perhaps for many years. Some families do not even manage to get out at weekends or to take holidays because of the difficulties of coping with the child or finding someone to look after him adequately.

If the child is incontinent or is physically handicapped or does not behave well when out, then shopping and travelling on public transport can be a nightmare if not impossible. Sometimes the husband or the other children in the family have to take on extra commitments to look after the child or to do the shopping, perhaps affecting the social life of the children or the husband's ability to arrange overtime work, for example. Shopping may be more expensive for the mother if she is unable to shop in large supermarkets but has to use the local small shop.

Especially if the child is incontinent, laundry may be time consuming, energy consuming, space consuming, and expensive. The child may wear out clothes very quickly because he crawls about on the floor or because the clothes have to be laundered so frequently, and this may become very expensive.

If the child does not appreciate danger, then problems of storage of breakables or knives about the house may be severe, as may problems of preparing and cooking meals, or doing the housework, while at the same time the mother keeps an eye on the child or takes him around with her. If the child is physically handicapped and bedroom and bathroom facilities are not available on the ground floor, then the mother may have to carry a very heavy child up stairs, with consequent effect on her health.

In addition to all these problems, the neighbours and relatives may or may not be helpful, and, as mentioned earlier, any of the problems and difficulties that arise in any family can arise in these families with equal or greater frequency: unemployment, other children, or babies to look after, etc.

Superimposed on all these difficulties is the fact that their child is different. Elizabeth Hall, a psychiatric social worker and the mother of a mentally handicapped child, has carried out an unpublished survey of parents from which it emerges very clearly that after the stresses of the initial telling of the news that their child is handicapped, the period when the child is aged 2–5 is particularly stressful. She writes:

"The parents with children over 7 years old were unanimous in their view that the first real stress point of their anxieties, after the initial telling, was when the child was about 2 years old. At 2 years, the retardation in their child's development had become apparent to them. It could no longer be concealed from other people. The needs of discipline and training demanded their attention. Should they rebuke him when he did wrong? Should they toilet-train? Other children were beginning to discard their nappies at 2 to 3 years old.

"'Can he understand?' grows very quickly into 'Will he ever understand?' At 3 to 4 years old, their friends' children are talking, walking, playing together, riding tricycles, throwing balls. Most mentally handicapped children are still unable to achieve any of these skills without constant encouragement or endless repetition.

"Eventually 5 years old looms on the horizon, and 5 means school. But which school, and where? The irrevocable step to the Training Centre is far from easy. Over the doorstep goes your rather helpless child to mix with and be labelled for life with the severely subnormal."

When the child is older other worries become paramount. What will he be able to do as an adult? What will become of him when we are no longer able to look after him?

The Future

It is to be hoped that there will be a vast expansion of services for the children and their families in the future. Certainly the future holds promise of this. Much more professional interest is being taken in the children and their problems by doctors, psychologists, educationists, and, not least, politicians.

The much-needed expansion of services for families may well mean that even more parents than at present will be able and willing to keep their children at home, and the formidable problems of those that do so will be greatly relieved. Recent changes in the structure of social service departments[16] should bring about much greater flexibility and co-operation between the various agencies that have provided the services in the past.

On the education front, much exciting work has been done in introducing special teaching techniques such as operant conditioning, especially in America.[17]

[16] Seebohm Report, *Report of the Committee on Local Authority and Allied Personal Social Services*, HMSO, London, 1968.

[17] See, for example, A. D. B. Clarke, P. Mittler, and P. Williams, Learning Processes in the Mentally Retarded, Symposium No. 4, Institute for Research into Mentally Retardation (in press); and L. A. Larsen and W. A. Bricker, *A Manual for Parents and Teachers of Severely and Moderately Retarded Children*, Institute on Mental Retardation and Intellectual Development Papers and Reports, Vol. 5, No. 22, Peabody College, Nashville, Tennessee, 1968.

The pattern of residential care, where it is necessary, will probably be radically transformed by the expansion of true "community care" in the form of locally based small units calling on specialists from a wide field to work with the staff and the children's parents in applying individual programmes of care and training.

Not least, this field of work offers tremendous opportunities for voluntary work, and for young professional people in child care, medicine, psychology, education, nursing, social work, and administration. It is a fascinating field that brings one in contact with a very wide range of problems and methods of solution that are generalizable to many other fields and other problems.

Acknowledgements

I am particularly indebted for many of the ideas presented in this chapter to Dr. Albert Kushlick, Director of Research in Sub-normality, Wessex Regional Hospital Board, and to Mrs. Elizabeth Hall, psychiatric social worker with Hampshire County Council.

CHAPTER 13

The English Law Relating to Children

KENNETH BRILL, OBE, LL B[*]

EDITOR'S INTRODUCTION

The standard English work on the law relating to children and young persons, that by Clarke Hall and Morrison,[1] is already in its eighth edition and runs to more than a thousand pages of statute and commentary. It has clearly been impossible in this context for Kenneth Brill to provide such an exhaustive survey of the law as it affects the younger generation. What he has done is to provide a commentary on those areas which are of particular interest to the social worker, that interest springing primarily from the basic problem of determining how society wishes to treat its children. What—to take one simple example—does the new entrant social worker feel about Kenneth Brill's short remark that "The Tattooing of Minors Act of 1970 makes it an offence to tattoo a person under 18"? One might consider first why 18 is held to be of such magical significance. One would wonder about the significance of tattooing itself. If a young person may hold a licence to drive a powerful motor-car at 17, is he not sensible enough to determine whether or not he ought to be tattooed? There are undoubtedly many extraordinary contradictions and illogicalities in the present law, and these may well reflect society's uncertainties about how much responsibility adolescents should bear, how much they should be protected from their impulsiveness, and so on. What is presented here therefore is not an exhaustive summary of law nor even an exhaustive com-

[*] General Secretary, British Association of Social Workers.
[1] W. Clarke Hall and A. C. L. Morrison, *Law Relating to Children and Young Persons*, 8th Revised Edition, Butterworth, London, 1972.

212

mentary upon it, but a stimulus to thought and an offer of terms in which social workers can re-examine themselves, their responsibilities to society, their identification with certain social controls, and, finally, the mechanisms and the language by which society expresses its concern for children and their families.

Origins

Before the middle of the nineteenth century the law did not take much notice of childhood, although some features of child law can be traced back to feudal times. Wardship, for example, probably originated in the right of the lord of the manor to control over the person and property of orphans, and the law against taking children from the possession of their parents has features deriving from the ancient crime of abducting an heiress. Under the common law a child had the same degree of protection against injury by a stranger as an adult had. In the field of employment a child had onerous responsibilities as an apprentice and some nebulous rights, the fulfilment of which depended on the goodwill of his master; those not in indentures were treated on the same basis as adult workers. Criminal sanctions applied equally to malefactors of any age once they had attained the age of 7: before that age there was no lack of informal penalties. Children were treated as possessions of their fathers and, as late as the 1870s, Lord Shaftesbury opposed the passage of a bill making it an offence for a man to ill-treat his child in his own home.

Pattern of Discussion

There is an element of artificiality about arranging the features of the law relating to children into sub-groups; e.g. the impact of the criminal law on children is referred to under more than one sub-heading. For convenience, this chapter follows the pattern set out below. Some legal concepts relating to children are very simple, e.g. the age at which a minor ceases to be such for the purpose of exercising a vote in parliamentary and local government elections. Others are complex and unclear, e.g. the nature of a parent's rights in relation to his child who has reached the age of 16 but not that of 18. Consequently some headings in this list can be dismissed in a few lines.

Where a topic is more complex it is dealt with in an elementary way and the inquirer is advised to look elsewhere for a more complete treatment.

1. Youthfulness as a factor limiting capacity and responsibility:
   - 1.1 Criminal responsibility
   - 1.2 Post Office savings banking
   - 1.3 Civil liability and capacity
   - 1.4 Discretion
   - 1.5 Employment in entertainment
   - 1.6 Employment generally
   - 1.7 Consent to intercourse
   - 1.8 Driving motor-vehicles
   - 1.9 Medical treatment
   - 1.10 Marriage
   - 1.11 Care or control
   - 1.12 Tattooing
   - 1.13 Full age
   - 1.14 Voting
   - 1.15 Military service
   - 1.16 Jury service
   - 1.17 Adoption

2. Care and custody exercised by individuals:
   - 2.1 Rights of married parents
   - 2.2 Rights of unmarried parents
   - 2.3 Guardianship
   - 2.4 Custody to a third party
   - 2.5 Custody vested in the court (wardship)

3. Care and supervision exercised by public authorities and voluntary organizations:
   - 3.1 By order of the juvenile court
   - 3.2 By order of other courts
   - 3.3 Voluntary reception into care
   - 3.4 Supervision orders
   - 3.5 Assumption by local authorities of parental rights

1. Youthfulness as a Factor Limiting Capacity and Responsibility

1.1. Criminal responsibility. This topic is treated first not because it is of paramount importance but because it marks the earliest age at which the law holds a child (as opposed to a parent or guardian) personally responsible for his actions. It was held under the common law that a child who had not reached his seventh birthday could not be found guilty of a criminal offence. The age was raised to 8 by the Children and Young Persons Act of 1933 and to 10 by the similarly named Act of 1963. A further Act of 1969 enables the Government with the authority of an order in council to raise the age as high as 14. In 1970 the Government of the day announced that they would postpone raising the age to 12 until such time as local authorities were in a position to make provision for badly behaved children in other ways and that they were not, in any case, intending to raise the age beyond 12. Meanwhile a survey made by chief officers of police and local authorities in 1965 had shown that no significant difficulties had followed the raising of the age to 10 a few years earlier. The 1969 Act, however, gives discretion to the police and to the local authority to bring an offender under 17 before the juvenile court as being in need of care or control instead of prosecuting him, for any offence excluding homicide. There are parts of the country where this discretion has rarely been exercised so far, but practice may change as experience broadens. The law presumes that wrong-doing between the age of 10 and 14 is not done with any criminal intention, and before finding a child guilty the court must be satisfied that he knew that he was doing wrong. Although this presumption is often overlooked in practice it can be crucial, e.g. though most children over 10 know it is wrong to steal many do not know it is wrong to help a friend by keeping watch while he steals, or to receive goods knowing them to have been stolen. A boy under 14 cannot be convicted of certain serious sexual offences and being under 24 entitles men to raise a special defence against prosecution for carnal knowledge. The courts are, of course, severely restricted as to the penalties they can impose on young people. A person under 16 cannot be convicted of cruelty to children.

1.2. Post Office savings banking. A child who has reached the age of 7 can operate an account with the Post Office Savings Bank.

1.3. Civil liability and capacity. An early case stated the principle: "an infant in all things which sound to his benefit shall have favour and preferment in law as well as another but shall not be prejudiced by anything to his disadvantage". Under the Family Law Reform Act 1969 this principle now relates to minors, i.e. to those who have not attained their eighteenth birthday. A minor cannot sue in his own name (except for his wages) but only through his "next friend", a person of full age, generally a parent or nearest relative. A minor cannot be sued for breach of contract except in special circumstances, e.g. to recover the price of necessary goods or services supplied, but he can be sued in tort: that is to say damages can be awarded against him for such wrong as trespass, defamation, embezzlement, or negligent injury. In practice it is rare to proceed against a minor since he generally lacks means to satisfy a judgement. A father is liable for the torts of his children under full age if he has authorized them or if the tort is committed in the course of the father's employment.

1.4. Discretion. The concept "age of discretion" crops up in several contexts: for example, in recent times the High Court has not required a boy of 13 to be consulted about his adoption by foster parents on the ground that he had not reached discretion. The age of discretion is said to be 14 for boys and 16 for girls, and it is argued that those who have attained years of discretion are free to choose where and with whom they shall live provided they have sufficient means and are not shown to be in need of care or control.

1.5. Employment in entertainment. Part II of the Children and Young Persons Act 1969 restricts the employment of persons under 16 in entertainment including broadcasting and making films for public presentation. Control is exercised by the grant of a licence by the local education authority, and there are relaxations and exemptions for runs not exceeding 4 days and for taking part, unpaid, in school shows. Licences are granted subject to restrictions and conditions contained in a statutory instrument made by the Secretary of State, the terms of which have been under discussion between the Ministry and representatives of the industry.

1.6. Employment generally. Part II of the Children and Young Persons Act 1933 as amended in 1969 forbids the employment of children under 12 and of children under 17 in street trading, and empowers local education authorities to make bylaws modifying this provision with respect to light employment by parents in agriculture, and also substantially extending the restrictions on employment contained in the statute. Because of this local option it is essential to consult the local education authority before employing any child under 14, or a person under 18 in street trading. Part I of the same Act makes it an offence to involve minors of various ages in activities on the fringe of commerce such as prostitution, brothel keeping, begging, sales of alcohol and tobacco, pawnbroking, and trading in old metal.

1.7. Consent to intercourse. It is an offence for a man or a boy over 14 to have intercourse with a girl under 16 regardless of her consent. The age of consent was fixed in 1885 when the average age of puberty in both boys and girls was substantially older than it is now. In practice the police exercise discretion in prosecuting.

1.8. Driving motor-vehicles. The right to drive may be of more significance to a young person than the older freedoms. The minimum ages vary according to vehicle and circumstance, being 17 for motor-cycles and motor-cars, and 21 for heavy vehicles on the highway. A child of any age may drive on private land except that he may not drive a tractor under 13. It is proposed to amend the law to allow disabled children under 17 to drive invalid carriages in public thoroughfares.

1.9. Medical treatment. Subsection 5(2) of the Mental Health Act 1959 provides that a person who has reached his sixteenth birthday has the right to decide whether or not to receive treatment for mental disorder regardless of the wishes of his parent or guardian. The position with regard to treatment for other disorders was clarified by section 8 of the Family Law Reform Act 1969 which provides for a minor who has reached 16 to give an effective consent to surgical, medical, or dental treatment, thereby specifically dispensing with any need to secure parental consent. This is taken to mean that a doctor must respect the confidence of a patient aged 16 or more. The decision, in March 1971, of the Disciplinary Committee of the General Medical Council that, in the special circumstances of a case they were hearing, the doctor was not guilty of serious professional misconduct in telling such a patient's parent that she had sought contraceptive advice does not affect the general proposition; rather does the publicity afforded strengthen the assurance that doctors will continue to be careful to preserve confidence.

1.10. Marriage. No person under 16 can contract a marriage in England and any ceremony purporting to marry such a person is void. A person under 18 must have parental consent, but the superintendent registrar can dispense with this if no parent or guardian is available. In cases of doubt, or if a parent withholds consent, the minor can ask the magistrates' court to consider granting consent. A person under 16 who has been married according to the laws of another country is recognized here as being married.

1.11. Care or control. A person who has not been married and who has not reached the age of 17 may be brought before the juvenile court if he is in need of care or control which he is unlikely to receive unless the court makes an order. This means that though a person has reached the age of discretion by the sixteenth birthday and is free to marry (with the appropriate consents), may live where he likes and (being a girl) has reached the age of consent, nevertheless the court can make an order after that age on the grounds that that person is "beyond control" or in "moral danger". A proposal in 1965 to reduce the maximum age to 16 was vigorously opposed by moralists and was withdrawn by the Government of the day.

1.12. Tattooing. The Tattooing of Minors Act 1970 makes it an offence to tattoo a person under 18.

1.13. Full age. By section 1 of the Family Law Reform Act 1969 a person attains full age at 18 (instead of, as formerly, at 21) for most legal purposes. The situations to which this change relates and those to which it does not relate are set out in schedules to the Act.

1.14. Voting. The Representation of the People Act 1971 provides that a person who has attained the age of 18 is entitled to vote in parliamentary and local government elections.

1.15. Military service. A person wanting to enlist under the age of 18 needs the consent of his parent or guardian if he or she is available and may not, in any case, enlist before the age of 16. Since 1970 the Government has not held a person recruited under the age of 18 to serve against his will after that age. Until compulsory national service terminated in the late 1950s, the age at which a man could be required to serve was 18.

1.16. Jury service. At the time of writing (July 1971) the minimum age at which a person is eligible for jury service is 21. A private member's bill to reduce it to 18 has been opposed by the Government on technical grounds. Since the ministerial opposition was not based on principle it seems probable that the age will be reduced to 18 in the foreseeable future.

1.17. Adoption. A person who has reached his eighteenth birthday cannot be made the subject of an adoption order. A person of any age, being the father or mother of a person under 18, can adopt him either alone or jointly with a spouse of any age. A relative of a person under 18 who has himself reached the age of 21 may adopt him either alone or jointly with a spouse who has reached the same age. A person who is neither a parent nor a relative of a person under 18 who has reached the age of 25 may adopt him either alone or jointly with a spouse who has reached the age of 21.

2. Care and Custody exercised by Individuals

2.1. Rights of married parents. Under the common law a father of a child born in wedlock was the sole custodian, virtually the "owner", of his children. There were some limited restraints against parental ill treatment: it was an offence for a father to kill his child or to cause him grievous bodily harm. As time went on the Court of Chancery exercised the inherent right of the sovereign as *parens patriae* to restrain the rights of a father over his children if he ill-used them, and the courts recognized limited rights for late teenagers to live their own lives (but not to manage their own property). The mother had no rights during the father's lifetime but might become the children's guardian after her husband's death.

Sir William Brett oversimplified the position in 1883 when he said: "The Law of England is that the father has the control over the person, education and conduct of his children until they are twenty-one."[2] In 1969 Lord Denning, speaking of that dictum, said: "It reflects the attitude of a Victorian parent towards his children. He expected unquestioning obedience to his demands. If a son disobeyed, his father would cut him off with a shilling. If a daughter had an illegitimate child, he would turn her out of the house. His power only ceased when the child became 21. I decline to accept a view so much out of date. The common law can, and should, keep pace with the times. It should declare, in conformity with the recent Report on the Age of Majority, that the legal right of a parent to the custody of a child ends at the 18th birthday: and even up till then, it is a dwindling right which the Courts will hesitate to enforce against the wishes of the child, and the more older he is. It starts with a right of control and ends with little more than advice."[3]

With legislation in the mid nineteenth century permitting divorce, provision had to be made for awarding the custody of a child to one of two

[2] *Re* Agar-Ellis 1883.
[3] *Hewer* v. *Bryant 1969.*

divorced parents. In the early years the father's common law right to a child's custody prevailed over any claim by the mother. In 1886 the Guardianship of Infants Act enabled a mother to apply for custody and required the court to have regard to the child's welfare and the parents' conduct, but it was not until 1925 that a similarly entitled Act required the court to regard the child's welfare as the first and paramount consideration and not to take into consideration any common law right of the father. Even now there are some circumstances in which, other considerations being equal, the father's wishes will prevail, e.g. if a child is entrusted to the care of a local authority and the parents are in dispute as to religious upbringing the court will be likely to give effect to the father's wishes. Furthermore, a father's signature is preferred to that of a mother on documents executed on behalf of a child. In May 1971 the Prime Minister announced the intention to introduce legislation to give husband and wife equal rights in respect of the guardianship of their children.

2.2. Rights of unmarried parents. At common law the illegitimate child was *fillius nullius* and had no legal guardian. With the growing recognition of women's rights the mother of an illegitimate child became his sole guardian. Parliament in 1926 provided for a child to be legitimated by the subsequent marriage of his parents—a proposition which the bishops first put to the lay barons at the Council of Merton in 1234. In 1926 legitimization was limited to children whose parents were free to marry at the time of his birth, but a further statute in 1959 extended the provision to a child whose parents at the time of his birth were not necessarily free to marry. A surprising consequence of subsection 3(1) of this Act was that the illegitimate father of a child acquired a special right to ask the court for custody. He still lacks parental rights *per se* (e.g. his consent is not required to the making of an adoption order) but he has a special right to apply for custody. This side effect of the Legitimacy Act 1959 became apparent in the famous "blood-tie" case of 1965 when the court awarded the custody of an 18-month-old child to his (Protestant) putative father after the child had been, since early infancy, in the care of a (Roman Catholic) couple at his mother's express request with a view to adoption by them. The mother opposed the putative father's application. The court then gave directions to avert in future the kind of delay in reaching a conclusion which was such a distressing feature of this case.

2.3. Guardianship. A parent may appoint someone other than his or her spouse to act as his child's guardian when he dies. This appointment may be made by deed or will and is, of course, revocable during the parent's lifetime. If the other parent is already dead or the child is illegitimate, the guardian acts alone. If the other parent of a legitimate child survives, the guardian acts jointly with him or her, and disputes between them may be settled by the court who may even award sole custody to the guardian, thus depriving the surviving parent of his rights. This is rarely done and only on most urgent grounds. If a child has no surviving parent or guardian, any person of full age can apply to the court to be made the child's guardian. This is a simple and inexpensive procedure in the magistrates' court and, unless the application is likely to be contested by other claimants for custody of the child, there is no need for legal representation. In a contested case legal aid may be granted to parties of limited means. Next of kin are not legal guardians. A grandparent, uncle, aunt, or grown-up brother or sister of a child whose parents are dead does *not* inherit the custody of a child on the death of the child's parents, but only becomes guardian if a parent has appointed him as such or by order of a court.

2.4. Custody to a third party. Both the High Court and the magistrates' courts have power to award the custody of a child to a third party, thus for the time being effectively excluding either parent from management of the child's upbringing. The court may take this step even if no person has put the child's welfare in issue but simply because one of the parents has made application to the court in a matrimonial case. Once the court is seized of such a case, regardless of the merits of the application or of the respondent's reply, it may award custody to a suitable third party who is willing to accept it. This action is, of course, rarely taken, and never capriciously. Custody orders can always subsequently be varied. Since 1969 juvenile courts have lost the power they previously exercised to entrust the care of a child to a "fit person" other than a local authority when a child was before them for the commission of a significant offence or as being in need of care, protection, or control. A few dozen such orders are probably still in existence and will remain effective until the child concerned reaches his eighteenth birthday.

2.5. Custody vested in the court (wardship). At any one time the custody of several hundred children is vested in the High Court as wards. The care and control of such a child is then undertaken by the person whom the court appoints, generally a parent. The court may then exercise control of the child's upbringing to the extent that it considers necessary and can, in particular, prevent his being taken out of the kingdom and from marrying and can also directly prohibit a third party from attempting to marry the ward or even from communicating with him or her on pain of imprisonment. The jurisdiction has become much less significant in restraint of elopement and marriage since the upper limit of wardship was reduced from the twenty-first to the eighteenth birthday in 1969.

3. Care and Supervision exercised by Public Authorities and Voluntary Organizations

3.1. By order of the juvenile court. Section 1 of the Children and Young Persons Act 1969 redefined the circumstances in which the juvenile court could order that a child should be placed in the care of a local authority by a "care order". At the same time it did away with the court's power to send the child to an approved school or to commit him to the care of a "fit person" other than the local authority.

A person between the tenth and the seventeenth birthday may still be brought before the juvenile court for an offence against the criminal law and, if the offence is one which is punishable in an adult with imprisonment, the court may if it thinks it is in his interests or in the interests of the community, commit him to the care of the local authority.

Side by side with this continuing criminal jurisdiction the court may entertain an application that anyone under 17 is in need of care or control and may make a care order provided it is satisfied on two separate issues:

(a)   that he is in need of care or control *which he is unlikely to receive unless the court makes an order*; and

(b)   that either: his health or proper development is being impaired or neglected or he is being illtreated or is in moral danger or is beyond control or is not receiving suitable education or has committed any offence (not necessarily an offence punishable in an adult with imprisonment).

On finding the case proved on both counts (a) and (b) the court has a choice of orders, including two relating only to the mentally disordered. In certain circumstances it can order payment of compensation by the child or his parents in respect of loss or damage caused in the commission of an offence and can order a parent to enter into a recognisance to exercise proper care or control (but only with the parent's consent). It can also make a supervision order (see paragraph 3.4).

The introduction of at least three important need concepts and the retention of one very old one can be identified in the new section.

First, a child may no longer be brought to court as in need of care or control unless it appears necessary to make an order to assure for him such care or control. This would appear to mean that if a local authority offers, say, to receive voluntarily into care a child who has committed a number of offences and the child and his parents agree to such reception into care, then the child should not be brought before the court. If by chance the child should already be before the court when these circumstances are revealed, the court should not make the order unless it thinks that the parent, the child, or the authority are likely to go back on the arrangement. The idea is to avoid court appearances if matters can be dealt with by agreement. But agreement between whom? Agreement, presumably, between the doctors, teachers, and social workers on the one hand; the possibly uninterested, illiterate, or even positively vindictive parent on the other hand; with the possibly inarticulate or even cowed child a very insignificant third. The clear assumption is that the expert local authority officers and advisors are likely to be right, and that there is no need for a court to check their decisions unless the parent has the nous to say "no" or the child has sufficient spirit to resist or to run away. Protagonists of the new system argue with justice that handicapped, sick, and disabled children are sent to residential schools, institutions, and hospitals on expert medical and educational advice provided parents do not resist. Against the new system it can be argued that parent and child suffer an intangible loss by the reception of a child into the care of the public authority; loss for the time being by the parent of the control and the presence of his child and loss by the child of the familiar experiences of his home life. Protagonists of the new idea want to silence for ever the poor law overtones implied by reception into care and to treat it instead as a positive therapeutic measure which the child and his parent will have cause to be grateful for in future years. Critics of the new system say that the enlightened attitudes of the professionals are unlikely to be viewed as such by the clients: that parents will be further impaired in their capacity to care by the implied judgement on their capacity and that the child will see removal from home as a punishment. Protagonists of the new system will retort that it is all the same in the long run because if court proceedings are introduced into what is essentially the exercise of professional judgement in the offer to a family of treatment for a child, the magistrates will inevitably be just as enlightened as the experts and will inevitably support their decision—an assessment of the characteristics of magistrates which is either a compliment or a calumny according to your point of view.

In 1965 the White Paper *The Child, the Family and the Young Offender* offered a *via media* between these two viewpoints. It borrowed from Scandinavia the concept of the "family council" which would have retained a measure of civil liberty for the child and his parents while cutting down recourse to the juvenile courts with all the overtones of criminal jurisdiction, uniformed police, incomprehensible formality, absence of an appointments system and a reception desk, squalid and overcrowded waiting rooms which unhappily characterize some juvenile courts and which are happily of rare or insignificant occurrence in some other juvenile courts. The family council would have been held in private, by appointment, at times when both parents could attend without losing wages and would have been conducted on the level, sitting round a table, with parent and child being shown such ordinary courtesies as explaining to them the role and identity of each of the persons taking part in the discussion and permitting them to intervene at relevant points in the discussion instead of requiring them to hold their tongues until the time came to make a speech for the defence or a plea in mitigation, perhaps preceded earlier in the proceedings by abrupt invitation to take once and for all the chance to examine, cross-examine, or re-examine a witness—a skill which some of the best barristers acknowledge they are still trying to improve after a lifetime in the courts.

The family council would at least have ensured to parent and child the knowledge that their views were of value and would be taken into consideration by people with names and faces instead of by decisions made somewhere in an office at the town hall and relayed to the families by social workers disposing of varying amounts of time and skill for the task. The idea of the family council was defeated by the juvenile court lobby who believed that by so doing they would preserve the elementary principle of a hearing before an independent tribunal when a parent's enjoyment of his child's presence in the family and of his day-to-day control over the child's upbringing and when a child's right to stay at home was in issue. The outcome has been exactly opposite to what the protagonists of juvenile courts intended. Unless parent or child digs in his heels he will have neither the formal procedure of a juvenile court nor the informal discussion of a family council to justify and dignify the immensely important and far-reaching decision to remove a child from home.

The second new concept introduced by the 1969 Act is the abandonment of parental inadequacy or culpability as a factor in deciding whether a child needs care or control. Henceforth it is to be what the child needs and not what the parent has done or failed to do which shall decide the issue.

The third new concept is that the court no longer has a say in what kind of care should be provided once it has reached a decision that a child may need to be cared for away from home and therefore should be subject to a care order. The court cannot even require that a child should be away from home at all if the authority decide to send straight home a child who had just been committed to their care, although it would be a brave Director of Social Services who authorized such an arrangement if the court had just expressed the view that to take such a course would not for the time being be in the child's interests. There is no longer a legal distinction between the approved school system and the remainder of the child care system. It is intended that the local authority shall decide in what way the child shall best be looked after for the time being, whether in his own home, in a foster home, lodgings, residential work including the merchant navy and armed forces, residential education, hospital, or in one of the forms of group care most (but not all of which) are now comprised under the general title of "community home" which includes what were formerly residential nurseries, children's homes, and reception and remand homes of various sizes, approved schools, and hostels for young people. Of course these establishments will not change overnight by reason of the change of name, neither is it desirable that each should give up those of its characteristics which minister to the special needs of the children for whom care in it is likely to be selected. At the time of writing this chapter (July 1971) the assimilation of the approved school system is incomplete: and certain difficulties (not unforeseen) are manifest. For example, the individual approved school is, under the present dispensation, no longer required to receive and keep a child who does not respond satisfactorily to the kind of care which the school offers: the local authority, on the other hand, is obliged to accept and care for every child in its area who is in need of care or who is committed to its care by a court. It looks as if the former approved schools may cease to be the institutions of last resort for children whom no one else wants. That role may be allotted to what used to be called children's homes. It is a role which they are imperfectly equipped to play.

The one old concept which has most markedly been carried forward with the new law of care and control is the distinction between the child who is alleged to have committed an offence and the child who is before the court on some other ground, the evidence for which may include sexual nonconformity ("moral danger") or aggressive and destructive behaviour ("beyond control"). The "offence", on the other hand, could be a venial one such as trespassing on railway property, or letting off a firework in the wrong place. The crudest adherents of this distinction between offenders and the offended describe the two groups respectively as the "depraved" and the "deprived". While acknowledging that the behaviour of some children in need of care is depraved and that many children in care bear the marks of deprivation, it is rarely possible to tell from an objective study of an individual child in care whether he has been accused of an offence and is therefore "depraved" or whether he came into care on some other ground and is therefore "deprived".

A child whose need for care is evidenced by the fact that he has committed an offence enjoys a higher degree of protection against a mistaken finding of the need for care or control than does a child whose need for care is founded on some other condition. If the case is based on an allegation that the child has committed an offence then the court must be satisfied beyond reasonable doubt that the child is guilty, whereas if some other condition is alleged the court may if it thinks fit base its decision on the balance of probabilities. Furthermore, evidence relating to moral danger, being beyond control, poor school attendance, or the like which has been unsuccessfully tendered at previous hearings may be used to support a subsequent application, whereas evidence of any specific act or omission constituting an offence may not be used a second time. This distinction goes a long way back in the history of child care. A hundred years ago there were two different kinds of residential school for children committed by the courts—one for those found guilty of offences and another kind for those found to be ill-treated or neglected.

A care order imposes a duty on the local authority to receive a child into their care and to keep him in care notwithstanding any claim by his parents. The authority then has the same powers and duties as his parent would have but for the order. The parent does not lose his parental rights but cannot generally effectively exercise them against decisions of the authority in respect of his day-to-day care unless the authority has allowed the parent to take over the child's care for the time being.

3.2. By order of other courts. The higher criminal courts have power to make care orders in respect of offenders under the age of 17.

Magistrates' courts and the High Court in the exercise of their matrimonial jurisdiction have the power to make orders committing children to the care of the local authority. These orders are not the same as care orders: they do not confer parental rights on the authority, but do provide that the child shall remain in the authority's care notwithstanding a claim by the parents. Matters requiring the consent of a legal guardian are reserved to the parent. The High Court may give directions to the local authority as to the way in which they should look after the child. Neither the magistrates' court nor the High Court may bring a matrimonial case to a conclusion until it has considered the welfare of any children of the family under 16.

The High Court can commit a ward of court to the care of a local authority in the same way as it can commit children of the marriage of persons involved in matrimonial proceedings.

3.3. Voluntary reception into care. The great majority of children in care of local authorities have been received voluntarily without the intervention of a court. The local authority has a duty to receive into care anyone in its area apparently under 17 who has no parent or guardian or whose parents or guardians are prevented by any circumstances from providing for his proper accommodation, maintenance, or upbringing. This is a very wide provision and has been taken to authorize an authority to receive into care, for example, children whose parents are able and willing to care for them but who have no house to live in. There is, however, a further requirement. The authority has no duty to receive a child into care even when the conditions so far mentioned exist unless they are satisfied that their intervention in this connection is necessary in the child's interests. Hundreds of difficult decisions have to be made every week in balancing these two provisions of the law, and the time may not be far off when professional social workers will decline to separate children from parents on grounds of homelessness, thus obliging the authorities to provide more houses and more temporary accommodation where parent and child can remain together. Social workers faced with this decision will have regard to the authority's duty to consider whether colluding in the separation of child from parent is, in a particular case, consistent with his welfare.

Once a child is in care under this section, the authority must keep him in care so long as his welfare requires it, but cannot keep him in care if a parent or guardian desires to take over his care, unless the authority has subsequently, for good reason, assumed parental rights. Furthermore, the authority must, in all cases where it appears consistent with the welfare of the child, endeavour to secure that his care is taken over by a parent, guardian, relative, or friend. Under a later Act (1963) the authority has a duty to make available advice and assistance directed to diminishing the need for him to remain in care. So long as a child is in care (whether voluntarily or by order of a court) the authority must further his best interests and afford him opportunity for the proper development of his character and abilities, and to this end may make reasonable use of facilities and services which are available for children in the care of their own parents. At 6-month intervals the authority must review the circumstances of his case. Such a review will include consideration of the continuing need for care and, in the case of a care order, the advisability of applying for it to be discharged.

Voluntary charitable societies also look after children at the request of parents, next of kin, or other persons having possession of a child. Such societies must register with the Secretary of State for Social Services. They are subject to inspection, and regulations relating to the administration of children's homes, boarding-out, and adoption apply equally to voluntary societies and to local authorities. Children entrusted by private individuals to the care of voluntary societies are not in care in the statutory sense. Parental rights cannot be vested in a voluntary society, and such a society has no legal duty to try to secure that a child's care is taken over by a parent, guardian, relative, or friend. The arrangement is an informal one which the parent or the society may terminate at any time. The practices of most voluntary societies, especially the larger ones, conform closely to those which are by law required of local authorities. The central government, in published statistics, sometimes differentiates between children in the *care* of local authorities and those in the *charge* of voluntary societies, thus making the legal distinction, but the Ministry's nomenclature has not been widely copied by the societies.

3.4. Supervision orders. Section 1 of the Children and Young Persons Act 1969 redefined the circumstances in which the magistrates may make a supervision order in respect of a child or young person. The duration of such an order may be specified but may not in any circumstances exceed three years. The court may select either the local authority or a probation officer to be the supervisor (subject to certain conditions and agreements in both cases). The duty of the supervisor is "to advise, assist and befriend the supervised person"; but it should be noted that if, while the order is in force, it appears to a juvenile court on the application of the supervisor that it is appropriate to make another order, or to insert in the order some other requirement, then the court may take that further action. In other words, should the child under supervision fail to respond in acceptable ways to the "advice, assistance and friendship" he is being offered, he may find himself again brought before the magistrates.

An interesting development in the treatment of children who appear to be in need of care and control is foreshadowed in Section 12 of the Children and Young Persons Act 1969. Under this Section magistrates may insert "requirements" into a supervision order. These requirements may be that the child must comply with such directions as the supervising officer may give on the following matters:

(a) to live for a specified period at a specified place;
(b) to present himself to a specified person at a specified place on a specified day;
(c) to participate in specified activities on that specified day.

The extent to which the child's freedom and choice of activity is thus limited is carefully controlled by the statute, and "directed" activities must not, broadly speaking, take up more than thirty days in any one year.

The treatment envisaged here is now commonly referred to as Intermediate Treatment. Under a supervision order a child generally resides in his own home; under a care order he generally resides away from his own home; as an intermediate measure he may be required to live away from home for a short continuous period or for a series of brief absences. Among forms of intermediate treatment might appear short courses of the "Outward Bound" or "adventure" type; intensive courses of vocational training; periods engaged in social service; attendance at evening courses arranged by Colleges of Further Education; or therapeutic groups.

Schemes of Intermediate Treatment are to be prepared by Regional Planning Committees and approved by the Secretary of State before the provisions of Section 12 are brought into effect.

3.5. Assumption by local authorities of parental rights. Section 2 of the Children Act of 1948 provides that, with respect to any child who has come into the care of a local authority under the provisions of Section 1 of the same Act, the local authority may resolve that the rights and powers of the parent or guardian shall be vested in the local authority. This power to assume by resolution the parents' rights is, however, strictly limited. It will be noted that the child *must* have been received into the care of the local authority and be still in care. In addition the circumstances or behaviour of the parents must be such as to satisfy the legal requirements. These were set out in Section 2 of the 1948 Act and further extended by Section 48 of the Children and Young Persons Act 1963; and under these Sections it must "appear" to the local authority that in respect of the child:

(a) his parents are dead and he has no guardian;

(b) a parent or guardian of his has abandoned him or suffers from some permanent disability rendering the said person incapable of caring for the child or is of such habits and mode of life as to be unfit to have the care of the child;

(c) the whereabouts of any parent or guardian of his have remained unknown for not less than twelve months, then the parent or guardian shall be deemed to have abandoned the child;

(d) the parent or guardian suffers from a mental disorder within the meaning of the Mental Health Act 1959 which renders him unfit to have the care of the child; or

(e) the parent or guardian has so persistently failed without reasonable cause to discharge the obligations of a parent or guardian as to be unfit to have the care of the child.

In circumstances where the whereabouts of the parents are known at the time of the Resolution is passed, the parents must be informed of the Resolution and its effect. They have the right to object to the action taken, in which case the local authority may if it wishes apply to a juvenile court for confirmation of the action that has been taken. If it does not so apply, the Resolution lapses. A Resolution once taken has effect until the child's eighteenth birthday unless the local authority has previously rescinded its action, or unless a parent has successfully applied to a juvenile court for the determination of the Resolution. Until such determination, the effect of the Resolution is virtually the same as the effect of a Care Order—i.e. the child cannot be removed from the care of the authority, or induced to run away, or harboured, on pain of a fine or imprisonment.

Appendix to Chapter 10

In July 1969 a Departmental Committee was set up under the chairmanship of Sir William Houghton to inquire into the laws and procedures governing the adoption of children. In November 1970 the Committee issued a substantial Working Paper ("The Adoption of Children", HMSO) with a long list of recommendations; this was widely circulated and discussion and comment were invited. Late in 1971 Sir William Houghton died and the chairmanship was taken over by Judge Frank Stockdale; and some twelve months later the final Report of the Committee was published—Cmnd. 5107 of 1972, HMSO, London. This Report may colloquially be referred to either as "The Houghton" or "The Stockdale" Report.

The final report contains no fewer than ninety-two recommendations, obviously too many to reproduce here, and in any case the majority of the recommendations would require legislative action before any change could be made. Many are so similar in wording to the recommendations in the Interim Report that Dr. McWhinnie's notes and comments in Chapter 10 are but little affected. Some of the recommendations apply more to children in the care of local authorities than to the adoption process.

The principal changes recommended by the Committee are:

(1) That all adoption placements should be made through an accredited adoption agency, by making "direct" and "third party" placements (referred to on p. 157 of this book) legal offences.

(2) There should be an extension of guardianship as an alternative to adoption in various specified situations.

233

(3) At an early stage—almost at a "pre-adoption" stage—the parent of the infant, usually the mother, should be required to satisfy a court that she had freely relinquished parental rights which would then vest in the adoption agency until such time as an Adoption Order were made.

(4) An adopted person over the age of eighteen should be entitled to a copy of his original birth certificate.

(5) An adoption service should be seen and organzied as part of a comprehensive child care and family service.

Further Reading

WHAT follows is an attempt at a guide to reading in the child care field. There is a very great deal of material now available, and any selection is bound to be arbitrary: this list is an invitation to go "on safari" across the great plains of social work literature, and perhaps does little more than suggest certain points of departure.

List I is intended for the real beginner, the committee member or the foster parent wishing to be better informed. List II is for those with some first-hand experience who wish to plunge deeper into the hinterland. List III suggests material which may most profitably be studied against a background of experience. But obviously these categories are arbitrary too: the real beginner, for instance, may well find much to interest him in List III.

But every man's safari is a personal affair.

List I

Report of the Committee on Local Authority and Allied Personal Social Services, HMSO, London, 1968 (The "Seebohm" Report).

BAUMEISTER, A. A. (ed.), *Mental Retardation: Appraisal, Education and Rehabilitation*, University of London Press, 1968.

Boss, P., *Exploration into Child Care*, Routledge and Kegan Paul, 1971.

BOWLBY, J., *Child Care and the Growth of Love*, Penguin Books, 1970.

BRILL, K., *Children, Not Cases*, Epworth Press.

FORDER, A. (ed.), *Penelope Hall's Social Services of England and Wales*, Routledge and Kegan Paul, 1969.

GOODACRE, I., *Adoption Policy and Practice*, Allen & Unwin, 1966.

HEYWOOD, J., *Children in Care*, Routledge and Kegan Paul, 1965.

HITCHMAN, J., *King of the Barbareens*, Putnam.

LASSELL, M., *Wellington Road*, Routledge and Kegan Paul.
PACKMAN, J., *Child Care: Needs and Numbers*, Allen & Unwin, 1968.
ROWE, J., *Parents, Children and Adoption*, Routledge and Kegan Paul, 1966.
SCHAFFER, E. R., and EVELYN, B., *Child Care and the Family*, Bell, 1968.
STEVENSON, O., *Someone Else's Child*, Routledge and Kegan Paul.
STROUD, J., *The Shorn Lamb*, Longmans, 1961.
STROUD, J., *Introduction to the Child Care Service*, Longmans, 1965.

List II

BALBIRNIE, R., *Residential Care with Children* (2nd edn.), Chaucer Press, 1972.
BEDELL, C., *Residential Life with Children*, Routledge and Kegan Paul, 1970.
BETTLEHEIM, B., *Love is not Enough*, Glencoe Free Press, Illinois.
BETTLEHEIM, B., *Truants from Life*, Glencoe Free Press, Illinois.
BURBURY, BALINT, and YAPP, *Introduction to Child Guidance*, Macmillan.
CAPLAN, G., *Prevention of Mental Disorders in Children*, Tavistock Press.
CLARKE, A. M., and CLARKE, A. D. B. (Eds.), *Mental Deficiency: The Changing Outlook*, Methuen, 1965.
CLEGG, SIR A., and MEGSON, *Children in Distress*, Penguin Books, 1970.
CLEUGH, M. F., *The Slow Learner*, Methuen, 1969.
DINNAGE and PRINGLE, *Residential Child Care: Facts and Fallacies*, Longmans, 1964.
DONNISON, D., *The Neglected Child and the Social Services*, Manchester Univ. Press.
ENGLISH and FOSTER, *Fathers are Parents too*, Allen & Unwin.
ERIKSON, E. H., *Childhood and Society*, Imago Norton, 1963.
FERRARD, M., and HUNNYBUN, N., *The Caseworker's Use of Relationships*, Tavistock Press, 1952.
GEORGE, V., *Foster Care*, Routledge and Kegan Paul, 1971.
GOULD, L. (ed), *The Prevention of Damaging Stress in Children*, Churchill, 1968.
HOLMAN, R. (ed.), *Socially Deprived Families in Britain*, Bedford Square Press, 1970.
HOLT, J., *How Children Fail*, Delta.
KORNITZER, M., *Adoption*, Putnam, 1970.
KUGEL, R. B., and WOLFENSBERGER, W. (eds), *Changing Patterns in Residential Services for the Mentally Retarded*, President's Committee on Mental Retardation, Washington DC, 1969.
LAYCOCK, *Adolescence and Social Work*, Routledge and Kegan Paul.
NATIONAL CHILDREN'S BUREAU, *From Birth to Seven*.
NEWSOM, J. and E., *Infant Care in an Urban Community*, Allen & Unwin.
PENROSE, L. S., *The Biology of Mental Defect*, Sidgwick & Jackson, 1963.
STORR, A., *The Integrity of the Personality*, Penguin Books.
TANSLEY, A. E., and GULLIFORD, R., *The Education of Slow Learning Children*, Routledge and Kegan Paul, 1965.
TIMMS, N., *Casework in the Child Care Service*, Butterworths, 1969.

TIZARD, J., *Community Services for the Mentally Handicapped*, Oxford Univ. Press, 1964.
WINNICOTT, C., *Child Care and Social Work*, Codicote Press, 1964.
WINNICOTT, D., *The Child and the Family*, Tavistock Press, 1957.
WINNICOTT, D., *The Family and Individual Development*, Tavistock Press, 1965.

List III

BIESTEK, F. P., *The Casework Relationship*, Allen & Unwin.
BION, W. R., *Experiences in Groups*, Tavistock Press.
BURMEISTER, E., *The Professional Houseparent*, Columbia Univ. Press.
CHARNLEY, J., *The Art of Child Placement*, Minnesota Univ. Press.
DRYSDALE, L., *Therapy in Child Care (Papers on Residential Work)*, Longmans, 1968.
HOLLIS, F., *Casework: Psychosocial Therapy*, Random House, 1964.
HUMPHREY, M., *The Hostage Seekers*, Longmans, 1969.
KING, R. D., RAYNES, N. V., and TIZARD, J., *Patterns of Residential Care—Sociological Studies in Institutions for Handicapped Children*, Routledge and Kegan Paul.
KLEIN, M., and RIVIERE, J., *Love, Hate and Reparation*, Hogarth, 1938.
KONOPKA, G., *Social Group Work*, Prentice-Hall, 1963.
LENNHOFF, F., *Exceptional Children*, Allen & Unwin, 1967.
McWHINNIE, A., *Adopted Children. How they Grow Up*, Routledge and Kegan Paul, 1967.
PERLMAN, H. H., *Social Casework: A Problem-solving Process*, Univ. of Chicago Press.
REDL, F., *Controls from Within*, Glencoe Free Press, Illinois.
SIMEY, T. S., *The Concept of Love in Child Care*, Epworth Press.

Biographies of Contributors

BALLANCE, GILLIAN, Lecturer in Social Work at Hatfield Polytechnic. Trained at the London School of Economics in social science and later took the Child Care Course at Liverpool University. Has worked residentially with maladjusted children and with girls on probation; and for thirteen years as Child Care Officer and Area Children's Officer for the Hertfordshire Children's Department.

BRILL, KENNETH, OBE, General Secretary, British Association of Social Workers; formerly County Children's Officer for Devon and Honorary Secretary, Association of Children's Officers.

Publications include *Children in Homes* (with Ruth Thomas), 1964; *John Croser, London Priest* (Ed.).

HAMMOND, PAULINE M., Senior Adviser, Social Work Services Group, Scottish Education Department, Edinburgh.

Publications include: Changing Practice in mental hospital social work, 1964; Supervision in professional development, 1965—both in the *British Journal of Psychiatric Social Work*; *Patterns of training in field-work*, 1966—Case Conference; *Some Thoughts for Older Students facing Training*, Accord, 1967.

HEY, V., Captain RAEC (Retired).BSC University of Durham. Superintendent, Boyles Court Assessment Centre, Essex. President of the National Association of Heads and Matrons of Assessment Centre. Physical Educationalist. Residential Social Worker. Lecturer and Consultant.

HEYWOOD, JEAN S., Reader in Social Administration in the University of Manchester.

Major publications include: *Children in Care* (Routledge) 1965; *Introduction to Teaching Casework Skills* (Routledge) 1964; *Casework and Pastoral Care* (S.P.C.K.) 1967; *Financial Help and Social Work* (with Barbara Allen) (Manchester University Press) 1971.

HOLMAN, ROBERT, Senior Lecturer in Social Administration and Social Work at the University of Glasgow, Member Gulbenkian Working Group on Community Work.

Major publications include: *Socially Deprived Families in Britain* (ed.), Bedford Square Press, 1970; *Unsupported Mothers and the Care of their Children*, Mothers in Action, 1970; *Power to the Powerless: the Role of Community Action*, British Council of Churches, 1972; *Trading in Children: A Study of Private Foster Homes*, Routledge & Kegan Paul, 1973.

HOWELLS, JOHN R., Diploma of Social Science, Diploma in Education. On completion of full-time education, John R. Howells entered the Approved School service as Assistant Master at Kneesworth Hall School in Cambridgeshire and after three years became Superintendent of Rheanfa Remand Home for Boys in Swansea.

In June 1965 he became Deputy Headmaster of Mile Oak Approved School for boys, a junior school in Portslade, Sussex, and took over his present appointment as Principal of Turner's Court, Benson, Oxfordshire, an establishment for deprived adolescent boys, in December 1967.

ILOTT, ROSEMARY, Homes Secretary, Church of England Children's Society. In charge of Residential and Day Care Establishments, Member of Nursery Nurses Examination Board and National Council Voluntary Child Care Organisations.

MCWHINNIE, ALEXINA MARY, Psychiatric Social Worker; Social Work Adviser in Substitute Care, Berkshire Social Services Department; previously Director, Guild Service, Edinburgh.

Publications include: *Adopted Children: How They Grow Up,* Routledge & Kegan Paul; *Adoption Assessments, A Team Approach*; *Group Counselling with 78 Adoptive Families*; *Unmarried Mothers*; *Are the Social Services Adequate?*

MONTGOMERIE, JANET, Residential Social Worker, studied Residential Child Care at Birmingham, having a particular interest in working with small groups.

PACKMAN, J. W., Lecturer in Social Work, University of Exeter.

Major publications include: *Child Care: Needs and Numbers*, George Allen & Unwin, 1968.

PRITCHARD, D. C., Professor of Education, University College of Swansea. Previously Head of the Sub-Department of Special Education, University of Liverpool. Chairman of Editorial Board *Special Education*. Fellow of the Royal Historical Society.

Major publications include: *Education and the Handicapped, 1760–1960* (Routledge) 1963; *Studies on the Mentally Handicapped Child* (with A. B. Boom *et al.*) 1968.

STROUD, JOHN, entered the field of child care in 1949 and after three years with Middlesex he moved to Hertfordshire where he has remained: he was Deputy Children's Officer from 1964 to 1971 and is now Assistant Director of Social

Services (Field and Domiciliary Section). He has written prolifically on social-work subjects, using both fictional and non-fictional styles.

WATSON, SYLVIA, Director of Social Services, Cambridgeshire, and Isle of Ely County Council. Children's Officer, Hertfordshire County Council, 1948–70. Former member of Central Training Council in Child Care and Central Advisory Council on Child Care. Member of Williams Committee on staffing of residential establishments, 1962–7. President of Association of Children's Officers, 1967–8. Has acted as professional adviser to County Councils Association since 1964.

WILLIAMS, PAUL, Tutor-Organizer, The Spastics Society, Castle Priory College, Wallingford, Berkshire; formerly Research Officer at Southampton University working on the Wessex project in mental handicap.
    Publications include: Industrial training and remunerative employment of the profoundly retarded, *Journal of Mental Subnormality*, 1967; Child care and mental handicap, *Developmental Medicine and Child Neurology*, 1969; Teaching processes in the care of severely retarded children, in *Learning, Speech and Thought in the Mentally Retarded* (editors A. D. B. Clarke and M. M. Lewis, Butterworths, 1972).

Index

243